Felix Ó Mur chadha (ed.)

Violence, Victims, Justifications

Philosophical Approaches

PETER LANG

Oxford · Bern · Berlin · Bruxelles · Frankfurt am Main · New York · Wien

Bibliographic information published by Die Deutsche Bibliothek
Die Deutsche Bibliothek lists this publication in the Deutsche
Nationalbibliografie; detailed bibliographic data is available on
the Internet at ‹http://dnb.ddb.de›.

British Library and Library of Congress Cataloguing-in-Publication Data:
A catalogue record for this book is available from *The British Library*,
Great Britain, and from *The Library of Congress*, USA

This publication was grant-aided by the Publications Fund
of National University of Ireland, Galway.

ISBN 3-03910-735-6
US-ISBN 0-8204-7998-5

© Peter Lang AG, International Academic Publishers, Bern 2006
Hochfeldstrasse 32, Postfach 746, CH-3000 Bern 9, Switzerland
info@peterlang.com, www.peterlang.com, www.peterlang.net

Printed in Germany

Contents

Acknowledgements

This collection emerged from a lecture series held at the Department of Philosophy, National University of Ireland, Galway in the Spring of 2002. I would like thank the head of department Professor Markus Wörner whose idea it was to hold a lecture series on violence and who encouraged me to publish a book on its basis. I would also like to thank the staff and students who attended those lectures. I have received moral and intellectual encouragement from a number of people, including all the contributors to this volume, to whom I ʳ ⅎ individually thankful. In addition to them I would like to acknowledge in this respect Dr. Ronald Bayne, Dr. Richard Hull and Dr. Mark Haugaard. To Dr. Ricca Edmondson I owe a particular debt of gratitude; without her advice and encouragement this book would probably never have seen the light of day.

Finally, for her constant loving support and engagement with this project I owe, as always, a special thanks to my wife Anne.

Felix Ó Murchadha

Introduction:
Violence, Discourse and Human Interdependence

Violence by definition has its victims. From bruises and scrapes to blood and body parts there abound the testimonies to beatings, assaults, bombings. Such testimonies are themselves embedded in discourses of grief and loss as well as justification and triumph. Violence is rarely allowed to 'speak for itself', but rather is expressed in different, often opposed, terms by victims, perpetrators and witnesses. This suggests that violence cannot be understood as an aberrant return to some inarticulate 'savagery', but rather as itself a social and cultural phenomenon. Violence articulates fundamental elements of human relations, specifically those of interdependence. Where there is vulnerability, the risk and the threat of violence is not far removed. To live within human society is to be vulnerable in relation to physical, emotional, intellectual needs, desires and aspirations. Without such vulnerability arguably human relations would not be possible, but by the same token violence responds to, and feeds upon, such vulnerabilities. From international politics to personal intimacy such relations of dependence and interdependence make possible violence, violations, victimisations. Relations of dependence make us vulnerable to violence and not surprisingly such relations are implicitly or explicitly a fundamental theme in the discourses of explanation and justification, of loss and grief, of shock and horror which surround it. The shock of violence is that it is embedded precisely in that without which human society and culture would be inconceivable: dependence on others and the discourses of justification and testimony.

Following the September 11th attacks there was a sentiment expressed especially in the United States that only the articulations of victims and certain witnesses should be countenanced: all justifications or even explanations were excluded from the outset. This stance has been repeated regularly since in the wake of 'terrorist atrocities'. But such a moratorium could not and cannot last, especially when this violence is matched by counter-violence (in Afghanistan, Iraq, Chechnya, the Occupied Territories). The same applies throughout the whole continuum of violent acts from random street violence to sexual assault to warfare.

The challenge for any philosophical approach to issues of violence is to come to terms with this interplay of force and discourse, violation and self-assertion. Such a challenge can only be met by remaining within this delicate interplay and avoiding the temptation either to dismiss violence as irrational[1] or to embrace it in a frenzy of political engagement.[2] Philosophical analysis must be applied to violence as it is manifest in diverse areas of human life, not be satisfied with stereotypes. Such stereotyping can be avoided by a readiness to imaginatively vary perspectives on the act of violence.[3] Three main perspectives are – at least ideally – constitutive of all such acts, those of perpetrator, victim and witness. No one of these perspectives is invariably true or right when it comes to violence. Philosophically one can view it consecutively from each perspective while remaining aware of the possible slippage between these viewpoints within the one act or series of acts of violence.[4] It is precisely to this challenge that the present volume responds. From various perspectives it questions the strategy of simple condemnation of violence by demonstrating the extent to which violence far from being an aberration is potentially, if not actually, a constant presence in human interrelations, from the bedroom to the battlefield. Furthermore, this volume brings to light the ways in which violence and discourse are ensnared in one another and are so from each of the three perspectives mentioned: perpetrator, victim, witness. This is not to suggest that there is a moral equivalence in these perspectives; but rather to argue that the moral right or wrong in situations of violence is generally contestable. The philosopher is not, however, condemned to moral neutrality on this issue: on violence no such neutrality is possible as the very schema of perpetrator, victim, witness suggests. However, what it does mean is that the philosopher has to come to terms with the complexities and ambiguities of the moral situation of violence. The contributions to this volume explore the intersections between violence and discourse in terms of justification, violation, explanation, identity and responsibility. In doing so, they underline the startling nature of the claim that violence is so far from being exceptional in normal human relations that we should see it as intrinsic to the interdependence which is constitutive of such relations and that questions of responsibility for violent acts can only be pursued in such a context. This in no way amounts to a facile social determinism. Rather, the claim is that violence must be understood concretely in that intersection between acts of force and discourse in which all social relations are in principle implicated. The contributors to this volume show that the moral and conceptual exploration of violence is even more urgent than is commonly supposed and that such an exploration is likely to be effective only when situated right at the heart of the matter with which it is dealing.

The justification of violence often takes the form of denying to one's own action (or the action of the side one supports) the pertinence of the very word 'violence' itself: *Our* legitimate use of force against *their* violence. Philosophically understood such a designation assumes the *prima facie* wrongness of violence: violence as the illegitimate use of force. To the extent to which one acts rightly then one is acting non-violently. This certainly corresponds to the commonsense meaning of this term in English (a meaning not, however, so obvious in other languages such as with the German word '*Gewalt*'). The difficulty with such a view is that it tends to favour the superior party in a relationship, whether between individuals or between communities and states. Such a strategy merely displaces the question from justifications of violence to justifications of force, understood in terms of law and right: justified force being lawful force. This, however, begs the question as to the justification of the 'force of law'.[5] The state monopoly of violence is a central tenet of liberal political thinking, but it assumes the legitimacy of the state. The syndicalist thinker Georges Sorel rejects such legitimist claims and argues for violence precisely when its aim is to undermine the state.[6] This rejection of the state amongst other things implies the possibility of a violence-free society. This assumption seems more aspirational than real although it animates the work of many philosophers, such as Jürgen Habermas, who argue for a communicative ethics and discursive rationality.

Habermas understands violence in terms of a disruption and violation of forms of communication.[7] Communication in this view is inherently non-violent. Such a position, underplays firstly the possibility that it may be necessary to employ violence to enter into equal communicative relations[8] and secondly the manner in which discourse can itself be violent. It serves to avoid precisely the problem violence poses, namely the interplay of force and discourse.

The common-sense understanding of violence often considers it as necessarily involving physical force. There seems, however, to be nothing characteristic of physical assaults which cannot be found also in psychological attacks: pain, harm, loss of self-esteem, or feelings of violation. The same dynamic of perpetrator, witness and victim is to be found in both. A more controversial issue is whether it is coherent to talk of structural violence.[9] The concept of structural violence, which can be traced back to the sociologist Johan Galtung,[10] is that all forms of social injustice are violent, whether inflicted intentionally or not, by individuals or by institutions. Likewise Pierre Bourdieu speaks of symbolic violence, i.e. the capacity of achieving a lasting hold on someone.[11] Emmanuel Levinas[12] understands violence as inherent in all identity, as the imposition of sameness on the other. The strength of such positions from Galtung through Bourdieu to Levinas and Derrida can be seen if violence is understood not so much from the point of view of the perpetrator, i.e. his intentions or aims, as from the point of view of the victim, his or her being violated. The contributions to this volume from Waldenfels, Enns, Bettcher and Liebsch demonstrate the fecundity of this approach.

It is characteristic of violence to enmesh perpetrator, victims and witnesses within the event of violence itself. A witness is not simply a spectator, she is someone who must bear witness, must testify, and who may suffer trauma. Violence does not begin with the perpetrator (whatever his responsibility), but precedes and envelops him. Nor does violence end with the victim, but in its very appeals to justification or in the taking of revenge continues past his victimisation. For that reason, as well as understanding violence in terms of act and agency, and in terms of structures, it may be equally important to conceive it as event. If rape is best understood in terms of agency and racial discrimination in terms of structure, much terrorist and military violence may be best understood as event. Returning again to September 11th – it was more than anything else an event. Indeed, much terrorist violence is conceived and executed consciously to take the form of events. One need only think of IRA 'spectaculars'. No matter how predictable, a violent event when it occurs is unexpected, it has a focus such as a bomb blast which breaks with the continuity of the everyday, it brings together perpetrators, victims and witnesses who would as individuals have no awareness of one another. Violence can be drab and dreary, it can also be immense and transforming. So much so that the stories of the victims of such attacks themselves become subsumed in the account of them. If the victimhood of the victim becomes lost in the justification of violent acts, their individuality becomes subsumed in the event of major acts of violence.[13]

It is the violation of victims, the feeling of victimhood and grievance, which gives an emotional intensity to questions of violence. Yet the extent of such victimhood is itself striking: violence is in one sense ubiquitous, in that there is no realm of human relations or activity from domestic intimacy to relations between countries which is in principle free from actual or potential violence.[14] Anyone who can be violated is a potential victim of violence. To be such a victim one has to have a claim to be respected and to be vulnerable to injury or harm which undermines that claim: if the person had no claims which should be respected no injury to him would be a violation, while if he were not vulnerable to injury it would not be possible to violate him. This vulnerability to violation is a function of the corporeality of human beings, whether as victims of rape or of cruise missiles. The place of violence is to be found where imperatives of morality, law, religion, converge with the needs, desires and penetrability of human flesh. This suggests that the ubiquity of violence is not accidental, nor too vague to be conceptualised, but rather is evidence of a specific interrelation of normative claims and embodiment, which is structurally constitutive of human relations themselves. Two correlative consequences follow from this. Firstly, the embeddedness of violence in discourse becomes more understandable: if violence is the violation of norms, then, unlike say natural disasters, it occurs within the realm of discourses of justification and outrage. Secondly, as the intersection of norms and embodiment seems inescapable there is, or appears to be, no place of non-violence from which to speak, either as a utopian projection or as a present possibility.

Violence most clearly seems to have to do with instrumental reason: the rationality of means and ends. Indeed, it is often considered exclusively in those terms.[15] While attempts at justifying violence in relation to means and ends are common, very often appeal is made to provocations, injustice suffered and past wrongs. In other words, those who justify violence do not generally – in the first instance at least – speak of the ends they wish to achieve, but the injuries, harm, injustices to which they or their associates were responding. In those terms violence is as much expression as means.[16]

If violence is constitutive of the structures of human relations and if it is in the nature of violence to enmesh perpetrator, victim and witness, philosophical reflection on this theme comes at a certain risk. Without pathos it is true to say, as from different perspectives both Honderich and Waldenfels do in their contributions to this volume, that philosophical reflection on violence is dangerous. It is a danger which cannot be evaded, however, without at the same time shirking responsibility.

The question of violence is one which draws responses from a wide spectrum of philosophical approaches, styles and methods. The attempt to understand the intersection of violence and discourse, of force and its justifications, of victimhood and its pleas for retelling, is to not the exclusive preserve of any one philosophical school. It is for this reason that this collection brings together philosophers from a number of traditions. Specifically the two main traditions of contemporary philosophy, analytic and continental, are well represented.

Ted Honderich opens the volume with a presentation of the central thesis of his recent book, *After the Terror,* namely that terrorism can be justified if the values which it aims to achieve are universal human ones. The essay, entitled *Terrorism for Humanity*, argues therefore that there can be no question of blanket assertions either that terrorism is always unjustified or that it is always justified, nor is the killing of innocent non-combatants in itself a compelling argument against acts of terrorism. Starting from this premise, Honderich goes on to outline a 'morality of humanity'. In terms of such a morality, we are obliged to take all rational and feasible steps to alleviate human wretchedness and other deprivations. Acts of terrorism, if they aim at getting people out of lives of wretchedness and deprivation, are acts for humanity in this sense. Honderich argues that the facts of the Palestinian – Israeli conflict show that Palestinian terrorism is aimed at such human betterment and can thus be termed 'terrorism for humanity.' This does not in itself make it right. That question can only be answered in terms of whether the acts of terrorism have a reasonable chance of success.

Honderich's thesis has caused much shock perhaps because he subjects terrorist violence to similar tests as the defenders of state violence employ. But does this mode of argumentation itself stand up to scrutiny? Bill Starr in his essay, *Can there be Moral Justifications for State Violence? The Case of America*, argues that it cannot. In the course of the article he claims that the prevalence of violence in American society both by the instruments of state and by ordinary citizens can be understood on the basis of the unique history of America. Having charted that history, he then explores whether any of the four main ethical theories, natural law, virtue ethics, deontology or utilitarianism, can offer justifications of American violence. Starr concludes that in fact a version of utilitarianism is often applied – if unreflectively – to justify violence perpetrated, for example, by police departments. According to this model of justification, violence committed against those engaged, or likely to be engaged, in crime is justified for the sake of the happiness of the greater number. According to Starr, such a justification is based on an implicit identification of community with the middle classes and as such does not succeed even on the basis of a utilitarian calculus.

Both the previous contributions dealt with justifications of violence, but the question remains what makes an act violent in the first place. Bernhard Waldenfels, in his essay *Violence as Violation*, conceptualises violence as the violation of another person or persons. He attempts to uncover the meaning of violence through oscillating between the perspective of the victim and that of the perpetrator. For the victim violence is a violation of a self-referential and integral being. On the side of the perpetrator there can be no question of clear distinctions between individual and collective responsibility:

individual actions are themselves structured by those collectivities to which such individuals belong. Methodologically this means that any discussion of violence must employ structural methods, without losing sight of the individual. Stressing the traumatic nature of violence for its victim, Waldenfels contends that there is a sort of singularity in violent acts which goes beyond every ordinary order of action and life. Violence irrupts within orders and this is not accidental. Violence is rationalised in the service of the existing order or orders, a mechanism, which Waldenfels compares to that of the *felix culpa*. Such a mechanism tends towards the justification and legitimation of the unjustifiable, a tendency to which no order can – in defence of its interest in self-preservation – pose a limit. But violence is not simply employed to defend an order, but lies at the origins of all orders, according to Waldenfels. This can be seen if the contingency of any specific order is taken seriously. All orders are contingent and hence their claims to justification rest on an ultimately unjustifiable and arbitrary exclusivity and selectivity, which implies a level of force and a consequent violation of individuals.

While Waldenfels places his emphasis on the suffering of violence on the part of the victim, the next contribution explores the responsibility for such suffering not so much on the part of the perpetrator as on the part of witnesses to acts of violence. Although violence is most often theorised in terms of acts, according to Vittorio Bufacchi in his *Violence by Omission,* there is a coherent way in which we can talk of violence in terms of omissions also. By omitting to aid someone when we are in a position to do so, we are doing violence against them according to Bufacchi. When omitting to act has the consequence of inflicting injury or suffering upon a person the omission qualifies as an act of violence. Nevertheless, the levels of moral responsibility vary and this depends on the possibility of alternative actions and the forseeability of the suffering resulting form omitting to act. While sometimes there is an equivalence of responsibility between acts of omission and acts of direct violence, this equivalence depends on the conditions of forseeability and alternativity, the latter meaning that it must both be *possible* and be *viable* to act in a different way Bufacchi argues that in certain cases these conditions do not apply and that we are less responsible and culpable for omitting to act in a certain way, than for acting violently, even if the consequences of both are equal.

Waldenfels' and Bufacchi's contributions both tried to extend our conception of what violence itself is, by linking it first with the phenomenon of social order, and secondly with the our everyday omissions. Both these approaches implicate *us* more deeply with violent actions than we might wish. Nonetheless, it seems clearly the case that the person who commits an act of violence is very centrally involved with it, and in the next contribution Eve Garrard discusses the moral psychology of the perpetrator. In her contribution *Violence, Cruelty, Evil* she analyses the relation between those three terms. Garrard understands evil to apply to the most terrible of deeds, those which seem to be more than simply wrong or bad. Violence is not always evil, although it figures in the paradigmatic cases of evil, such as the Holocaust, Rwanda, the Brady and Hinley murders. Nonetheless, Garrard argues that violence is not even a *prima facie* wrong. This is so because in certain cases, as in the overthrow of a tyrant, violence may in fact be good-making. In the light of this she turns to cruelty as a concept which may fill out the account of evil and one with which violence may be significantly connected. Unlike violence, cruelty is a 'thick' moral concept: cruel acts always involve unjustified suffering. In that sense cruelty is *prima facie* wrong, it is a wrong-making property of an act. In the case of evil acts the agent is impervious to the weightiest reasons against acting as he does. The cruel person is impervious to the reasons which the suffering he is causing give for him to desist. Cruelty may not always be violent, but it has a strong tendency to be so. In this sense, she concludes, it is the cruelty involved in certain acts of violence which tend to make them evil.

However it is to be conceptualised, all the contributions to this volume share an understanding of violence as that which can best be understood as constitutive of human relations rather than as aberrant behaviour. This entails that the claim to a violence-free position is itself denial of responsibility for violence, a responsibility which goes beyond the more obvious perpetrators of violent acts. Questions of freedom and responsibility in relation to violence must be placed in such a context if unthinking responses to it are to be avoided. It is to this theme that Burkhard Liebsch devotes his contribution, *Freedom versus Responsibility? Between Ethical Indifference and Ethical Violence.* He begins by arguing that violence begins with the exclusion of others and indifference towards them. Such phenomena provoke the question of responsibility. The concept of responsibility is however one which comes into conflict with a notion, deeply rooted in the western tradition of political and ethical thinking, that of 'radical freedom.' According to such a view, freedom is essentially unrelated to responsibility, rather responsibility – if it is at all – is rooted in freedom. Arguing against such a notion, Liebsch maintains that conceptions of 'negative freedom' make sense only within relations of embeddedness with others in which we learn the meaning of freedom in responding (or failing to respond) to them. Drawing on the work of Emmanuel Levinas, he discusses the complexities of such relations with others arguing against both Hobbesian and Neo-Aristotelian accounts. Denying the cogency of a Hobbesian ethical indifference, Liebsch shows that nonetheless a return to a pre-modern communitarian universe is impossible. It is rather the case that even in a Hobbesian universe the alterity of the other cannot be obliterated and that alterity calls me to responsibility. Following Levinas, Liebsch argues that freedom begins with such responsiveness to the other. But he goes on to show that Levinas's notion of responsibility contains within it its own sources of violence in the form of an excessive, indeed unlimited, responsibility for the other.

This ambiguity in the Levinasian approach to violence is a core concern of Diane Enns in her contribution, *At the Limit: Violence, Belonging, and Self-Determination.* Drawing on the autobiographical accounts by Susan Brison (of sexual assault and attempted murder) and Jean Améry (survivor of Auschwitz) and the theoretical writings of Levinas, Foucault, Butler and especially Agamben, Enns proposes two apparently contradictory concepts of violence: on the one hand, a violence of totalisation, identifying, naming, delineating borders, and on the other hand violence as shattering, fragmenting, dehumanising, un-naming. In this context she problematises the notion of belonging. She details Brison's account in which as a result of suffering violence she feels displaced and alienated from the world. This feeling discloses a fundamental contingency in one's belonging to the world and in consequence the necessity of carrying on without the illusion of certainty and predictability. Enns brings this account into dialogue with Agamben's attempt to build political philosophy from the figure of the refugee. Recovery in this context becomes a non-teleological process, which points to the possibility of a community without belonging in the sense of conditions of belonging such as borders, strict identities and whole narratives. In effect she is proposing a new understanding of belonging, one not so much free of violence as taking seriously the lessons violence teaches us.

In her conclusion Enns distinguishes between those of us who have not been the victims of traumatic violence and those who have. Talia Bettcher's contribution, *Appearance, Reality, and Gender Deception: Reflections on Transphobic Violence and the Politics of Pretense,* discusses the phenomenon of violence against transgendered people. Her concern is specifically with people who, having male or female sexual organs, identify themselves, dress and act as the opposite gender. The issue she addresses here is that of deception as a justification of violence: if a person appears as a woman although 'really' a man, then violence against that person may seem at least understandable, if not justifiable. Bettcher demonstrates that, the charge of deception notwithstanding, transgendered people are in the double bind of either appearing as being engaged in pretence or seeming to deceive. This amounts to a basic denial of authenticity to transgendered people. In the course of a thoughtful discussion of the binary model of gender she concludes that even if we recognise the social constructedness of gender, we must recognise too that transgendered people are systematically constructed as frauds. For this reason the calls to authenticity and the correlative call to visibility are deeply problematic for transgendered people and may indeed add to the possibility of violence against them.

Questions of authenticity and of responsibility are discussed in a different context in Felix Ó Murchadha's contribution *On Provocation: Violence as Response.* Ó Murchadha begins by charting the development in legal history of the defence of provocation showing how it is mainly an excusatory plea, with however certain implicit justificatory elements. He explores the structure of motivation implicit in provocation and argues that violence is a response to provocation

for which the one provoked is in part responsible – in the sense that
to be provoked by something is to be that type of person for whom
that thing is provocative. Responsibility in this sense is understood to
refer in part at least to that in a person which cannot, or indeed ought
not, be changed. Certain things ought to provoke a person, but that
person is still responsible for being provoked and as such contributes
to the provocation. To explore this idea Ó Murchadha engages in an
extended phenomenology of anger. Anger he understands as a perception of being wrongly injured. Anger contains a certain reflective
moment – on the wrongness of the injury – and is for that reason
neither an essentially irrational response, nor one which always
dissipates with time, both of which are assumed in the standard legal
understanding of the plea of provocation. Anger aims not at the injury
itself, but at the – culpable – source of the injury and refers the self
back to its own vulnerability as the angered party. It is a violent
response, which might then be articulated in retaliatory acts of
violence. The source of violence as response to provocation is a
person's own vulnerability to the other.

This collection covers some major themes in relation to the
question of violence. It does so from a variety of perspectives, but
with a constant concern to understand violence as that which both
calls forth and silences discourse, as that which is constitutive of
human relations and yet threatens to destroy them. The richness of the
contributions to this volume make it necessary to reflect on the diversity of approaches, arguments and conclusions in a relatively open-
ended manner. This is the task which the editor seeks to fulfil in the
Afterword. The Afterword begins with an extended discussion of
Honderich's article and in doing so bring to the fore as central themes
those of innocence and vulnerability in the issues of justification and
of victimhood. It then brings the different contributions into dialogue
in relation to these themes. To the extent to which violence imbues
human relations, the claim to total innocence seems questionable; in
the same way vulnerability to violence is a basic human condition. All
the contributions to this volume argue in different ways for gradations
of innocence or more correctly gradations of *lack* of innocence. In this
sense pure victims, pure perpetrators or pure witnesses are rare. The
Afterword shows that the contributors to this volume present an

understanding of violence as rooted in a vulnerability which is inherent in human interdependence. Practically, this means that strategies for combating violence will remain ineffective so long as its embeddedness in the everyday reality of what we do and who we are is not acknowledged from the outset.

This volume originated in a series of lectures organised by the Philosophy Department, National University of Ireland, Galway in the second semester of the academic year 2001–02. Of the seven papers which made up that series five are published here along with an additional four papers, which have been collected with the aim of offering some further perspectives on the key themes of the series. The volume reflects accurately the variety of approaches and yet the constancy of key themes of the original lecture series. It took place less than six months after September 11th and during the war in Afghanistan. Undoubtedly within sight of the building in which it took place overlooking the river Corrib, which flows gently past the University, countless acts of violence, countless cases of violations, and perhaps a few dozen violent events took place. There is a certain presumption in discussing violence in relative isolation and insulation from its worse excesses. Yet, mindful of that presumption, hesitant to claim any great discoveries, or any final truths, the contributors to this volume have set their intellectual nets far and have captured more than one insight to further the discussion of one of the few truly universal human phenomena.

Endnotes

1   As for example Karl Popper does in 'Utopia and Violence', *Conjectures and Refutations: the growth of scientific knowledge* (London: Routledge, 1989), pp. 355–363.
2   As arguably Sartre does in his Preface to Frantz Fanon's *The Wretched of the Earth* (London: Penguin, 1967), pp. 7–26.

3   The notion of imaginative variation is taken from Edmund Husserl. Cf. Husserl:
     Experience and Judgement, (Evanston: Northwestern University Press, 1973),
     pp. 193f.
4   This distinction between points of view on violence is taken from the work of
     the sociologist David Riches. Cf. his 'The Phenomenon of Violence', in Riches,
     D. (ed.): *The Anthropology of Violence,* (Oxford: Blackwell 1986), pp. 1–27. I
     am employing it for more philosophical ends than he had in mind however.
5   Cf. Derrida, J.: 'The Force of Law', in Cornell, D. (ed.): *Deconstruction and the
     Possibility of Justice* (London: Routledge, 1992), pp. 3–60.
6   Sorel, G.: *Reflections on Violence,* edited by J. Jennings (Cambridge: Cam-
     bridge University Press, 1994)
7   One could refer to any number of Habermas' texts for this, but as a
     representative text cf. Habermas, J.: *Between facts and norms: contributions to
     a discourse theory of law and democracy,* translated by William Rehg
     (Cambridge: Polity Press, 1996).
8   A criticism made by E. Balibar. Cf. his *We, the people of Europe?* (Princeton:
     Princeton University Press, 2004), p. 131.
9   Many theorists and philosophers reject the coherency of this notion. Cf. Coady:
     'Violence' in Craig, E. (ed.): *The Routledge Encyclopaedia of Philosophy* vol. 9
     (London: Routledge, 1998), pp. 615f.
10   Galtung, J.: 'Violence, Peace and Peace Research', *The Journal of Peace
     Research* 6.2, 1969, pp. 167–191.
11   Bourdieu, P.: *Outline of a Theory of Practice,* translated by Richard Nice
     (Cambridge: Cambridge University Press, 1995), p. 191.
12   Cf. Levinas, E.: *Totality and Infinity,* translated by A. Lingis (Pittsburg:
     Duquesne University Press, 1969), passim, esp. pp. 21–25; cf. for a critique
     Derrida, J.: 'Violence and Metaphysics' in *Writing and Difference* (Chicago:
     Chicago University Press, 1978), pp. 79–153.
13   Cf. After, D.: 'Political Violence in Analytic Perspective' in *The Legitimation
     of Violence,* p. 4: 'victims become roles rather than persons'.
14   Cf. Kappeler, S.: *The Will to Violence,* p. 1: 'Violence is a ubiquitous reality in
     our society.'
15   Cf. Arendt, H.: *On Violence* (London: Penguin, 1970).
16   Cf. Riches, D., op. cit., pp. 11f.

Ted Honderich

Terrorism for Humanity

1. Some Moral Propositions

Our failing to save the lives of Africans now living, 20 million in one
sample, is wrong. Israel's taking Palestine from its people is wrong, as
is our support of this new Zionism. Suicide-bombings by the Palestinians are right. 9/11 was wrong. The war on Iraq was wrong, unlike
other wars that did not happen because we overlooked reasons for
them. It is wrong for new Zionists in and around the American government to conceal their divided loyalties, not to declare an interest
that is other than American. African terrorism against our rich
countries would be right if it had a reasonable hope of success. In our
rich countries, those do wrong who bring it about, by way of the
media they own, that many people out of ignorance believe what is
wrong is right.[1]

These are some particular moral propositions that many people,
probably a majority of humans who are half-informed or better, now
find it difficult to deny. My purpose in what follows here is to look
mainly at some philosophical issues that come up with a more general
proposition than the one about Palestinian suicide-bombing. This has
to do with what has the name of being *terrorism for humanity*.

You may ask, given my purpose, why propositions about more
than terrorism have been mentioned.

It is the practice of courts of law not to let the jury know of the
accused's previous offences, if any. His record, however, *is* read out if
he is found guilty of the charge in hand. Among the good reasons is
one that may be overlooked. It is that previous offences give confidence in the particular judgement of guilt that has been made on him
by the jury. More obvious is the reason that previous offences give

further basis and confidence with respect to the sentence to be passed by the judge.

No doubt the previous offences should be kept from the jury while they are deliberating on the present charge. But is absurd to say that these past offences have nothing to do with the question of whether he has committed the offence with which he is now charged, and in particular his culpability in it, say his degree and kind of intentionality. Of course they do. A man previously convicted of five rapes is very much more likely to have committed the one now being considered.

It is not only terrorists who are accused in our world. We are too. You have only to get on an airplane to another sort of country to be reminded of it forcibly, in more ways than one. And the accusation, for the sort of reason just noticed with the court of law, has more that is relevant to it than just the charge in hand against us, say complicity in the wrong done for decades and still being done to the Palestinians.

Do you allow this different kind of guilt by association is part of the natural fact and practice of morality, but strictly speaking a mistake, a kind of human weakness or failure? How is that? Records about X change probability judgements about Y, if X and Y are instances of some Z. And probabilities about Y alter moral judgements about Y. To ignore this is to lose touch with the reality of moral judgement. You can see that some complicity in a wrong, or a war, is an instance of a pattern of excessive self-interest and delusion. It is not something with special or unprecedented features, maybe historical, maybe a war on a monster, to which a lesser or excusing response is in order.

It is also to forget our own practice. It is to forget that we ourselves do most certainly include the previous records of terrorists in judging their last wrongs. We also include their whole cultures, and in particular their religion.

Do you still wonder if it is already a mistake, before we get around to the guilt by association, to attend to something other than terrorism, to attend to charges against us rather than charges against terrorists? We disagree there. Even if there were *no* connection between any of our guilt and any of theirs, it would be natural enough and no mistake to think about the two things together. Asking a moral question about *X* can indeed get you thinking about the morality of *Y*, get you thinking about the whole of life rather than a part, particularly when *X* is taken as a kind of global event.

To disregard our own records, furthermore, even if there were *no* connection between them and terrorism, would actually be mistaken. A comparative viewpoint must enter into thinking about any such issue as terrorism, and terrorism for humanity in particular. Morality does indeed have what can be called *data* in it, and general truth, and certainly consistency. But it is a matter of more than reports and consistency tests. It is a matter of judgement, and such judgement cannot be decently made in isolation or self-deception. You will get a part wrong if you don't know about the whole. You will feel differently about the dirtiness of killings by others if you remember that you have had to wash your own hands regularly, and notice that there is a need to do so right now. A proper reaction of the guilty to the guilty plays some part in morality.

That is not all. It is not just that we stand accused ourselves of particular offences to which more offences are relevant, and that pieces of moral and political philosophy do indeed have chosen subjects, sometimes with a natural unity, and that judgements need to keep the judges themselves in mind. That is not all. It is only persons of certain committed minorities who can suppose for a minute, or pretend to suppose, that there is no connection between any terrorism and charges against us. There must be the possibility, to say no more than this, that some of what we do, say with respect to Palestine, enters into a justification for some terrorism. Blair, the leading politician of my country, says otherwise, but that incidental proof of the proposition is not needed.

2. Killing Innocents,
and the Problem of an Impulse About It

Contemplate two acts of killing. The first is by a young Palestinian suicide-bomber of an Israeli in Israel, a passer-by. The second killing, by a crew-member of an Israeli helicopter gunship, is by rocket. Those who die, in Palestine, are a terrorist leader of the Islamic Resistance Movement – Hamas – and a Palestinian passer-by. You may recoil from such examples, maybe humanly. But you cannot simply recoil and also do well in thinking and feeling about our subject matter. It plainly calls for more rather than less engagement. Also a wide human sensitivity rather than a narrow one.

The victim of the suicide-bomber and the second victim of the crew-member in the gunship, two passers-by, are non-combatants, civilians, and, as at least their own people say, innocents. If they are children they *are* innocents, even if they are or have been throwing stones. We might think about trying to improve on these categories a little, by replacing them with the categories of non-combatants, un-engaged combatants, half-innocents, clear innocents, and civilians.

Non-combatants are not armed or otherwise personally life-threatening at the time of their deaths, and are not in the army or police or any other life-threatening organisation, say a terrorist one. We could decide to add that they are not officers of state or certain organisations either.

Unengaged combatants are not armed or personally life-threatening at the time, but are in the army or other life-threatening organisation. Maybe they make bombs or maintain helicopters. We could add that they may be officers of state, overwhelmingly more responsible for wrongs than engaged combatants.

Half-Innocents are not armed or otherwise personally life-threatening at the time of their deaths, and not in the army or the like. These non-combatants and unengaged combatants, however, are by choice or consent benefiting or profiting from wrongful killings by their state or their people. They are as well-named as being *half-guilty*.

They may be settlers on the land of those they are not personally threatening.

Clear innocents are not life-threatening at the time, not in the army or the like, and are not by choice or consent benefiting or profiting from wrongful killings by their state or their people.

Civilians, for what this fifth category is worth, may be non-combatants, half-innocents, or clear innocents. They may be none of these, but rather combatants and not half-innocents or clear innocents.

Very clearly these five categories need work in order to be made more determinate, particularly in connection with choice and consent. If they can be improved, they may still not be of great use, since we are likely to be unable to say who was or is in what category at the time of a conflict.

Since the beginning of the current *al-Aqsa* intifada in Palestine in September 2000, a total of about 2,100 Palestinians, of a population of about 3.4 million, have been killed. A total of about 700 Israelis, of a population of about 6 million, have been killed.

Of the 2,100 Palestinians killed, about 1,650 are said to have been 'innocent civilians' by a good Palestinian source.[2] About 100 were children under 12.[3]

Of the 700 Israelis killed, about 500 are said by a good Israeli source to have been 'civilians'.[4] How many of the 500 were also non-combatants etc. is left open. An exact number for the very many fewer Israeli children killed is not readily available.

The figures are not merely dwarfed, but are made trivial or insignificant numerically, when compared to numbers of deaths, in the very many millions, owed to genocides and politicides carried out by states and governments.[5] In particular, the deaths owed to the Palestinians, these deaths owed to non-state or non-governmental action, are barely anything numerically to the numbers of deaths in state or governmental genocides and politicides. The deaths owed to Palestinians are yet fewer, relatively speaking, when compared to state or governmental killings in war generally as well as genocides and politicides.[6]

Do these comparisons matter? They do not matter at all to the Israeli family whose daughter and sister is killed by a bomb. This brings into focus a reason why the comparisons cannot matter to us in these reflections either. There is a fundamental moral or human sense in which a death by killing does not become of less consequence when it is one of few or many such deaths. With a death, a world goes out of existence. This remains true despite the fact that to place the Palestinian killings in the wide context of genocide and so on may give pause to one's feeling, as in the case of the Israeli killings. Despite that pause, we cannot possibly put our questions aside.

One question is whether it is possible to judge Palestinian and Israeli killings by staying at the level of the five categories – non-combatants and so on, however improved. One way of trying to do so is by announcing, as a properly-respected philosopher of peace of my acquaintance does, that killing innocent people is wrong.[7] In his view, as it seems, that is all there is to say. A human impulse, certainly.

Would he persist in this if asked for the rationale of killing non-innocents in his sense rather than innocents? Could he say that his announcement is of a moral truth that needs no rationale? Well, there is no avoiding the usual question about a terrible choice between killing one or a few innocents or killing many innocents. Does what we choose not matter? There is no avoiding a question, either, about the choice between killing a few innocents and allowing another horror, say the starving to death of many thousands of innocents, or a million of them.

If these are distasteful and conceivably dangerous questions, they are necessary ones. To his credit, I doubt too that the philosopher of peace would say, in effect and obscurely, that he cannot be faced with such choices, and thus the need for a rationale, because he would not be responsible for the choice-situations – or just that his own life's inner purpose precludes his doing any killing with his own hand.[8]

The fact of the matter seems to be that we cannot seriously even try to stay only at the level gestured at. There must be a reason for embracing the simplicity of the equivalence of very diverse and differently consequential killings of innocents. There must be a reason for the supposed non-comparability of killings of innocents and the other horrors.

Some reason is necessary for going against the distinctions written into the whole course of civilisation, including its religion. We ourselves have defended immense numbers of killings of innocents –

in the naval blockade of Germany in World War One, in the terror bombing of Germany and the destruction of Hiroshima in World War Two.[9]

Certainly, despite a common utterance to the contrary, *some* killing of innocents does not lead to more of it. Even if it does, to repeat the question, are there no circumstances, no human hells, that rightly call it up? Would a world without killing, no matter what else it contained, be better than any other world? No society has ever thought so.

Surely we cannot condemn Israel just on the ground of its killing of innocents, or on the ground that it is killing more innocents than the Palestinians. Further moral thinking is unavoidable.

3.   The Morality of Humanity

It is no easy thing to see what ordinary morality comes to in all of its nature. It is easier to see what should be in an adequate morality – a philosophical morality or the like. Such a morality is a proposal or recommendation for a possible or an actual world. An adequate morality must contain a single principle or summation or idea, or can have one put on it, and also secondary proposals or recommendations of parts or sides of life, say politics or business. It very likely needs to have in it moral data or moral touchstones, and also a preferred clarification of our shared moral concepts and their relations, say those of right actions, morality, responsibility, and decent persons. Such a morality must contain, finally, particular moral propositions like the eight with which we began.

Separate from all these elements will be reasons for them, propositions of fact, larger and smaller, general and particular, of various kinds. These are as essential to the enterprise. No adequate morality is unreasoned. There will be propositions of fact at every level of the enterprise.

It is not being assumed, of course, that the more particular parts of adequate moralities are *deductions* from the more general. The generalisation or summary is a way of getting the whole thing in view, and a particular kind of check on other elements, as they are on it. This picture of adequate or reflective moralities, I take it, covers those of Aristotle, Aquinas, Kant, Bentham, Nietzsche, Marx, and Rawls.[10]

It also covers the morality of humanity – which we need to get back in mind. It rests on our human nature and mainly on our desires for the great goods, six according to one classification and variously interdependent. The goods, under one description, are a decent length of life, say 78 or 79 years rather than 37, bodily or physical well-being, freedom and power, respect and self-respect, goods of closer and wider relationship, and such goods of culture as knowledge.

That brief list is so unenlightening as to the human importance of the things in question as to be a parody. It is as unenlightening to gesture by implication at lives *deprived* of the great goods, lives very different from those of well-being and perhaps satiety, sufferings of great evils, lives of wretchedness and other distress.

Morality of humanity also rests on other truths. A second, more or less implicit in the first, is that humans, or wonderfully more than enough for the purposes of argument, are alike in another way.[11] Consider yourself, and a certain judgement you will make. Consider a conceivable conflict between (1) you or your family escaping from wretchedness and (2) a further improvement for me or my family in my or our existing well-being, perhaps my having more of the great goods to the point of satiety. You will certainly judge there is greater reason for (1) the help for you or your family. You know that now. There is reason for the help, you will judge, that is greater than any reason offered by me for my self-indulgence.

Say my reason of private property, or a morality of relationship and non-relationship, or a supposed categorical imperative about treating people as ends as well as means, or some theory about the need to help the wretched *in general*, as distinct from you in particular, maybe the trickle-down theory in political economics.

You will not be moved either by an invocation of any political morality or moral politics, say liberalism in its obscurity, or of course conservatism, or indeed socialism if it can be made use of in this unlikely cause, or of course the amorality of national self-interest, what is called political realism. Nor will you take your or your family's wretchedness to be a lesser reason than any so-called *ethical* as against merely *moral* reason of mine for self-indulgence, say my integrity, or my life-project, or a kind of personal necessity, or an absence of responsibility for what I can in fact prevent, let alone my moral luck and yours.[12]

Nor is this truth of human nature about distress and indulgence only a matter of contemplated or imagined circumstances. There are almost certainly analogues of it in actual conflicts in your own lived life. Consider life-threatening situations. You do not give more weight to the ambulance-man's not caring enough because he is badly-paid than you give to your need to get to the hospital. You do not put the understandable self-concern of unrespected teachers ahead of your child's being saved from ignorance.

A third truth, never successfully denied except in practice, is that reasons are general. For you to be committed to the rescue of yourself or your family, in a contemplated or an actual circumstance, is for you to be committed to actual rescues in actual circumstances around us, say African and Palestinian circumstances. This is a rationality that cannot be avoided, whatever response of obfuscation is made to it.

Finally, there is the relevant truth of human nature that we have some dispositions of character that support this latter rationality. To act on it is to do what is also sympathetic, human, generous, and comes out of fellow-feeling. Those are not terms that describe nothing in us. If there are also clear wants of humanity in our natures, so demonstrated by conventional morality, there *are* the facts of sympathy and the like. Philosophical moralities that recommend themselves as *undemanding*, as realistic in that way, overlook or understate these human facts. To my mind, they must be under suspicion, along with the political tradition of conservatism, of wanting to reduce these facts in the aid of personal comfortableness.[13]

The morality of humanity owed to these four truths, to state its summative principle quickly, is that we must take actually rational steps, which is to say effective and economical ones, to get people out of defined lives of wretchedness and other deprivation. This is what it comes to. It is different from all other moralities and utterances in which the given truths of argument can be taken to issue, including the passionless vacuity of the Golden Rule.

The main rational steps can be put into a few policies. These have to do with rescuing people from bad lives by means that do not affect the well-being of the better-off, with rescuing them by means that do affect that well-being, with reducing inequality-demands, and with violence – the latter policy allowing for less exception than other policies against violence. The grounds of the morality of humanity are clear and simple. As against liberalism, say, it is a flood of light. As against morality of relationship, it has not merely consistency but has the consistency of humanity, the consistency that matters more than any other.

Of the rest of what might be remarked here about the morality of humanity, let me say only that it is more engaged in the world than alternative philosophical moralities, and by its nature not embarrassed to be so. For good reasons, it is more political. I take it to be more committed to factual truth than alternatives are. It thus speaks not only of the *violation* of Palestine by the Israelis, but also of Palestinian *terrorism*, of killing that rightly has that name. It does so despite this killing's also being *resistance, resistance to ethnic cleansing, self-defence*, a *liberation struggle*, an *uprising*, which of course it also is, quite as much.

As you will have anticipated, I take the morality of humanity to issue, of course by way of various additional propositions of fact, some of them historical, in the particular moral propositions about the 20 million Africans, Palestinian terrorism, and so on. Or rather, because moralities can differ fundamentally in more than what can be called bare propositional content, and can have their distinctive nature in their kind of commitment, affirmation, mildness, resignation or pretence, it is better to say something else. It is better to convey the principle of humanity's resistance to a *consensus of civility*. It is better to say this morality issues, for present purposes, in roughly the following group of particular moral propositions.

Letting 20 million fellow human beings die makes the American way of life, say, into an evil giving rise to an evil. The Israelis have violated not only principle or law but another people and their homeland. The Palestinians do indeed have a moral right to their terrorism, and would have even if it were not a response to state terrorism – to say they have a moral right is to say that their terrorism has the support of a moral principle of force, indeed the moral principle more capable than any other of justifying actions. 9/11 was hideous and monstrous in its moral irrationality. Nothing else can be said of it. The invasion and occupation of Iraq, if conceivably rational in terms of a certain end, was another attack on humanity. Bush and Blair are moral criminals, whatever their capability of realising it. They would be criminals in international law if that thing was what all victors and some lawyers pretend it to be. Blair is a liar, a liar with ends about which he is confused himself and which he seeks to obscure. Such information-providers as Murdoch who make for or add to the stupidity of a society have a guilt as awful as their self-deception.

4.   Whether some terrorism is for humanity

There are more things to be said of how the morality of humanity can issue in or contain, in particular, a support for the kind of terrorism of which the Palestinian is an instance.

Terrorism for humanity is terrorism with the aim of the principle of humanity. That is the aim of getting people, including whole peoples, out of lives of wretchedness and other deprivation, bad lives, lives of great evils. Do you think there is room for a certain question? Do you think there is room for the question of whether the killings by the Israeli in the helicopter-gunship, rather than the killing by the Palestinian suicide-bomber, is terrorism for humanity?

It would be reassuring if the question of whether some terrorism has the end of humanity were always open to a confident answer. That is not so. There is often difficulty about deciding if a line of action, terrorism or whatever else, has, as we can quickly say, the end of humanity.

The matter comes into view by way of the invasion of Iraq. It was not in my view terrorism, given its large scale, despite being against what there is of international law and therefore akin to terror-ism reasonably defined.[14] Was this war aimed at saving people from bad lives owed to a dictator? Was it a war for humanity? Americans were told by their politicians that something like this was its justifying aim. The British, differently, a little more affected by international law, had to be told by their principal politician that the justifying aim of the war was not bringing down Saddam but rather disarming Iraq of weapons of mass destruction that existed as an immediate threat against us.

Did the war in fact have the end of humanity? The best sort of answer, perhaps, consists in pointing out that the war, like many such endeavours, plainly had a considerable number of aims.

One was trying to deter terrorism, including terrorism for humanity, by a demonstration of power against a suitable country. For this aim it was not essential that Iraq itself had carried out 9/11, or even contributed to it in any material way whatever – although that belief by half or even two-thirds of the American people was useful, and largely owed to its politicians and other leaders. It was not necessary to the anti-terrorist aim that Iraq had done anything more than half the world does with respect to terrorism for humanity – *understand* it, as some say.

The war aims also included control of oil supplies, certainly the removal of a possible defender of the Palestinians, the removal of an otherwise anti-American leader of great audacity, wider American interests and strategies, and the removal of one of the world's ruthless and anti-American dictators. These aims were not greatly less signifi-cant than the aim of deterring terrorism. There was also something less obvious. This was an ideological aim, the assertion of ideology as an end in itself, killing as assertion.

This needs to be distinguished from aims having to do with the satisfying effects of imposing an ideology, some of them just re-marked on, including profits to American corporations. Killing as assertion is announcing what is right in such a way as to get attention, having the reassurance of being heard. It is also aimed at the comfort of having fewer moral critics in the world, fewer moral judges, or anyway quieter ones. It is related to what is known as the justification of punishment in terms of communication or expression, different from deterrence or other prevention.[15] Other forms of such self-expression, without the killing, are common enough.

The war on Iraq also had the aim of putting in place new international deferences and expectations, no doubt under the name of international law, and of course a significant aim having to do with American domestic politics. Not for the first time, people were killed in anticipation of an American president's election campaign. There was also, on the part of an English prime minister, a lawyer-politician's view of England's material self-interest in maintaining an alliance, and his own careerism.[16]

If you now ask again what counts as terrorism for humanity, one short answer is that it is terrorism whose aim is more clearly the rescue of people from bad lives than was our war against Iraq. The war against Iraq serves as an excellent ostensive definition of what terrorism for humanity is not.

We get a further answer to our question by returning to Palestine. The state of Israel ought of course to have been constructed out of a part of Germany after the genocide of the Jews. But that it had to be established somewhere is a kind of moral datum, certainly in accord with the principle of humanity. So too, to my mind, given what seemed to be the necessity and the particular possibilities at the time, was it right that Israel was set up where it was, partly by way of Zionist terrorism for humanity, and despite its being an historic injustice to another people.

That is consistent with the fact of the violation of Palestine by the new Zionism of Israel since 1967. This is indeed an offence of moral viciousness. It is an offence of both new Zionists and also those who travel with them, in Israel and the United States above all. It has the disdain of all Jews who are within that current of compassion in Jewishness, so free from legalism and divine revelation, clear and strong in its intellectual and other contribution to the struggle for humanity. This is the current of compassion of the Jewish Left, to be honoured without reservation.

That the great goods have been wrongly denied to the Palestinians is made clear not by political history, let alone casuistry about who did what when, but rather by the figures for Arab and Jewish populations in Palestine since about 1876.[17] There is only room for merely partisan dispute as to the proposition that one people took over the land of another.

To speak more generally of the great good of a people that is their freedom and power in their homeland, its value has been better demonstrated historically than any other good. That it is one of few things that can be said to have formed our human history is a proof of this desire and the human worth of its satisfaction. It would be childish to try to disdain the worth of what our nature gives this proof.

The elucidation and explanation of the pain and suffering of its denial must include its being necessary to other great goods, respect and self-respect above all. It is no surprise that Palestinians can now be made the objects by some Jews of a racism of which Jews themselves have had unique experience. Things of the same sort can be said of the necessity of freedom and power to other great goods.

It is my own view, importantly as a result of these facts, that the terrorism of the Palestinians is a paradigm case of terrorism for humanity, terrorism with the aim of humanity. The most salient of these facts is the established necessity of this terrorism, the clear absence of *any* alternative policy whatever for dealing with rapacity. The terrorism of the Palestinians is their only effective and economical means of self-defence, of liberating themselves, of resisting degradation. It is to me ludicrous to contemplate Israeli state terrorism, whatever else it may be called, has the end of humanity.

But that this or any other terrorism is terrorism for humanity is not enough to make it right. The thought that all terrorism with the aim in question is right would be absurd, as absurd as the thought, sometimes inexplicitly and viciously relied on, that more or less any policy or action of a democracy is right. The proposal, rather, is that the only terrorism with the *possibility* of justification is terrorism for humanity, as the only war with such a possibility is war for humanity.

5.   Innocents, Our Fundamental Moral Concepts, Double Effect

It was maintained earlier about the two killings in Palestine and Israel that we cannot think about them only at a certain level, the level of a simple absolute about the kind of action in question, killing innocent people somehow defined. That is not to say that the only reflection that is needed is well above that level, at the level of such a general moral principle as that of humanity. Of course there is need for further thinking on killing the somehow innocent, and of how to approach it. To do so is of course not to join those spokesmen of democracy on television whose concern for the innocent is only for their innocent, not for the innocent killed by their democracy. This may actually be merely a concern for the innocent, their own innocent, in the enterprise of taking more land or keeping more land already taken.

Is it the case, in particular, that further thinking on terrorism for humanity in connection with innocents can establish that although terrorism for humanity has a unique possibility of being right, it nonetheless is not right, or that some instance of it, say Palestinian terrorism, is not right? That there is a disproof of its rightness?

Our fundamental moral concept is that of *the right thing* to do or bring about – the right action, policy, kind of life, institution, society. The right action or the like is a matter of rationally anticipated consequences. It is at least in large part a matter of the six great goods – a decent time to live, bodily well-being rather than pain, freedom rather than subjection and impotence, respect in place of disdain and contempt, connection with others rather than isolation from them, knowledge and the preservation of the history of one's people.

To this concept of right action we add that of a person who gets *moral credit* for a particular action or the like, someone approved of for his or her moral responsibility for it. This is importantly a matter of his or her intentions. Thirdly, we tend to distinguish a person's *moral standing* over time, maybe a lifetime. Perhaps this is the result of both rightness in actions and moral credit for them.

That right actions are fundamental, these being a matter of certain consequences of actions, is in a way provable, in the following way.

A certain world is conceivable. It has in it only persons who persistently or even consistently get moral credit, at bottom for good intentions and effort. As a result, their standing over time is high. But they are very ignorant and unlucky, and produce a world of misery. Another conceivable world has in it persons who get less moral credit and are of lesser standing – a matter, let us say, of their mixed intentions. For whatever reason, however, their world is not one of misery but of well-being. Maybe almost all people in it have all of the great goods.

Does anyone, save an occasional moral philosopher with another agenda, hesitate when asked which world it would be right to bring into existence? An intention, after all, is not a spiritual mystery, a funny reality that is a source of obscure rightness. It is a mental event including desire and belief that both represents or pictures and gives rise to an action then or later, which mental event gets the person credit or not. Does anyone say it would be right to bring into existence a world filled with the agony of torture as against the good things of which we know, in order to have the world with better intentions in it?

That is not to say that moral credit and moral standing are irrelevant or unimportant. We want persons of credit and standing because they are more likely than others to do the right thing. Very differently, it may be that we need the many conceptions of credit and standing in order to have an adequate view of precisely the rightness of actions – effects are typically characterised by likely causes, or indeed seen by way of them. But, as good as indisputably, these are but qualifications or elaborations of the truth that our fundamental concern is with how the world is in so far as we can affect it, not with certain personal antecedents valued for themselves.

This ordinary moral thinking, hardly at the level of moral philosophy, is typically forgotten or passed over in a salient condemnation of some killings of somehow innocent people. I have in mind such as the killings, by the Israeli crew-member in the helicopter gunship, of the passer-by as distinct from the Hamas terrorist leader. This is contrasted, in terms of intention, with the Palestinian suicide-bomber's killing of an Israeli passer-by. The first killing is said to be right, the second wrong.

It is said the killer in the helicopter in some sense does not *intend* the death of the innocent passer-by, but only that of the Hamas leader, while the suicide-bomber *does* in this sense intend the death of the innocent Israeli. Of the two effects of his firing the rocket, the killer in the helicopter intended only one. There is therefore a difference in the two acts, the first being right and the second wrong. This is the doctrine of double effect.

It is easily and rightly objected that the intention ordinarily conceived of the man in the gunship represents both the death of the Hamas leader and another probable death or deaths. For a start, we need to take him to be aware of the incidence of deaths of more or less innocent Palestinians – perhaps, as indicated earlier, that there have been about three times as many deaths of more or less innocent Palestinians as against more or less innocent Israelis.

The probable death is of course a foreseen consequence. *Foreseen probable consequences*, as against foreseen absolutely certain consequences, are not rare or unusual, let alone suspect. They are by far the most common sort of foreseen consequences, the ones we are mainly concerned with in life, the ones we generally act on. The probabilities may be high. An innocent death owed to a rocket fired into a busy street is about as probable as the consequence of playing Russian roulette with someone else's head.

Therefore, in terms of intention as conceived in the rest of adequate morality, and presumably in every legal system in the world, the killer in the gunship *did* intend more than the death of the Hamas leader. He knowingly did and can be held to account for more than that – the death of the passer-by. So too, incidentally, does he add to the proven criminality against humanity of Sharon, the leader of his country.

Of course it can be maintained that there is a different sense in which the helicopter crew-member did *not* intend the death of the passer-by, also a clear one. *If* he could have killed the Hamas leader without killing a passer-by, we are to understand, he would have done this. But of course it is false that the suicide-bomber does not have such an intention. It must be taken as just as true of the suicide-bomber that *if* she could have acted effectively to try to liberate her people without killing a kind of innocent, she would have done this. The distinction, if different in detail from the other case, is as real and relevant.

No one can quarrel with this kind of refutation of the casuistic doctrine of double effect, so often put to such unspeakable use by ignoring facts of identical intentions. My aim is to add something to the refutation.

In brief, what is to be added is that while there are uses of our conceptions of moral credit and moral worth, mentioned above, there are also misuses of them. It is a misuse of the conception of moral credit to suppose that one can really begin to justify as right the action of the crewman in the helicopter by assigning to him the credit that if he could kill the one person without killing the other, he would do so. This is not our ordinary morality, but rather a self-serving misconception of it. It is not as if a double effect argument may fail because of its intrinsic weakness or indeed chicanery, but that it *begins* from a mistake.

Even if it were the case that the crewman lacked an intention had by the suicide-bomber, it does not at all follow that he would have been doing right, and that the suicide-bomber was doing wrong. There are no such connections. For example, there is no connection between having an intention that represents or pictures an *unidentified* human being rather than a *seen and nearby* person and the action's being right. Hosts of ordinary examples establish the contrary. And of course there is no significant general difference in intention.

There *is* reason to reflect at more than one level about particular questions, one about innocents, that face any morality and are answered by particular moral propositions. That is to be granted, as it is also to be granted that it is insufficiently clear how things at different levels are related. But there is the overriding fact that what is right is at bottom a matter of our actions to change or keep the world in which we live, and that matters of credit and standing are no sure guides to this.

Any arguable morality will be like anything that deserves the name of being a court of law. It will disdain the defence of a killer that what he did was right because in a secondary sense he did not want to do what he did and what he knew he was doing. From the horror of killing the somehow innocent, there is no conclusion to be drawn except with the aid of or in the context of an adequate morality. Anything else is childish or at least suspect. It may be viciously self-serving.

6. Conventional Views

It is also my conviction, as you have heard, that there is a possibility of rightness with respect to terrorism for humanity, and thus Palestinian terrorism, and no such possibility with other terrorism. If that has not been proved for you, you have most of the elements that can go into an attempt at proof – the sort of proof possible in morality. Consider now another large thing that enters into resistance to any such thing. It is surely more effective than such propositions of argument as double effect.

In some societies, most importantly the United States, as already implied, it can seem that there is little or no assent to the possibility that terrorism for humanity is justified, let alone its actually being justified. So too with the others of the particular propositions with which we began, and which, as you have heard, give collateral support to the proposition about Palestinian terrorism and terrorism for humanity in general. It can seem that a large majority of people find them or say they find all but the one about 9/11 outrageous. There seems to be no assent, if there is a little lip-service, to the general morality in which the propositions are at home. Instead, a large majority of people appear to give assent to what can be labelled *conventional views*.

Whatever this fact really comes to, it contributes to a presumption. This is the presumption that what most people in our own societies think is right does at least have something to be said for it. In the fact of numbers and whatever goes with it, we are to suppose, there is a reason for thinking something right. There is no doubt this presumption has a grip on us. Anyway, it has had a grip on me.

Convention in moral thought, feeling and language, generally speaking, is a sameness or congruence in a society about what is right or who is to be credited with responsibility or who is decent. It seems a natural thing since it is not a code, and since people may follow it just because it has been followed before. The fact of convention is as old a society. So is the perception and valuation of it, and of how it comes about. Thrasymachus spoke of it to Socrates when he exposed the alternative truth, as he thought, that justice consists in the interests of the stronger. At the present moment of language in my own country, Britain, one part of the fact of convention is talked of in terms of governmental *spin*, which term in its tolerance is itself an instance of it. Spin is typically lying, maybe lying in order to get a people into a war or to increase your personal anticipation of a place in history.

Bacon, Burke, Mill and Marx gave different accounts of convention, Burke approving much of it under the name of *prejudice*. It is one thing clarified in detail by the great moral judge of this time, Chomsky. The fact of it has been properly studied by way of many related social facts. These are the facts of authority, legitimacy, legitimation, illegitimation, naturalisation, consent, ideology, norm-construction, indoctrination in education, mystery and mystification, influence, propaganda, sacralising, and demonising.

To engage in the study of convention by these means is partly to engage in conspiracy theory. Plainly there have been and are conspiracies, which is to say secret plans to achieve or keep something about which at least a question arises. To deny all or even most conspiracy theory is to oblivious of the history of monopoly, government and business, church and state, international trade-offs, hidden or obscured alliances, and so on. What is more important with respect to the fact of convention is its being owed to the self-interest of dominant groups whose members act together not out of secret plan but partly out of a want of self-awareness, an excess of self-deception, and self-serving illusions having to do with the common good and the just society and the like. They have no need of a plan. Their interests fall together, which is the main fact about their endeavours, and these are served by their common convictions. They are more like a mob than a plot, if a mob with some decorum and with the rules on its side.

Is convention a larger fact now than it was in the past? Consider our culture of the past few decades, since about 1979. It has had in it, increasingly, profit in place of public service, competition and the pretence of it in place of cooperation, a new greed, the manufacturing of wants in place of satisfying them, buying raw materials and commodities from poor societies by victimisation, market as morality, corporate engrossment, a sexualisation of life that makes prostitution secondary, and so on. This culture, which does not have truth as its aim, is now a larger part of morals and politics. Governments are unable to see outside of it. So too, since about 1979, has there been a further domination of mass communications, which domination also does not have truth as its aim. It is rather an engine whose products are authority, legitimacy, and so on. These two developments, at the very least a greater imbalance between sides of life, between commerce and the other sides of life, and more of self-serving control or management of information and attitudes, may make the fact of convention a more consequential social fact now than it has ever been before.[18]

7. Factual and Moral Truths

Despite the explanations given of conventional morality, in terms of authority, legitimacy and so on, the presumption that what most people think is something like right can have a grip on you. The presumption itself is very likely more efficacious, as already remarked, than any other attempt to resist most of the eight propositions with which we began.

The presumption first faces the necessity and difficulty of making clearer and qualifying the actual fact of numbers on which it depends. Generally speaking, that was said to be most people, maybe a vast majority, finding certain moral propositions mistaken or outrageous, and presumably the reasons for them mistaken. The generalisation runs up against, for example, the public opinion polls showing that half the British people were somehow against the idea that war on Iraq was right.[19] It runs up against the fact that international charities such as the Red Cross and War on Want can effectively appeal to our bad conscience about Africa as well as our concern. It is also plain, about my own country, that the Palestinians have the sympathy of much of the population in their resistance to an army of occupation and suppression. The sympathy issues in such politicians' plans as the one current in 2003, called the road map to peace.

Despite these several qualifications, it remains true that there is a fact, not simple, of kinds of majority-opposition in our societies to certain moral propositions. There are kinds and degrees of congruence in opposition to them or at least withdrawal from them. This is true of Palestinian suicide-bombing, which we have uppermost in our minds. It is true, somehow, of the killing of kinds of innocents. Why should the fact trouble those of us who are inclined to or committed to the morality of humanity and all the eight propositions?

The presumption of its moral importance, some say, in one way or another, has to do with the fact that two heads are better than one, and more heads are better than fewer. The community of scientists may be offered as an analogy. There are other expressions of the thing. Is the idea that more heads rather than fewer are a guide to relevant *truths of fact* as distinct from what can seem to be moral truths? Well, to be on the side of the common people is of course not to be committed to any such piety with respect to relevant propositions of fact. Science itself is the first of overwhelming obstacles to such piety.

No doubt, consistently with the realism about truth that traditionally has issued in the Correspondence Theory, there is pretty good evidence that it is raining in Texas if most Texans say it is. But there is extensive ignorance of the factual proposition about our natures that makes (1) anybody's wretchedness a stronger reason to him or her for something than (2) somebody else's satiety a reason for something else. It is more relevant than anything else with respect to the questions before us. To ignorance is to be added falsehood. That Iraq perpetrated 9/11 is not made less idiotically false by the fact that a majority of Americans believed it. So too with the wretched lie by Blair that we were under immediate threat from Saddam, half-believed by many in my country for a while, and that this was the aim of the war.

In place of continuing this reminder of ignorance and mistake, absolutely necessary though it is in other contexts, let me qualify my scepticism about majorities or congruences and factual truths, and quickly draw a conclusion.

By way of qualification, can we not do more than *hope* that people come to believe factual truths about their politicians eventually, see whether they are straight or not? Have the British people not seen, differently, that the expropriation by privatisation of their railways was not at all in their interest? Have they not seen, in general, that what were called the public services were overwhelmingly in their interest? You may say that my hopeful examples of public knowledge are true to my politics, which is no surprise. But they serve as well as any to indicate a conclusion.

Taken together with what was said before, about kinds and degrees of public support or tolerance of radical propositions, we have the cautious conclusion about factual propositions that there is *no* clear, well-supported and significant generalisation connecting majorities or congruences with morally-relevant truths of fact. I suspect a less cautious view is true, but it is unnecessary in order to defend the morality of humanity against conventional morality.

Are so-called *moral truths* different? We can have in mind not only such conventional denials of my particular propositions on Africa, Palestinian suicide-bombing, Iraq and so on, but also the recommendatory views and doctrines from which denials of the particular propositions issue. Here we face another reminder. It is a kind of consideration that could as readily have been used against the supposed recommendation of majority support for relevant propositions of fact.

It is not as if the many who hold the conventional moral propositions have thought them out or inquired into them. Nor have they been educated into them if education is different from indoctrination. They have not heard what can be said both for and against them, put them in

a structure of argument, clarified the relevant concepts, or even heard
an actual exposition of the conventional propositions by those who
for whatever reason defend them. Those who hold the conventional
propositions, as you have heard, have no adequate grasp of morally
relevant factual propositions. They are unpractised in the rationality of
consistency. They have had no such instruction worth the name in the
bits and pieces of patriotic language that help to identify what you can
call a national consciousness. Nothing calls out for more analysis than
talk of *freedom*, unless perhaps it is *the American way of life*.

What the many who incline to the conventional propositions
have had, rather, is an induction into morality that indubitably is to be
studied, in large part, in terms of all those ideas mentioned earlier –
authority, legitimacy, legitimation, illegitimation, naturalisation, consent, ideology, norm-construction, indoctrination, mystery and mystification, influence, propaganda, sacralising, demonising and so on.
There can be little doubt about this.

The *forming* of Americans, to continue to speak of them on
account of their importance, is owed in large part to an ongoing history of which the basic fact is economic power. To describe it more
enlighteningly, it has to do with different grasps on the material means
to well-being, the most important means to the great goods, and in
particular on political power. The basic fact of economic power is that
the top tenth of Americans have 17 times the incomes of the bottom
tenth, and a few hundred times the wealth of the bottom *four* tenths.[20]

Again it is not hard to draw a cautious conclusion, in this case
about moral propositions. There can be no clear, significant and well-
supported generalisation connecting majorities or congruences with
moral propositions that have the recommendation, in brief, of *moral
intelligence*. This moral intelligence is a matter of judgement owed to
knowledge and of practice in inquiry, not watching television.

Add in some historical episodes, including the German population's tolerance of the genocide of the Jews. Add the discomfiting and
indeed destructive thought that different societies existing now have
different and inconsistent conventional moralities, including different
attitudes to terrorism. They can't *all* be right.

It can seem to be a kind of *dream* that there is a decent presumption that what most people in a society think is right at least has

something to be said for it. And yet the dream lingers, in more heads than mine.

8.   Democracy, and a Conclusion about Convention

Does the lingering of the dream have a lot to do with democracy? Democracy is also about majorities, and it docs certainly have a re-commendation over most of the actual governments it has supplanted. If the outcomes of democratic elections have a recommendation, then so too, you may say, do the factual and moral beliefs that issue in the votes of the people – i.e. conventional morality. Indeed any defence of democracy must assign *some* recommendation to the input-beliefs.

You may take the view that the main recommendation of demo-cracy is that it leaves a people politically freer, or less politically unfree, than they are under certain alternative forms of government. More people get more of what they want – whatever happens to other peoples. But that recommendation is less impressive if conjoined with the admission that democracy is about as likely as not to derive from mistakes of fact and morality, including mistakes about wants. That the democratic election gives you freedom takes a knock from one of them issuing from such factual and moral beliefs that it produced Hitler as the winner.

You will guess that at least a general scepticism about demo-cracy, or rather *our* democracy, is basic to a general scepticism about conventional views, and to support of the eight propositions with which we began. To stick to the present point, it is indeed possible to think that recourse to our democracy is of little use in trying to explain why conventional morality should be accorded a significant respect. Indeed the history of reflection on illegitimation, mystifica-tion, sacralising and so on is mainly reflection about our democracy.

To me, for the reasons you know having to do with income and wealth mentioned earlier, the most important means to well-being, our democracy is *hierarchic democracy* at best, indeed *oligarchic democracy*. By proper comparisons it is government of, by and for in-equality rather than for equality.[21] It is specifically not a decision-procedure that recommends the decisions made. In brief, it is not truth-governed.

You will anticipate that it also seems to me that the fact of convention, often but not always the fact of convergence on views that have a long history, gets no recommendation from the ideology of conservatism. An analysis of it in terms of its commitments to con-serving things, its superiority to theory, its perception and promotion of a certain human nature, and its selective attachment to freedom and so on, can issue in a certain conclusion. That is not that it is uniquely self-interested, but that no recognisably moral principle supports that self-interest.[22]

Even so, does the dream still linger that there is sense in what most people think is right? I confess to having hoped to find some-thing or other of interest to say about this, something more or less philosophical. Perhaps some cautionary light on the obvious excep-tions to principles and nostrums about the value of *any* rules as against none. Perhaps some stronger generality about working to change the rules rather than breaking them, or something about giving up vio-lence as a precondition to negotiation, or about negotiation now because you will have to negotiate in the end. Perhaps some toleration of the people's deference to governments and states, which things in their genocides and politicides have, as remarked before, killed so many people as to make deaths by terrorism numerically trivial.

But *is* there any more to be said of majority views in our demo-cracies? Is there any more in popular perception and wisdom than that those with bad lives know what those lives are like and see through our shams? In the absence of some clear thought about the recom-mendation of conventional views, about the people and truth, it is hard to resist a boring conclusion. It is that the dream that there is sense in what most people think is a dream that itself is part of the convention. The convention applies to and gives to itself an authority, legitimacy and so on. The convention, for which there is so little to be said, is not only about Africa and Palestine and so on, but also about itself. We philosophers and the like remain victims of what we only *see* a little better.

9.   Actual Justification of Some Terrorism for Humanity

Of what else can be said here, one thing was more or less anticipated when it was remarked that from the felt horror of killing the innocent, no conclusion can be drawn but by way of some adequate morality.[23] This sort of morality was gestured at still earlier[24] – it consists in articulation of a whole view as to how the world ought to be. It is to be added, or made more explicit, that there is the same need for such a morality in any strong reflections on killing the innocent. This comes into focus immediately, by the way, with respect to both half-innocents and clear innocents – they must be understood in terms of *wrongful* killings by their own state or people. To know an innocent, you have to make a reflective judgement on a state or a people.

It is plain that something general and clear has to be thought about our basic moral concepts – right actions, moral credit, moral standing. It is as plain, to come up to where we are, that the only re-commendation that conventional views could have is that they some-how express an adequate morality. Is it even conceivable, on final reflection, that we could have found a reason for going along with a majority if we did not have a hold on an adequate morality somehow to assign to them? The same question arises about trust in our demo-cracy, indeed any democracy. It arises, more generally, about a residual inclination, despite the genocides and politicides, to support or accept state or governmental action, *official* action, as against other action.

Finally here, it is my own judgement that those who stand against most of the particular propositions with which we began cannot ex-plain themselves by way of an adequate morality. But my present point is that nothing else will suffice. If you disagree with the propos-itions, what is the adequate morality by which you do so?[25]

The question of whether a campaign of terrorism for humanity is not only possibly but also actually justified comes down to whether it will work – whether it has a decent probability of gaining the end in question, or more likely one of a range of related ends, at a cost that makes the result worth it. Those of you who are superior to what is misconceived as *consequentialism,* and is sometimes absurdly under-stood as the idea that an end justifies any means,[26] will do well to reflect that the reasoning in question is of just the form recommended by the orthodox theory of the just war.

The terrorism for humanity that is most likely to pass this final test of rationality is liberation-terrorism, which calls up human and moral resources greater than any other terrorism. Palestinian terrorism, for example, was of the strength to see through and disdain the dog's breakfast of a Palestinian state on offer during the presidency of Mr Clinton. It will, I think, see through and disdain any other dog's breakfast.

You have an idea of most of the materials for what proof can be given, in my view, of the moral right of the Palestinians and other peoples to their terrorism for humanity,[27] I myself have greater con-fidence in it than before the war on Iraq. The lies on which that war was predicated, or at the very least the culpable stupidity of self-deception, has strengthened my confidence. I refer to that consider-ation of guilt by association mentioned earlier. To be against Blair is to be reassured.

Still, and sadly, this matter of confidence has more to it. It is not easy to escape contradiction, not easy to get to consistency. There is great reason to take terrorism as *prima facie* wrong, as a good defini-tion makes it. It is possible to think that the factual questions in terror-ism – centrally the question of whether and how it will work – are of yet greater difficulty than the moral questions. What of those terrorists for humanity who will never give up, not because they will win, but so that others may one day win? The moral questions, to revert to them, cannot be taken as entirely clear and readily manageable. You can understand a man who says his head blows up when he brings together the viciousness of the new Zionism and the murdering of an Israeli child.[28]

Do you, in the end, ask me how it is possible to contemplate rising over the horror of the killing of a child? How it is possible to rise over the horror to a justification of the killing? Well, I would like to have more confidence than I have, more than the war on Iraq has given me. But some things are clear, indeed obvious. There is also the horror that is the rape of a people. To avoid the shock of it, to be half-lulled by the unspeakable spokesmen on the television mouthing stuff about democracy and terrorism, is also to be in a state that is appalling.

Do you say that to assert a moral right to some terrorism is to give up a hesitancy that is part of proper moral philosophy?[29]

Well, claims of moral right, as watching television can remind you daily, are not abstract propositions, so to speak, or not only abstract propositions, but ordinary parts of conflicts, ordinary means to an end, weapons made use of to the fullest extent possible. If the side of humanity has always been served better by truth than the other side, it needs also to say the most for itself that can truly be said. To do less, in the face of those against it, is to fail in a kind of realism.

Is there arrogance in all this?

Well, there is not much sense of personal ability or importance. There is a sense of the importance of the greatest of moral principles, that of humanity, the one not deformed or tainted by self-interest. As it seems to me, it stands alone.

Endnotes

1   This paper is a revision of a lecture under the same title to the 20th International Social Philosophy Conference which took place in Boston in 2003. My thanks to Ingrid Coggin Honderich for comments, which demonstrate that we are not in complete agreement. The present paper is to be printed in the conference proceedings and as the substance of the revised paperback edition of my *After The Terror* (Edinburgh University Press: Columbia University Press, 2002). There is more on several of this paper's points in 'Palestinian Terrorism, Morality, and Germany', published in English in a German journal of law and philosophy, *Rechtsphilosophische Hefte*, vol. x (2005). The sample of 20 million lost lives has to do with the worst-off tenths of population in Malawi, Mozambique, Zambia and Sierra Leone. See my *After the Terror*, Ch. 1.

2   Miftah (Palestine Initiative for the Promotion of Global Dialogue and Democracy) website: www.miftah.org , accessed 15 March 2003.

3   Palestinian Red Crescent Society Website: www.palestinercs.org, accessed 30 June 2003.

4   B'Tselem: The Israeli Information Centre for Human Rights in the Occupied
      Territories website: www.btselem.org, accessed 31 May 2003.
5   Barbara Harff, 'Toward Empirical Theory of Genocides and Politicides:
      Identification and Measurement of Cases since 1945', *International Studies
      Quarterly*, 32.3 (1988): pp. 359–371; 'No Lessons Learned from the Holo-
      caust? Assessing Risks of Genocide and Political Mass Murder since 1955',
      American Political Science Review, 97.1 (2003): pp. 57–73.
6   On war and terrorism, and on such other matters as the definition of terrorism,
      killing the innocent, and humiliation as a cause of terrorism, see the absolutely
      exemplary lecture by Virginia Held, 'Terrorism as Small War', forthcoming in
      the proceedings of the 20th International Social Philosophy Conference.
7   Prof. Ed Kent, personal communication.
8   Cf. Bernard Williams, *Utilitarianism: For and Against* (Cambridge University
      Press, 1973). See also my *Violence for Equality: Inquiries in Political Philo-
      sophy* (London: Routledge, 1989), ch. 1, or a revised edition under the title
      Terrorism for Humanity: Inquiries in Political Philosophy (London: Pluto,
      2003).
9   Jonathan Glover, *Humanity: A Moral History of the Twentieth Century*
      (London: Jonathan Cape, 1999), chs. 10, 11, 12. The ordinariness of claims of
      moral rights to killing, indeed moral rights to state terrorism, as in the case of
      neo-Zionist Israel, is considered in 'Palestinian Terrorism, Morality, and
      Germany' on the world-wide web: www.homepages.ucl.ac.uk/~uctytho.
10   There is more on the general nature of morality in *After the Terror*, ch. 2.
11   Cf. 'After The Terror: A Book and Further Thoughts', *The Journal of Ethics*,
      7.2 (2003): pp. 161–181, which piece is reprinted in *Political Means and Social
      Ends* (Edinburgh: Edinburgh University Press, 2003).
12   Cf. Bernard Williams, *Utilitarianism: For and Against and Moral Luck*
      (Cambridge: Cambridge University Press, 1982) and *Ethics and the Limits of
      Philosophy* (London: Fontana, 1984). As footnote 9 also indicates, I have lately
      been struck, incidentally, by the wider implications, political and social, of
      moral philosophy primarily concerned with private lives.
13   Cf. Tim Mulgan, *The Demands of Consequentialism* (Oxford: Oxford Uni-
      versity Press, 2001).
14   Violence is physical force that injures, damages, violates or destroys people or
      things. Terrorism is violence with a political and social end, whether or not
      intended to put people in general in fear, and necessarily raising a question of
      its moral justification because it is violence – either such violence as is against
      the law within a society or else violence between states or societies, against
      what there is of international law and smaller-scale than war. For more on this
      definition see *After the Terror*, pp. 91–100, and 'After the Terror: A Book and
      Further Thoughts', op. cit.
15   Cf. R. A. Duff, *Punishment, Communication and Community* (Oxford: Oxford
      University Press, 2000).

16 There is more on such a view of the Iraq war in chs. 7 and 8 of an enlarged and revised edition of my *Conservatism*, entitled, *Conservatism: Burke, Nozick, Bush, Blair?* (London: Pluto Press, 2005).

17 There were about 365,000 Arabs and about 7,000 Jews in 1876 in Palestine, then a recognised Arab homeland with the same boundaries recognised by the Western powers mandate after World War 1. There were about 500,000 Arabs and 50,000 Jews in 1900 in Palestine. After World War 2, if both states called for by the United Nations had come into being, there would have been about 750,000 Arabs and 9,250 Jews in the Arab state, and 479,000 Arabs and 498,000 Jews in what would be the Jewish state. See *After the Terror*, ch. 1. The given figures and others come from *The World Guide 2003–4* (New Internationalist Publications, Instituto del Tercer Mundo, 2003). Cf. Justin McCarthy, *The Population of Palestine: Population History and Statistics of the Late Ottoman Period and the Mandate* (New York: Columbia University Press, 1990), and Norman G. Finkelstein, *Image and Reality of the Palestine Conflict* (London: Verso, 2001).

18 It is reassuring and a pleasure to record the full extent of the convergence of views in this article with views of Noam Chomsky, the moral judge of our centuries, he who has made better use of truth and consistency than anyone else. See, for example, *Necessary Illusions: Thought Control in Democratic Societies* (London: Pluto, 1989). For a summary of his thinking, see *What Uncle Sam Really Wants* (Cambridge MA.: Odonian Press, 1992), and in particular pp. 86–91, where there are specifications of what democracy as we have it and so on comes to. The main difference between us, as I see it, is in what we advocate instead. He speaks of the socialism that is control of production by the workers themselves, not owners and managers who rule them and control all decisions, whether in capitalist enterprises or an absolutist state. That strikes me as the description of a means rather than an end, or a description of an end that could and should be more explicit. What I advocate is the end of the Principle of Humanity. I am also tempted to greater approval of the means of a more organised socialism than is suggested by speaking of workers' control. Cuba is a good example. It would be a finer one except for the pressures brought to bear on it about which Chomsky and I agree.

19 A Guardian/ICM opinion poll published in *The Guardian* on 19 March 2003 was that 51% of Britons were against war and only 35% supported it.

20 For a consideration of this and related facts, see *After the Terror*, ch. 1.

21 See also 'Hierarchic Democracy and the Necessity of Mass Civil Disobedience', *Conway Memorial Lecture*, 1994, republished in *On Political Means and Social Ends*, and also *After the Terror*, Ch. 4.

22 See *Conservatism* (London: Hamish Hamilton, Westview, 1990; London: Penguin, 1991 or the revised edition, London: Pluto Press, 2005).

23 See above, p. 41.

24 See above, pp. 31f.

25   For a consideration of several candidates, see various essays, several pertaining
      to liberalism, in *On Political Means and Social Ends*. The demand that an
      adequate morality be provided in argument is my principal reply to at least
      intemperate Israeli critics of such views as the one in this chapter. Prof. Jacob
      Joshua Ross of Tel Aviv-University, in his spoken paper on it at the conference
      mentioned above, said it was like the Nazis' anti-Semitic instruction to Ger-
      mans, derived from Bismarck: 'think with your blood'. For an account of the
      furore in Germany about the alleged anti-Semitism of *After The Terror*, see
      'The Fall and Rise of a Book in Germany', on the world-wide web:
      www.homepages.ucl.ac.uk/~uctytho/. There is more on this subject in 'Pales-
      tinian Terrorism, Morality, and Germany', also at the mentioned web address.
26   'Consequentialism, Moralities of Concern, and Selfishness', *Philosophy*, 76
      (1996), reprinted in *On Political Means and Social Ends*.
27   See also 'After the Terror: A Book and Further Thoughts', op. cit.
28   Dr Jeremy Stangroom, personal communication.
29   Cf. *Violence for Equality: Inquiries in Political Philosophy* (London:
      Routledge, 1989), revised as *Terrorism for Humanity: Inquiries in Political
      Philosophy* (London: Pluto, 2003). It is true that my convictions have become
      both more confident and more resolute, partly as a result of violation of
      Palestine.

Bill Starr

Can there be Moral Justification for State Violence? The Case of America

Violence in America has a long, mostly inglorious history. This paper will consist of two main parts. First, I will go through the history of violence in America and develop the notion that this has occurred from a complex of factors. Second, I will offer some philosophical reflections which may provide the conceptual underpinnings for both an attempted explanation and even a justification of some forms of violence in an American context.

I would like to make a preliminary point at this juncture. Philosophers often get bogged down in discussions of definitions. In their quest to be clear a tremendous amount of time can be spent in developing a definition of a given concept, in this case that of *violence*. The idea is to provide a definition that exhaustively captures the necessary and sufficient conditions for a given term. Then the idea is to apply the term. This strategy will not be attempted here for two reasons. First, to attempt to do this will take too much time away from the task at hand, which is to discuss violence in an American context and suggest what philosophical theories are lurking behind much of American violence. Second, it is simply a fruitless enterprise. Language is simply too rich and complex to button hole into rigid definitions with strict parameters.[1] I believe no matter what definition of violence is offered, clever readers will come up with counter examples to the definition, and thus the definition will not be successful. I do not wish to play that 'language game.'

It will simply be stipulated here that violence discussed in this essay will be restricted to physical violence, either real or virtual as expressed in, say, video games. That is, the notion of the use of physical force to the extent that it damages the recipient of the physical force will suffice as a working stipulation of what constitutes violence.[2] Other forms of violence that are expressed in the literature include such concepts as psychological violence, structural violence, economic violence, political violence, etc. which do not actually result in physical violence will not be discussed here. Sissela Bok states quite articulately:

> One of the quickest ways to short-circuit serious reflection about any form of violence is to insist that it is impossible to define it specifically enough for policy debates. After all, some people define 'violence' so broadly as to include all injustice, even as others have claimed that all fiction is lying, all property theft, all sexual intercourse rape.[3]

Whether these sorts of things are legitimate extensions of the term *violence,* I leave for others to decide.

Let me make one final point about my discussion of violence. As much as possible an effort is being made to be descriptive, not evaluative. It does not follow that violence is automatically bad or ethically indefensible, although most of it surely is. Consider the following example. American football is a game in which 22 players, 11 on each team attack each other in an extremely hard-hitting physical manner for the three hours that the game takes place. It is a very violent game involving a great deal of damaging physical force. Yet the players freely consent to both acting violently on the opposing players and being the recipient of violence by them. The game is enjoyed by literally millions of Americans every weekend from August to January, and both players and fans accept and thoroughly enjoy the violence as an integral part of the game. Hume's ghost, the is/ought issue, rears its head here. To say X *is* violent is one thing, to say the same X is *desirable* or *undesirable* is to say something quite different.

1.   Violence in America

Recent statistics do not present a pretty picture regarding violence in America. Homicide rates are far higher in the United States than in other western countries. This is especially true for African-Americans who, for example, had 65.6 deaths by homicide per 100,000 populations in 1990. The same rate for American whites was 15.5 per 100,000.[4] The rate for homicide per 100,000 in England and Wales was 0.6 while in Scotland it was 4.0. In the 1990's about one third of all homicides were gang related.[5] While violent incidents can occur anywhere, in the United States this is more an urban phenomenon than a rural one.[6] Of course, it may be the case that rural acts of violence are more underreported than in urban areas. Violence can occur for a plethora of reasons. These reasons are not restricted to the United States of America. However, what makes America stand out statistically with respect to acts of violence is the use of handguns. According to data provided by Handgun Control Inc., based in Washington D.C., in 1992 deaths due to handguns were the following: Australia had 13 deaths, Great Britain 33, Sweden 36, Japan 60, Switzerland 97, Canada 128, the United States of America had 13,220.[7] This is staggering. Handgun violence in America has a dramatic dimension of its own not matched by other western countries. A sketch of how this occurred will be developed shortly. About two thirds of all murders in the United States appear to be from guns.[8] In spite of these horrific numbers, there may be a ray of hope. Violent crime in the United States does seem to be going down since the 1990s, in fact from a rate of 10 deaths by homicide per 100,000 in 1991 to 6.4 per 100,000 in 1996.[9] Of course this overall rate in America makes the death rate by homicide for African-Americans that much more shocking. Also, it is worth mentioning that in 1995 the United States was not the most violent country or even in the top three based on reported incidents. That dubious honour went to Colombia, South Africa, and Russia.[10]

What are the historical roots of American violence? Here the paint brush will be stroked very broadly indeed. American, as opposed to Native American, history started in the seventeenth century. Consider for example puritan New England in the seventeenth century. There were small tightly-knitted homogenous groups controlled by village elders who were also religious leaders. In other words small theocracies ruled in New England in the seventeenth century. There was even a flavour of natural law in the New England air of the time. The idea was that these religious leaders who also were legal judges were representatives here on earth of God. As such, it was their solemn duty to enforce God's law upon God's subjects, that is, the citizens of the village. This resulted in the judicial system beginning to write down God's or natural law and codify it into positive law. The puritans were not gentle when it came to punishment. From their perspective physical punishment was a perfectly appropriate way to properly enforce God's will. Punishment was also public, swift, and filled with the justificatory language of moral righteousness. Friedman captures this quite nicely. 'Whipping, branding, and pillory were public displays of the fruits of crime designed to warn the immoral. In a face-to-face society, public rituals of this nature strengthened the legitimacy of criminal proceedings.'[11]

> Guilt or innocence was not the only point of criminal process; the judges were also concerned with the willingness of the accused to submit to authority. This trait, of course, runs like a scarlet thread throughout the story of American criminal justice.'[12]

Whipping developed into the standard punishment of colonial America in the eastern states from New York to Maryland as well as in the south. The special concern in the south was to keep slaves submissive and in the non-slave states to keep servants and lower classes in line as well. Punishment could get quite ugly. For example mutilation was another form of punishment. As one commentator put it, 'Dozens of detached ears [...] litter the record books.'[13] The upshot of all this is that violence became institutionalized and internalized by the authorities at a very early stage in American history. And it was often used.

In 1776 the American Declaration of Independence was written, signed, and declared to be a statement that America was no longer a colony of Great Britain. Several years later the new country won on the battlefield and Great Britain's soldiers went home in defeat. In 1787 the new United States constitution was written and a year later it was approved by the 13 former colonial states, now new states in the new federal United States of America. The memory of Britain and its soldiers were very fresh in the minds of the citizens of the new country and its constitution. The constitution was a formal document that spelled out how the new government was to be set up and run with its separation of powers and three separate but equal branches of government. However, there was no detailed statement explaining what rights its new citizens had. After all, there is not much point to fighting for independence simply in order to form a new government although from the American perspective not having a king was already a distinct advantage. A powerful concept of individual rights is something worth fighting for. The constitutional framers realized this and in 1791 wrote the first 10 amendments to the United States constitution. These rights are known as the Bill of Rights. Most of these rights are the sort of things one would expect in such a document, e.g. the right to freedom of expression and assembly, the right to freedom of the press, the right to freedom of religion, the right against unreasonable searches and seizures, the right against self-incrimination, the right against double jeopardy, the right against cruel and unusual punishment, the right to reasonable bail, the right to a trial by a jury of one's peers, etc. A quirky right was included in the Bill of Rights partly in fear that the British might return, partly in fear among those in frontier areas that they may be attacked by the indigenous population, and partly because the owning of arms had been internalized and was now a part of the culture of the new American society. This right became the second amendment to the United States Constitution. It says: 'A well regulated militia being necessary to the security of a free state, the right of the people to keep and bear arms shall not be infringed.' Gun owning is a right for Americans enshrined in its own constitution. From the time the country was formed as a new nation, both violence and gun ownership were an integral part of American culture.

Urban growth occurred in the new America at an extremely high rate in the mid-nineteenth century. There were two main factors which caused this phenomenon. They were, internally, the move from the

farm or rural area to the city; and externally, the move from other
lands to the United States. This put tremendous pressure on the cities.
The response was to emulate the new London police department
formed in 1829 and start formal police departments in the cities of
America. This occurred from the 1840s through the 1870s. Before the
development of formal police departments, law enforcement was
loose, informal, ad hoc, not well organized, and surely not professional. This began to change in the mid-nineteenth century. The
role of these new police departments was to enforce law and order.
How law and order was to be maintained was for the most part not of
much concern to the public. The charge to the police was not subtle. It
was 'just do it.' Citizens in urban America at that time were concerned
that they would be overrun by new uncouth, uneducated, immoral,
violent, shiftless, aimless transients, or 'masterless men' as they were
known at the time. 'And for God's sake, some of them can't even
speak English.' I'll return to these sorts of issues later. The idea of the
police acting roughly with the lower classes, beating confessions out
of the accused, using physical force when necessary, has been a well
established part of law enforcement in American police departments
for a long time. It is still with us today although the accused are far
more likely today to assert their legal rights than in the nineteenth
century. Friedman states in writing about the American experience,
'police brutality has a long, dishonourable history, not only on the
street, but also in the station house'.[14] He continues:

> Thousands of nineteenth-century tramps and thieves were beaten, coerced,
> arrested, thrown into jail, all without lawyers. They confessed after long
> stretches of the third degree, and almost nobody uttered a murmur of protest –
> certainly not the tramps and thieves [...]'[15]

The United States has had a special relationship with its African-
American citizens, much of it quite horrible. This was especially true
in the American south where a new form of 'law' was created and was
known as 'lynch law'. This is a special type of vigilantism in which
mobs of 'good decent people' apprehend one they believe to be a law
violator and instead of turning the person over to legal authorities take
the law into their own hands and mete out justice on the spot. This

usually results in executing the alleged criminal, traditionally by hang-ing. This is what has become known as 'southern justice.' In a great majority of lynching white citizens lynched black citizens. It was racism of the vilest kind, pure and simple. It was an extraordinarily violent sort of activity committed by a mob against a generally defenceless victim who was executed without any sort of legal trial whatsoever. Lynching was especially likely to take place in the south if the alleged perpetrator was a black man and the alleged victim was a white woman. Friedman captures this quite well as he writes,

> lynching was part of an 'unwritten code'. Southerners distrusted the state, and preferred, in these cases, 'personal justice'. They believed strongly that com-munity justice included both statutory law and lynch law; indeed, lynch law was perceived as a legitimate extension of the formal legal system.[16]

America was a big country with wide open spaces. It was impossible for these areas to be adequately patrolled by law enforce-ment authorities. While organized police departments made sense in the urban east and Midwest, the few sheriffs and marshals in the western part of the country had no chance whatsoever to track down and arrest most law violators in this huge sparsely inhabited mass of land. So, individual citizens or groups of people felt the need to en-force the law themselves. These extra-legal law enforcers became known as vigilantes. The idea here is a bit Hobbesian in the sense that a fundamental need is for society to live together in peace and security. Since the official authorities are incapable of providing this need, 'we' have to do it ourselves. In the absence of authorities to en-force the law effectively, if we, the good citizens of the community, don't do it ourselves, we will revert to a state of nature in which we will be in perpetual war of all against all. Hence, there is the need to revert to vigilantism and the attempted moral justification for such a practice.

Three more factors need to be added to complete this picture of violence in America as the twentieth century began. First, American prisons for the most part were quite awful places. Too many people, mostly men, were thrown together in overcrowded conditions often supervised by poorly trained guards who believed physical abuse of prisoners was quite appropriate. 'After all, these lowlifes are barely human beings, the bottom of the barrel. Maybe I can knock some sense into them. In any event, the only language they know is no nonsense, make it hurt, physical treatment. That's just what I'm going to provide.' And a number of prison guards did just that. Of course, there was at times a high level of violence among prisoners themselves. No one cared all that much about that. The attitude was that it was just a bunch of animals going after a bunch of other animals. Let them have their fun. Second, by the nineteenth century Americans had become extremely mobile people. The seventeenth-century Puritan model of small tightly-knitted religious communities was cast aside into the dustbin of history. Except for slaves, Americans could now pretty much move about as they pleased. One could move from farm to city, city to frontier, town to town. One could move to escape one's past, to start a new life. When this internal migration was supplemented by huge number of immigrants coming into the United States it became clear that the country was in a perpetual state of flux. From the perspective of geography, it was and is a most dynamic, not static, society. An unfortunate consequence of this new mobility was an increase in crime and violence. America developed a new anonymity. Now it was not the case that everyone knew each other in a given area. It may be virtually impossible to physically abuse your neighbour or friend, but for some it was not so hard to act that way toward a stranger when stealing from him or becoming involved in a brawl in the bar. Some even became full time criminals. With the new mobility, one could physically attack someone, perhaps even kill another, and get out of town quickly and move on to another place. One might even have a decent chance of escaping the clutches of the law. To put this more sociologically, the bonds of family, church, and community had broken down for a number of people. Some of them turned to violent crime and other acts of violence as a result.

Third, women are well connected to the history of violence in America mostly as victims. Women had few legal rights until well into the twentieth century. Until very recently it was legally impossible for a husband to rape his wife. Unless a woman was married or a virgin it was virtually never the case that the legal system took seriously any claim of rape. Traditionally police officers did not respond to domestic abuse cases on the theory that 'this is private stuff, not something for the police or the criminal justice to become involved in.' Occasionally women became violent themselves, particularly with the crime of infanticide. The stigma of having a child without a husband was so great that desperate women would kill their infants and somehow hope no-one would notice. However, for the most part, women were victims of violence, not perpetrators. As one writer stated, 'women in large numbers were robbed, murdered, beaten (often by their husbands), seduced, cheated, and raped.'[17]

It is worth adding two twentieth-century phenomena to round out the sketch of the historical roots of American violence. First, the phenomena of organized gangs are largely a feature of the twentieth century.[18] Today gang murders account for over a third of all homicides in America's second most populous city, Los Angeles. Contemporary culture has produced disaffected, angry, rebellious, alienated youths. Combine these factors with the illegal American drug culture and violent behaviour is an inevitable consequence of these forces coming together. Friedman eloquently makes this point.

> Violent crime is a product, by and large, of male aggression. But that aggression can take many forms, and seek all sorts of outlets, many of them quite benign. Somehow, macho honour and swagger have generalized; they have worked their way down the social ladder. They take forms that are, at times, violent, vicious, and perverse. A gang member has to be tough, has to be a man, has to be willing to fight, to shoot, to avenge. In neighbourhoods without exit or hope, this terrible code mixes with drugs, drug money, the weakness of the family, the decline of traditional authority, the exaltation of individualism and choice, the vulgarity of media messages, the rampant narcissism and consumerism of American society, and the easy, cheap arsenal of guns, to form a witch's brew of crime, social pathology, and violence.[19]

This passage is chilling and is supplemented by other studies in the literature. The emergence of gang/illegal drug life has clearly increased the prevalence and viciousness of violence in America in contemporary times.

A final factor which greatly impacts upon violence in America is psychological in nature with a bad philosophical grounding to support it. This is the notion of self-expression. Discussion of this issue will be deferred until part two of this paper, to which I shall now turn.

2.   Moral Justifications?

Is there any philosophical perspective or combination of philosophical perspectives that can help us understand violence in America? Or is philosophy so disconnected from the violence that has come about and is presently practised in America such that violence in America and philosophy simply go their separate ways? This second possibility if actualized would be most unfortunate and once again would provide data for those who claim that philosophy has nothing to say about issues in the real world. Happily, this is not the case.

I suggest that historically there have been four great moral theories that have stood the test of time. They are natural law ethics, virtue ethics, deontology, and utilitarianism. Of course there are contemporary candidates of ethical theories such as care ethics, discourse ethics, and the environmental ethic of deep ecology which if accepted would cause a radical ordering of our ethical priorities. However, here I will restrict my analysis to the traditional four theories. Now there is not much to say about natural law ethics in an American context. I mentioned natural law ethics, employed quite poorly, was a basis for the Puritan order in seventeenth-century colonial New England. However, since the eighteenth century the United States has been a secular country. To claim a natural law ethic is not supported by the data. There is not a tradition that law is created by God and is 'out there' to be discovered by humans. The United States Supreme Court does not claim to be a representative of God upholding natural law and imparting it to humans. This Court consists of nine members who are appointed by the President and confirmed by the Senate to rule on legal matters based on written positive law. Thomistic natural inclinations whether nutritive, animal, or truly human[20] do not seem to play an active role in American public discourse, although private religious traditions may well advocate and practice natural law ethics. So, it is not a promising enterprise to attempt to explain violence in America by reference to natural law theory.

Can American violence be explained from a Kantian or to put it more broadly a deontological framework? I think not. Kantian ethics holds that consequences are not determinate of what one ought to do. What one ought to do is to follow the categorical imperative which is how a person of purely good will should act. Such a person should act in accordance with doing her duty, which is precisely obeying the categorical imperative. Whether one prefers the universalizability or the respect for persons version of the categorical imperative is not relevant here. It is beyond credibility that virtually anyone acting violently towards others or even contemplating violent behaviour is wondering whether such behaviour can be universalized or wondering if such an action would be showing respect for the intended victim as an end in herself. That is not what is occurring when one is thinking about violence.

Perhaps more importantly, when considering Kantian ethics as applied to violence, there is more than a psychological claim being made. Philosophically, Kantian ethics cannot justify the vast majority of violent acts that actually do occur. Some forms of violence in the legitimate name of self-defence would be permitted assuming there was no other means available to defend oneself or others under threat of violence and the violence was a proportionate response to the attack. Proportionate violence in a just war may well be acceptable on Kantian terms as well, perhaps, as certain sports contests. However, the great majority of acts cannot under coherent interpretation pass muster from a Kantian perspective. This includes the notion of violently punishing people because it is God's will or torturing others through violent means for any reason. On Kantian grounds it is not acceptable for police to act violently toward others to get the alleged criminal to confess or to somehow maintain public order or to keep the 'lowlifes' in line. The categorical imperative does not allow one to act violently by lynching another or in the name of vigilante justice. It does not justify or even excuse violent behaviour in a gang, sexual, or religious context. It does not justify violence on grounds of 'I was just expressing myself.' So, both psychologically and philosophically Kantian ethics is not going to be helpful in our quest for providing a philosophical grounding for violence in America.

Can virtue theory, Aristotelian or contemporary versions such as that of MacIntyre or Pence, provide a philosophical foundation for violence in America?[21] In a limited manner there is a connection between violence and virtue theory, mostly negative. Courage is one of the most important of the Aristotelian virtues. Surely there are times when the soldier, police officer, or good citizen does a good deed by acting violently to protect others when non-violent alternatives are simply not available. In these sorts of cases the person in question is acting neither rashly, an Aristotelian excess, nor cowardly, an Aristotelian deficiency. This is a clear case of applying an Aristotelian virtue to the use of violence. There are attempted uses of virtues to justify violence as well. For example, the vigilante mob may say: 'Look, we applied justice when we beat up this person. He viciously attacked three women, the authorities refused to take action, and we had no choice.' Justice was served in the traditionally Aristotelian sense in that the attacker received what he deserved. This applies the Aristotelian mean and is neither excessive nor deficient. Now this sort of justification needs to be looked at on a case by case basis. It is quite likely most of these cases of violence will not be justified. Vigilantes do not generally take due process or constitutional rights very seriously. Trials by vigilantes, when they exist at all, are not impartial. Often the vigilantes act as prosecutor, judge, and jury which are anathema to any fair sense of justice. The absence of constitutional protections virtually guarantees that more innocent persons will be 'convicted' than when traditional rules of evidence, trial behaviour, due process, and constitutional safeguards are taken seriously. So, the vigilante justification for grounds of violence on grounds of justice, a crucial Aristotelian virtue, is dubious at best. Of course, most forms of violence are performed with no thought of applying justice at all.

However, the preponderance of evidence shows that the vices are enhanced and the virtues diminished by acts of violence. Sissela Bok shows quite convincingly that those who act violently and learn violence from early childhood, often from the entertainment industry, develop the vices of aggression, fear – especially of becoming a victim of violence – desensitization, and uncontrolled appetite. That is, having aggressive tendencies to strike out at others, living in fear of others, becoming insensitive to oneself and one's community, and not being able to act in a moderate manner are not good ways to live. If the cornerstone of virtue ethics is proper character development which will enable one to live a life of human flourishing in a happy state of mind, then the four characteristics above will severely impede the ability for one to live such a virtuous life. Consider the virtues of resilience, empathy, self control, and respect for self and others. These virtues, Bok argues, are impeded by a culture that thrives on violence. This is just the culture, Bok believes, that exists in contemporary America.[22] The withering away of these important virtues for a culture is tragic. Virtue ethics can be brought to bear upon an analysis of violence in America. However, virtue ethics at best plays a marginal role, e.g. the vigilante claiming justice, when it comes to actually providing a philosophical explanation of violence in the United States.

One factor which is helpful in explaining a part of violence in the United States rests in the concept of self-expression. The explanation is philosophical in nature only that it badly misapplies both utilitarian and Kantian ethics. Consider the person who acts violently toward another by viciously hitting him in the face with a club. When asked why he did that, he calmly replies, 'it's the way I express myself, I just like doing that sort of stuff. Besides I needed some money, and the guy looked like he had a lot of money on him.' Consider an actual example from Friedman:

> Crime, supposedly, does not pay, but this is not obvious to the naked eye. Many crimes, in fact, look like they do pay – and quickly, too. Drug dealing is one; robbery is another. Theft produces money which, if not effortless, is at least not earned by hard work in the usual sense. Theft is a way for young kids (males, almost exclusively) to make quick money, instant money. In 1990, a group of young men in New York tried to rob a family of tourists from Utah; in the scuffle that followed, they killed one family member, a 22 year old man, who was trying to protect his mother. The point of the crime was to get money to go dancing. Which is exactly what they did after the crime. They went dancing.[23]

What went badly wrong philosophically is that while it is true that Kant's categorical imperative does include the notion of respecting oneself as an end and never merely as a means, it does not allow you to not respect others as ends in themselves.[24] It does not allow you to violate your perfect duty to yourself to not violate the law nor the imperfect duty to yourself to act in harmony with the community. Such behaviour surely cannot be universalized as a law of nature, another requirement for the correct application of the categorical imperative. Self-expression, a good when properly applied since it enhances a person's self-worth as an autonomous being, has parameters which those who commit acts of violence such as those described above clearly transgress.

Self-expression is an important component in utilitarianism such as John Stuart Mill's which notes that utility is ultimately grounded on the principle that it enhances the notion of 'man as a progressive being.'[25] Why is it so important for the development of a human being to be allowed to progress in the best way possible? Because if that occurs, the community will be better off and utility will be maximized. This is why liberty plays such an important role in Mill's philosophy, when he writes in *On Liberty*:

> The object of this Essay is to assert one very simple principle […]. That principle is, that the sole end for which mankind are warranted, individually or collectively, in interfering with the liberty of actions of any of their number, is self-protection.'[26]

The key here is that one is not allowed to harm others even if this represents one expressing oneself. Harming others makes it impossible for them to progress as human beings and is extremely injurious to maximizing utility. On both Kantian and utilitarian grounds using the issue of self-expression, most violence has no justification whatsoever.

It is not yet time to despair. There is one philosophical attempt to justify much violence as practised historically in the United States, which does seem to at least pass the threshold of plausibility. It is a version of utilitarianism taking the utilitarian credo of the greatest happiness for the greatest number head on. Utilitarianism holds that one ought to maximize the best consequences for the community, often cashed out as happiness. Whether one is discussing or advocating act utilitarianism, rule utilitarianism, preference utilitarianism, hedonistic utilitarianism, pluralistic utilitarianism, or any other version, the notion of consequence maximization for the community is common to all versions. There is an intuitive appeal to utilitarianism. Consider the role of the legislature. Is not the role of the legislature to enact legislation which will maximize the general welfare of the community, that is, maximize the most desirable consequences for as many members of the community as possible?

However, there is one issue largely overlooked in discussions of utilitarianism which has a direct bearing on the attempted justification for violence in the United States. Just what community is being considered when it is stated that we ought to maximize the best consequences for the community, maximize utility? My thesis is this. The community that police departments, vigilantes, lynch mobs, or gangs have in mind is their own constituency, which can include themselves, plus those they believe they represent, plus one. The 'plus one' is the victim of violent action by the community in question. Let us see how this plays out from the perspective of an American police department. The police are told by the community to maintain law and order and 'do whatever it takes to get the job done.' Now this is too strong as stated since the community wants constitutional legal protections to be taken seriously as well. This serves as a constraint to condoning the most blatant use of violence against alleged criminals. Nonetheless, it is clear that the charge of the police is to keep the streets safe, and if they have to get a bit physical to do so, so be it. 'They're not dealing with angels, after all.' The community will certainly understand if some legal niceties are not followed to the letter of the law.

The key here is what constitutes the community in this situation. My thesis is that the community as described here consists of the good middle class citizens who want safe streets. It also consists of the politicians, businesspersons, and those with influence and power to whom the police department has to answer. It consists of the police department themselves who are generally under enormous pressure to provide adequate security for the community just described. It also includes the criminal who may be the victim of violence. And that's it. It does not include the poor, the underclass of criminals, those who are not part of mainstream respectable society, for the most part those who are not members of the middle or upper classes. To put this crudely but not inaccurately, the unit by which utility is to be measured is a combination of 'the good people of the community' plus the person whom the police believe is engaged criminal behaviour. Applying the utilitarian model of pleasure and pain, it is easy to see that the amount of pleasure gained by the community just described in getting a criminal off the street and into jail is inevitably going to be greater than the pain suffered by the criminal even if he is slapped around by the police. Here there is a serious attempt to provide a moral justification for violence, it is utilitarian in nature.

At the end of the day the moral justification does not work for two reasons. First, even if this utilitarian move is accepted, it shows something disastrously wrong with utilitarianism. Acting violently toward a criminal to get a confession, to find out who his partner is, or 'just to teach him a lesson' shows a clear lack of respect for this individual as a human being. This is important. The utilitarian model of decision making is not cashed out as an individual one. Every person in the collective is part of the collective. For example, if the community is better off with one person in jail because of police brutality, or the lack of constitutional safeguards during his trial, and hence the happiness of the whole collective, including the accused criminal, is raised, that's the way it should be for the utilitarian. But this is not what morality is supposed to be about. The bottom line of morality is that *each individual counts*. Surely this Kantian notion captures what the core of morality is all about as opposed to the utilitarian model.

Second, even taking utilitarianism on its own terms, note the artificially contrived community necessary to make the justification work. Once we actually include in the community society at large, the likely utilitarian calculus changes dramatically. Consider the fear, alienation, and distrust that those in the community who have not passed the threshold of entry into the middle class are likely to feel knowing that they may be victims of police intimidation and violence if the police believe that one is doing something out of line. The amount of pleasure in this larger context may well outweigh the pleasure the middle class community has at knowing the police will do what it takes to keep their middle class neighbourhoods safe. Once the community is included to be all the citizens of the community instead of the artificially contrived community, which is the middle class and upper class community plus the one accused criminal, the results will change dramatically once constitutional safeguards are overridden.

Even if it is granted that there are some cases in which violence is acceptable, far more often it is not. This is especially true of any attempted moral justification of institutionalized violence practiced by the government as shown above. The fact that these attempted ethical defences and justifications of violence fail in such contexts is quite a good thing. After all when it comes to violence, less is better.

Endnotes

1   C.f. Searle, John: *Speech Acts: An Essay in the Philosophy of Language* (Cambridge: Cambridge University Press, 1969).
2   C.f. Bradby, Hannah (ed.): *Defining Violence, Understanding the Causes and Effect of Violence* (Aldershot: Ashgate Publishing, 1996), pp. 1f.
3   Bok, S.: *Mayhem : violence as public entertainment* (Reading, Mass.: Addison-Wesley, 1998), p. 6. For examples of the wide use of the term 'violence', see Engels, F.: *The Condition of the Working Class in England*, tr. & ed. W.O. Henderson and W.H. Chaloner (Stanford: Stanford University Press, 1958), p. 108; Robert Paul Wolff, 'On Violence,' *Journal of Philosophy*, 66 (1969): pp. 601–616; Johan Galtung, 'Violence, Peace, and Peace Research,' *Journal of Peace Research*, 3 (1969), pp. 167–181, from Bok, S. op.cit, p. 160.
4   Weiss, Billie: 'Violence in the United States' in Bradby, op. cit, p. 86.
5   Ibid., p. 90.
6   Ibid., p. 88.
7   Ibid., p. 90
8   Friedman, L.: *Crime and Punishment in American History* (New York: Basic Books, 1993), p. 454.
9   Bok, S. op.cit, p. 8.
10   Ibid.
11   Friedman, L. op. cit., p. 26.
12   Ibid.
13   Ibid., p. 40.
14   Ibid., p.361.
15   Ibid., p.303.
16   Ibid., p.190.
17   Ibid., p. 210. For a good overview of the status of women in American history see Peck, E.: *Domestic Tyranny: The making of Social Policy Against Family Violence from Colonial Times to the Present* (Urbana, Ill.: University of Illinois Press, 1994).

18 Although exclusively a twentieth-century phenomenon, consider the popular movie released recently *The Gangs of New York* about gangs in New York City in the 1860s, cf. *Gangs of New York*, dir. by Martin Scorsese, 2002.

19 Friedman, L., op. cit., p. 455.

20 Thomas Aquinas: *Summa Theologica* 1–II Q94 A2

21 See Aristotle: *Nicomachean Ethics* (London: Penguin, 1976); Alasdair MacIntyre: *After Virtue* (Notre Dame:U. Notre Dame Press, 19842); Gregory Pence: 'Virtue Theory,' in Peter Singer (ed): *A Companion to Ethics* (Oxford: Basil Blackwell,1991), pp. 49–58.

22 Bok, S. op. cit, pp. 49–89.

23 Friedman, L. op. cit, p. 441.

24 C.f. Kant, I.: *Grounding for the Metaphysics of Morals* translated by James W. Ellington (Indianapolis: Hackett Pub. Co., 1983), Section 2.

25 Mill, John: *On Liberty* (Oxford: Oxford University Press, 1992), p. 14.

26 Ibid., p. 12.

Bernhard Waldenfels

Violence as Violation*

Our following reflections are based neither on the assumption that violence is something which has its own essence, nor do they presuppose that there are normal acts of violence which have a certain meaning and follow certain rules, as if violence simply belongs to our being in the world. On the contrary, violence seems to be something strange. It resembles phenomena such as love and death, phenomena traversing various domains of life, striking us as something ungraspable, insoluble, extraordinary, questioning all order, something with no proper place. The peculiarity of violence is shown by the fact that in antiquity it appears in a mythical form as do Kronos, Eros and Thanatos. With no secure place of its own, it gives rise to peculiar aporias. In Hannah Arendt's words, violence confronts us with the task 'of thinking the unthinkable'.[1] If violence could be conceived as something which simply belongs to the life of individuals and peoples, it would affect us like a virus. To think violence means to think against it.

Such a difficult issue requires a proceeding which approximates the phenomenon in an indirect way, marking the aporias we are confronted with. Hence, I shall begin with a selection of topics which encircle the phenomenon, taking into consideration various points of view and taking a look into the corresponding linguistic field. What seems to be especially important is to see that violence is a cultural phenomenon which cannot be transposed to some kind of brute nature. However, the leading idea will consist in the assumption that violence has to do with a violation that befalls somebody. This leads us to further questions concerning the state of the perpetrator and the state of the victim. As to the first we have to ask to what extent the actor can be regarded as responsible, and as to the latter we have to take into account a sort of singularity which exceeds the different paths of normalisation such as legalisation, medicalisation, moralisation or historisation. Our reflections will end by testing different ways of legitimisation which all seem to miss the strange character of violence.

The way we proceed can be characterised as phenomenological in so far as we go beyond categories, regulations, arguments and evaluations of all sorts, raising the question as to how violence appears, how it invades the field of experience and how it is expressed in language. Phenomenology is not as naive as some people pretend. It does not presuppose that what appears is completely outside of language, but it does presuppose that what happens and appears to us is more than what can said about it and what can be argued for or against it. The crucial point is not to assume that there is something given outside of language, but to concede that language precedes itself. Seeing and saying and even saying and doing will never coincide. These general considerations directly touch our issue of violence. If philosophers skip the genealogy of violence and, in a broader perspective, the genealogy of morals they simply beg the question, preserving their good moral consciences and leaving the rest to judges, doctors and the military.[2]

1.   Topics of Violence

Violence arises at the intersections of various orders. Thus, it transforms our own *body* into a sphere of vulnerability up to the point of violence against life and limb. *Technology* originates as body technique, and from the very beginning it creates not only tools with which we work on things, but also weapons with which we attack beings like ourselves. Tools are in themselves double-edged things. It was an axe with which Cain killed his brother. 'I wish David had killed Goliath with a lyre,' says the contemporaneous Polish aphorist Stanislaw J. Lec. Just as the body functions as the first instrument, it also functions as the first weapon. Our hand clenches to a fist, our elbow moves forward like a club. But nowadays, relying on modern weapons of destruction which are no longer used or operated as instruments or machines, but turned on and off as an apparatus, we have moved a considerable distance from bodily violence. Violence can be so clean that traces of blood have an atavistic or even an obscene effect. Nor are *games* exempt from violence even if we think of the largely ritualised and regulated jousting of the knights at chivalrous tournaments or of boxing matches. *Religion* is just as deeply impregnated with violence in terms of sacrifices which are offered to a higher power. The ritual or ascetic character of human or animal sacrifices, circumcision, mortification and castigation set these apart from the violence of simple fighting. In Freud's view joint patricide is a primal event in which the community of brothers is founded. The ambiguity of *sacrificium* and *victima* belongs to the semantics of 'violence' and gives it explosive features. Finally, there is our *language*, which not only speaks *about* violence, but also speaks the language *of* violence. The linguistic scale extends form verbal acts such as insult or threat through bearing witness to violence up to its legitimisation. It is almost superfluous to mention the official domains of law, morals and politics. Crimes of violence, the state monopoly on the use of force and violence and the oscillation between using and exploiting labour force and natural forces all belong to the traditional problematic.

On the conceptual level violence is difficult to demarcate.[3] The German word *Gewalt* is ambiguous. It covers a double meaning including on the one hand *potestas*, the authority vested in public office (*Amtsgewalt*) and controlled by the separation of powers (*Gewaltenteilung*), and on the other hand *violentia*. In its immediate vicinity we find the term 'power' (*potentia, dynamis, Macht*), and its environment includes items like 'force' as effective power which runs into counter-force, 'constraint', which is characterised by impediments and coercion, 'conflict' as the clash of forces and interests, 'repugnancy' as the incompatibility of experiences and attitudes, and a sort of 'polemics' without which politics would be a mere epiphenomenon. As to the use of language we must say that too narrow a concept would be apt to curtail the horizon of the problem, whereas too broad a concept would tend to water down the problematic.

Furthermore, we shall have to distinguish special modes of seeking access to violence and of dealing with it. The classical distinction between participation and observation falters. On the one hand, should we assume that the victim of violence 'takes part' in the act of violence, perhaps by lack of resistance? On the other hand, is there anything like 'pure observation'? We know that to do nothing more than to take note of what is going on could be punishable, for example as failure to lend assistance or as condoning a crime. And where are the limits of what can be reasonably required of the third party who is expected to run a risk by intervening? What about the system-theoretical distinction between drawing a distinction and observing it? To what extent is it possible to describe violent acts in terms of merely systematic procedures? These questions suffice to indicate to what extent our everyday and our academic ways of thought can be shaken by violence.

Finally, I would like to raise an objection on my home ground which mutatis mutandis may also be applied to analytical philosophy. Phenomenology and hermeneutics are dominated by the category of *sense* or *meaning*, which originates from processes of intending, understanding and rule-following. And here the question is whether violence has a sense and whether acts of violence have a meaning which could be explicated, interpreted and appropriated. Should we not rather assume that violence appears as something out of place, as a sort of *foreign body,* which disturbs and interrupts the economy of sense? This is where a particular dispute among historians will break out. What seems to be at stake is not the divergence of historical perspectives, trends of interpretation and methodological approaches, it is rather History as such (something which does not exist for the ancient Greeks or for far-eastern cultures) that has to be put to the test. The questions arising here do not inevitably lead to a dubious sort of *posthistoire.* They may just as well lead to an alternative historiography which would no longer be prepared to eliminate every sort of rupture and irruption by means of interpretation and explanation. The 'stumbling logic', inherent in the course of history,[4] would find its counterpart in a stammering sort of historiography.

2. Violence between nature and culture

There is a certain trend which is difficult to stamp out. I mean the attempt to locate violence in a pre-historical state of nature which we are so lucky to have left behind us. The repeated irruptions of barbarity into civilised regions are reduced to mere forms of relapse. We act as if we could contemplate the waves of violence from a safe haven. Such attempts to stem violence go back to the beginnings of our cultural history. *Kratos* and *Bia*, force and violence, which in Aeschylus' *Prometheus Bound* appear in a personalised form, yield their power to the imperium of *Techne*. Cicero's *De officiis* presents two ways to overcome conflicts: the human way of dispute (*disceptatio*) and the animal way of blind violence (*vis*). Regarded from the perspective of world history, the well-known path from darkness to light, from brute beginnings to moral sophistication is opened up. But this does not silence dissenting voices who contradict this all too beautiful and simple fable.

Dissenting voices, which since the days of Rousseau increasingly contest thinking in terms of progress, suggest that violence finds its place, or better its non-place, on the *threshold between nature and culture*. As our dreams demonstrate every night and every day, this threshold will never be definitively crossed. As far as our issue is concerned, this means that violence displays certain features which cannot be banished to the beginnings or to the dark corners of our history. Wherever real progress takes place in the course of history, the old saying bears repeating: *corruptio optimi pessima*.

Thus, we have to consider some basic features of violence. First, there is the *cultural* character of violence, in contrast to a mere brute or natural sort of violence. Wars and revolutions are completely different from the avalanches or volcano eruptions to which they often are compared. In the last century this naturalisation often had a rather vitalistic air, for example when we listen to the fanfares which accompanied the outbreak of World War I.

Further, the violence which human beings do to each other takes on *symbolic* forms. It is mediated by artificial signs, rituals, practices, tactics and interpretations. It may be sufficient to consider the discourse of war which includes things like the law of war, the declaration of war, war enemy, prisoner of war and war crime. Wars are waged, they do not simply occur. Supposedly brute and naked violence always appears well formed, dressed and armed, and so-called brute force (*Brachialgewalt*) is assisted by head and heart. There are no violent basic actions unless one abstracts rather artificially from the semantics and pragmatics of the violent event. As Hobbes already stresses, violent acts are *deemed to be* manslaughter, an act of self-defence, an interrogation under torture and so on. Politics, which is permeated by violence, starts with the act of naming prior to acts of decision-making and judging. To take an example from our contemporary history, it makes a great difference whether the events of 1954 in Budapest are classified as a counter-revolution or as a popular revolt. The difference begins with the right to a burial (which is so important in Sophokles' *Antigone*), and it ends with the legal rights of the surviving dependants. Similar remarks could be made about more recent events. The question as to whether the bloody events in Bosnia should be classified as an ethnic conflict or as a genocide had considerable consequences. The first alternative only called for a neutral intervention, whereas the second one required that the process be stopped by all possible means. The fact that Srebenica (the place of violence, quickly cast from mind, that returns from time to time like a nightmare) became a kind of turning-point certainly does not imply that things happened before in a more moral way. The declaration of the French Parliament in June 1998 that 'France officially recognises the Armenian genocide of 1915' belongs to a highly delayed politics of language. The fact that only 29 of the 580 deputies were present makes the symbolic value shrink. But linguistic politics also includes extraordinary attempts to lend words to the singular suffering which nonetheless remains unspeakable, it includes attempts to snatch from the jaws of silence events which cannot be simply classified. Thus the genocide committed on the Armenians and Jews has been given names such as *Grand Crime, Grande Souffrance, Catastrophe, Holocaust* or *Schoa*.[5]

3. Violence and violation

After this first circumscription of the phenomenon, we have to ask what is at issue in the case of violence. What is at stake when violence occurs? What are we speaking about when we speak of violence? Is there a semantic nucleus which criss-crosses the multiple variations of violence? In what follows I shall pick out a central motif which is suggested in particular by the Latin word *violentia* and its derivations in the Romance languages. Violence will be shown to be a sort of *violation* which under certain circumstances will increase to para-lysing and long-lasting forms of traumatism. But at this point we are showered by questions.

1. From the victim's point of view the question arises: *Who* or *what* can be violated? There are three possibilities: something, some-body or a general rule. Let us start with the possibility that something is violated. If we adhere to everyday and even legal usage, we must admit that simple things can be damaged or destroyed, but certainly not violated. Violence presupposes a certain *self-referentiality* and *integrity* which does not exist in the case of simple function bearers. Something which exists for the sake of something else and not for its own sake cannot be injured in its being, it may only be impaired in its function, for example if a chair looses a leg or a tube leaks. When certain functions are impaired we only speak of damage, which may be light or grave. The German word *Kriegsbeschädigter* tends to blur this distinction in opposition to the English expression *disabled veteran* or the French expression *mutilé de guerre*. If we accept the proposed distinction, it seems reasonable to interpret what is called violence against things as an indirect violence against persons.

Let us go on to the second possibility. A general *rule* is infringed or violated if somebody does what is forbidden or does not do what is prescribed. But this provides no more help in grasping the full meaning of violence. It is true that murder or manslaughter are re-garded as legal or moral crimes, but it is not true that every case of breach of a rule, for example failure to observe the proper period of notice when terminating employment or giving false evidence in court, is taken to be an act of violence. Moreover, there are legal forms of deprivation of freedom, execution or killing in war. What makes them acts of violence must be something different from a violation of law.

There remains the third possibility, ascribing the violation to somebody *to whom* it is done. Thus, violence has an addressee, someone from whom life is taken, to whom death is given or to whom something is done. This form of dative has been called addressee dative by Karl Bühler.[6] This means that verbs like 'murder', 'insult' or 'rape' are used as three-valued predicates: *somebody* does *something to somebody*. This aspect of the dative, which belongs to the deep structure of doing to (*Antun*) just as it belongs to the deep structure of speaking to (*Anrede*), is dissipated when we reduce acts of violence to legal or moral cases. In doing so we judge such acts from the position of a third party, and we take it as something which somebody (in the nominative) has done on his or her own initiative or on behalf of others. However, the victim of violence puts a limit to the processes of legalisation and moralisation which both tend to make the victim of a deed (*Tat*) disappear behind the legal definition of the crime (*Tatbestand*) under which the deed is subsumed. Moreover, we should avoid identifying somebody to whom violence is done with a person to whom certain rights and duties are ascribed. There are pre-legal and pre-moral claims which demand to be listened to and to be looked at, which provoke a responsive mode of hearing and seeing. Such claims arise before they are subjected to the binary criteria of right or wrong.[7] The famous slogan 'My country, right or wrong', pronounced by myself, should be balanced by the prior saying 'My face, right or wrong', heard from the Other. If it is transposed into a general legal or moral claim, the Other's situated claim would be nothing more than a particular case. Finally, we should take the possibility into account that there are not only human but also non-human addressees of violence.[8]

This use of the difference between something and somebody is far from trivial. A wide-spread form of violence is based on the transformation of somebody into something or on the transformation of the addressee into a goal-object. Let me cite some famous examples. Aristotle defines the slave as an 'animated tool' which is only made use of and not spoken to, except in the computer-like language of directive orders. John Locke, an honourable, liberal man, does not hesitate to declare: 'One may destroy a man who makes war upon him, or has discovered an enmity to his being, for the same reason that he may kill a wolf or a lion [...]'.[9] The slave has never been human, the enemy stops being human, in both cases violence is done *to something*. By mixing the features of thing and person we generate hybrids which belong to a special grammar of violence.

2. With regard to the course of a criminal act, the question arises: *In what form* has somebody been violated or injured? Here we run into dubious distinctions such as *bodily* violence and *mental* cruelty. *Symbolic* violence, which is implemented by calumny, threat and insult, is distinguished from real violence, which leads to robbery or killing. But such distinctions always tend to play off one form of violence against the other, as if for example an attack on the Other's dignity were less offensive than a punch. Once again the ordering hand intervenes before violence finds its own language. Such faults of prejudgement can be avoided if we start from an integrated sphere of life, namely *bodily existence as a sphere of vulnerability*. The old proverb according to which we learn by suffering refers to the fact that there are experiences, *Widerfahrnisse*, which occur to us or befall us before we take the initiative.[10] These strong experiences are accompanied by forms of violation which we only become aware of afterwards. The ambiguous character of bodily experience, which is never completely harmless, finds complex expression in the Greek word *pathos*. Our body must not only be resurrected as a 'great reason' as in Zarathustra's speech against the '*Verächter des Leibes*' (the despisers of the body), it must also be understood as the place of an all-penetrating violence. Because it is visible, tangible and open to attack, even to mortal attacks, our body forms a territory which opens the door to violence. Our body spreads through the world. It has its surroundings, formed by clothes, everyday tools, dwelling, home country, property and relatives. That is the reason why the requirement to wear a uniform or degrading forms of nakedness, burglary and trespass, expulsion, ban of language and collective liability of the members of a family are the home grounds for indirect forms of violence, which affect the Other detrimentally by a sort of

Mitleidenschaft (co-suffering). Blackmail always takes such an indirect path. Instead of dividing the field of violence into a dualistic pattern, we should look for finer distinctions. Thus, we could distinguish between a *peripheral* and a *central* form of violence, referring to a scale which extends from the insistent gaze through lewd remarks and offensive conduct to torture, rape and murder. Making the further distinction between *direct* and *indirect* violence enables us to trace the evasive manoeuvres of violence as in the case of reprisals. Similarly to how Freud separates the *Triebziel* (drive goal) from the *Triebobjekt* (drive object), we can distinguish between the more steady goal and the more variable object of violence. Finally, there is a difference between *on-going* and *structural* violence. The fact that this distinction may be used to denigrate institutions as a whole should not lead us to personalise violence excessively. In this context it may be helpful to consider the acting and the habitual side of our body. Violence occurs momentarily when we suffer from disregard, attack or injury. But it can also be deposited in our body. There are numerous examples of this: forced labour, which engraves its traces into the body day by day; military drill, which bends the body into shape and makes it interchangeable; the diffusion of an atmosphere of fear, which represses free utterances; discriminating administrative rules or practices, which infringe on the rights of equality; stigmatisation, which extends to the extreme forms of branding slaves or imposing the yellow star of David on Jewish citizens. Whereas structural violence, when restricted to forced labour, preserves a minimum of community, it turns into pure terror when victims are used as deterrents, and it ends with extermination when all victims are equalised by technically and hygienically constructed killing machines.[11]

3. From the side of the perpetrator we have to pose the question: *Who* or *what* is responsible for the violation? Do we have to do with acts of violence or with a simple occurrence of violence? What about the originator of violence? The first answer should be: events become actions or deeds by being ascribed to somebody as his or her action. Everybody can more or less participate in what happens. The eclipse of the great subject also undermines the position occupied by the great holders of power and violence, by all sorts of *Macht-* and

Gewalthaber. Responsibility appears in dosed forms, and the dose is measured in accordance with the different orders of action, of society and of life, which all distribute chances and allow for initiatives, but in different ways. However, if nobody were personally involved in committing violence and if nobody were addressed by it, there would be nothing left other than pure operations to be observed and controlled from the neutral position of a third party. The participation perspective would be simply replaced by the observation perspective. This would be another form of violence. The complete incapacitation, the *Entmündigung* of the perpetrator would simultaneously incapacitate the victims by taking even the word of complaint out of their mouths.

4. Collective, individual and anonymous character of violence

Questioning the functioning of violence we are confronted with further questions, first with the question of the *collective* aspect of violence. John Ladd, who represents an individualistic approach, defines collective violence as 'that kind of violence that is practised by one group on another and that pertains to individuals, as agents or as victims, only by virtue of their (perceived) association with a particular group'.[12] In opposition to the *private* form of violence, the collective form cannot be explained by personal motives like profit-seeking or vindictiveness; such an attempt would be guilty of an 'individualisation fallacy'.[13] Such a broad definition of collective violence allows us to include not only war and genocide, but also criminal assassinations when individually committed, further lynch justice with an individual victim or a ritual duel. Concerning the institution of violence there are sharper qualifications at hand: a *massacre* takes place when perpetrator and victim are in a one-sided relationship to each other, a *war* when several hostile groups fight against each other, a *genocide* is given when whole populations are exterminated. However, in general it seems to me more appropriate to oppose private to *public* violence, corresponding to the distinction between private and public law. This permits us to avoid confusing the institution of violence with its organisation.[14]

Further we must ask how the actions of those who are actively or passively involved in the event of violence are organised and to what extent they can be found guilty in the moral or in the legal sense. In this context we are faced with the alternative of an individualism which reduces the whole event to individual actions and a holism which introduces wholes like people, mass or class as collective agencies. Even if this distinction has to be understood only as a methodological option, the prestige of a corresponding social ontology persists. This ontology is severely shaken by a genealogical approach which takes both, individuals and societies, to be the result of a simultaneous process of individualisation and socialisation, and which presumes that such a process can happen in different ways and to different degrees. A medieval craftsman or a family-bound Japanese does not show the same individual features as a modern bourgeois or a hypermodern single. Pascal's ascription of all disaster to the fact that we are unable to remain quietly on our own room presupposes a high degree of independence and self-sufficiency. When Foucault raises the question of the author he does not ask, 'Is there an author?' but rather, 'What is an author?' Merleau-Ponty's assumption that there is a sort of corporeal-social anonymity at the heart of our being and that we will never be absolutely individualised[15] also undermines the alternative of individualism or holism. Finally, this view is complemented by the inner polyphony of speech we encounter in Mikhail Bachtin's literature studies.[16]

Let us now ask about the consequences which all this has in respect to the authorship of violence and the alternative of individual or collective guilt. If we follow Merleau-Ponty or Norbert Elias and accept the anti-Cartesian and anti-Humean presupposition that there is an intertwining of own and alien, that is, that there is an *Ineinander* (intermingling) of speech and counter-speech, of action and counter-action, based on an original form of intercorporeity, then the single person finds his place within a social field which is not only, but also a field of violence. This entanglement does not only connect victims and co-victims, perpetrators and accomplices, it does not even come to a halt before the relation between victim and perpetrator. Jorge Semprun, who certainly is far from glossing things over or covering up injustice, shows very clearly how infamous it is when victims are transformed into accomplices, not only in order to save their own lives, but also in order to prevent things from becoming worse.[17] This is not to blur all distinctions, leading us into the night when all cats are black, in which every kind of responsibility would be extinguished. Rather, it creates a *clair-obscur*, a manifold spectrum of variegated perpetration and complicity, occupying one and the same social field in which forces are unequally distributed up to the point of polarisation into power (*Macht*) and powerlessness (*Ohnmacht*).[18] Moralists who want to make the situation of violence less ambiguous than it is by strictly separating light and shadow, good and evil, do not only falsify what is going on, they also harm the victims. They demand from them an excess of morality, selflessness or heroism – as if not even victims had a right to normality. Victims are not victims because they are saints or heroes. The fact that there are extraordinary men and women who have taken a greater risk and have given more of themselves than others awakes and merits our admiration. But even the 'ordinary' victim deserves our respect.[19]

The anonymity of violence is based on the embodiment of our body which will never be completely our own body, but has something of a *Fremdkörper, a foreign body*, something of a body out of place. This genuine anonymity is reinforced by an excess of technologisation which increasingly transforms violent acts into mechanisms and operations of violence. The history of war is full of striking examples. Pressing a button or remotely controlling a movement are far removed from a thrust of the bayonet or from the gun smoke of trenches. Decisions calculated by computer require computer-like implementations. Actions resemble distant stars which are already extinguished when we see them. It may be that technological processes need tele-morals which take into account instant long-distance effects and '*Fernstenopfer*' or distant victims, and not only later effects. But such morals would be rather schematic and would vanish in technological networks, if we fail to become at the same time 'good neighbours of the nearest things'.

5.   Normality and singularity of violence

The anonymisation of violence is accompanied by another problematic which could be called the normalisation of violence. I shall not unfold this problematic in its full length, but I want to exhibit what has an immediate effect on violation by violence. I begin with a methodological alternative which plays an important role in the human and social sciences with regard to the question of collective violence. An anonymity of violence which cannot be reduced to individual intentions and interests calls for a *structural* method. In accordance with this method, individual positions, actions and ideas are treated as variables which even allow for statistical registration and which are far removed from the *Haupt- and Staatsaktionen*, the pomp and circumstance, about which Marx makes ironic comments. With such preconditions, it is not impossible to speak of a normal concentration camp guard and vice versa of a normal concentration camp prisoner, although they have a horrible and frightening normality,[20] and although the 'banality of evil' is far from being banal itself. However, the structuralist treatment does not preclude the complementary possibility of taking account of individual modes of experience which can be explored by means of oral history, using biographical evidence and, assuming it is not too late, narrative interviews. Both approaches, the structure-orientated and the experience-bound, have their own right, and there is no reason to play off subjects against structures.[21]

The problem seems to arise elsewhere. A structural-functionalist or systemic approach would have to treat even victims as typical or as statistical cases. Consequently, the suffering of victims would pertain to the functional equivalencies which sustain or threaten a system. Nothing against this, just as there is no reason not to draw up lists of crime rates or accident statistics. Anomalous states, which due to their character as crime or illness deviate from normal feeling or behaviour, can be normalised. We do so whenever we speak of a normal *Gestapo* officer, a normal *Stasi* (former East German secret police) collaborator or of a normal heart attack. Further, in the face of such generalisations

it is not sufficient to insist on *individual* victims, suffering and violations. The individual as something of which something is predicated
without being itself a possible predicate (the Aristotelian definition)
appears as a *Dies-da*, a this-here (τόδε τι); but that already sheds the
light of general determinations on it. In terms of modern thinking, the
individual forms the intersection of different rules, or it presents itself
as a deviation within a social field. The individual is something or
somebody else, that is all; it will never be totally other because in this
case it would fall out of the frame of determination. The debates about
the victims of the Nazis take a completely wrong track when on
the one hand they remain on the level of general conceptualisation
and on the other hand insist on the uniquity and incomparability of
Auschwitz. A concentration camp can of course be compared to a
Gulag or to the Inquisition and the persecution of witches as long as
violence is considered as something which finds its place (where
else?) in some region of the world and in the field of history.

If we claim that suffering is unspeakable this must not be
understood in the sense of the old dictum: *individuum est ineffabile*.
This sentence means only that nothing which appears here and now is
exhausted by general determinations. The old statement, 'the concept
of dog does not bark' finds its equivalent in a corresponding
statement, 'the concept of victim does not suffer'. If we consider the
victim of violence there is much more at stake, namely the fact that
the other's claim is violated and not only a general law infringed. First
of all the act of violence is *not a topic about which* we talk with
others, but an action, directed at an *addressee to whom* it is done. This
action lives on in one's own witness and in that of others. Bearing
witness does not only mean speaking *about* an event, but rather *from*
an event, making it known. The witness does not give a direct account
of what is the case, rather it pronounces the way in which something
comes into view and is expressed, and this is something that can only
be shown and said *afterwards*. This is the origin of the belatedness of
traumatic experiences which since Freud has received such strong
emphasis,[22] and the same holds for the entanglement of forgetting
and remembering in which the horrible events persist. Traumatic
events which are impregnated with violence are not marked merely
by individuality, but by a sort of *singularity* which goes beyond every

ordinary order of action and life. This uniqueness is not only expressed
in an excess of suffering, but in outbursts of hatred. These have to be
regarded as irrational not only because they run out of control (they
can indeed be stimulated and provoked, as we all know), they are irrational because they surpass all measure and generate an affective
surplus which is acted out in acts of annihilation. The extraordinary
that makes itself felt here is not located in a celestial or infernal after-
world, it is something strange within this world. Just like other forms
of the extraordinary it takes place by disturbing and interrupting the
various orders of our world. We call something singular that in the
process of 'comparing the incomparable'[23] proves to be incomparable;
and this does not mean that the victim's suffering is completely other
or different, but that it is 'other than Being', far removed from the
reign of ordinary speaking and calculating. It will never find *its place*
in the world and it will not find *its place* in history which – despite
Hegel's averment – is not able to heal all wounds without leaving
scars.[24] It is in this sense that Auschwitz, a name standing for innum-
erable other places of violence, is incomparable, beyond every comparison, a black hole in the web of history. Singularity occurs in the
plural.[25] One does no injustice to the victims of the Nazis by also
conceding singularity to the victims of the Gulags or to the victims
of the Armenian or Bosnian genocide. On the contrary, those who
elevate Auschwitz to the *summum malum* of history themselves make
use of a comparative scale.[26]

6.   Violence under the sway of order

Assuming that violence is culturally and historically variable according to the orders in which it appears and assuming that this is what
gives it its collective shape, then the genealogy of violence forms a
junction with the genealogy of orders. This association of order and
violence will be our last issue. It is only in this context that violence
takes on a clear shape and its historical colouring. We can distinguish
different strategies of rationalisation.

Violence against order, violence against reason and right means that one opposes to non-reasonable violence a non-violent reason. Consequently violence seems to be pure *disorder* and lack of reason. This antithesis is too beautiful to be true. Reason and violence encounter each other within this world, they intermingle, and they cannot be assigned to an upper world of light and to a underworld of darkness.

Violence in the service of order makes it possible to sanctify and rationalise violence to some extent. One relies on a *felix violentia* which, similar to the *felix culpa*, is on the path towards a non-violent order and derives its justification from this fact. The integration of violence into a process which surpasses it leads to the well-known distinctions between just and unjust war, revolution and counter-revolution, or progressive and regressive violence. These distinctions are themselves sources of violence because they lower the threshold of violence. In Western history in particular, violence tends to be ideologically charged and veiled. There is no appeal against *legitimated* violence. The trend to justify violence increases in the nineteenth century because the demarcation line between legitimate and illegitimate is increasingly transposed into the immanence of history, with the effect that there is no longer a backdoor for reprieve and forgiveness. Things prove to be more modest in the liberal tradition where since the time of John Locke violence is taken as the *ultima ratio*,[27] as *emergency violence* or as *counter-violence*. Whereas the former remains in contact with *Notwehr*, self-defence, the latter starts up a machinery of legitimisation which will not come to a stop because in each case the other's violence is declared to be violence, whereas one's own violence is counter-violence.[28] Things become even more modest when this material debate is replaced with formal procedures whose correctness is the only criterion in questions of legitimacy and illegitimacy of violence. What remains could be called *procedural* violence. Violence manifests itself as a source of friction or noise within the machinery of functioning orders which are fighting for their own existence.

The over-rationalisation of violence which tries to justify or legitimate what is unjustifiable will never cease to provoke reprisals in terms of *violence in revolt against every order*. The over-rationalisation corresponds to a militant irrationality which explicitly adopts an anarchic form of violence. Oscillating between a utopia of non-governance and the pure destruction of structures of dominion, this kind of violence leads into a dead end.

7.   Violence in the shadow of orders

Is there any way out of this vicious circle of power on the endless path of self-intensification and self-preservation? It would be a considerable help to take the *contingency of all order whatsoever* seriously.[29] If all order can be different than it actually is, no order will ever be completely legitimised. The inevitable selectivity and exclusivity, inherent to the character of every order that it is 'thus and not otherwise', implies a certain measure of force. Just as we say of an interpretation that it 'does violence' to what is interpreted, or as we speak of trenchant measures, we must assume that there is something violent about order. There is no speech, no action, no gaze, no communication which does complete justice to the claims of those who are involved. There will always remain something which is alien (*fremd*), extra-ordinary because it does not find its place within the given order. *Fremdheit* (otherness and alienness) and violence are very close to each other as is suggested by the meaning of *hostis*, which oscillates between *hospitality* and *hostility*. Just as we should assume with Merleau-Ponty that 'there is' (*il y a*) rationality and sense or with Foucault that 'there is' order, but that reason *as such*, sense *as such*, order *as such* do not exist in the sense of a *singulare tantum*, we should admit that *there is something* violent, which is the reverse of order. The adjective form 'violent' (*gewaltsam*) may suggest that violence takes place in a parasitic form and not in the substantive form of 'violence' (*Gewalt*), not as a substance of violence which would lead us back onto the tracks of Gnosis.[30]

Apart from the violent aspect which results from the contingency of order, violence is to be found in every form of apparent legitimisation and exaggerated sense-giving that we have mentioned. Every attempt to derive the fact that there is violence, a fact that depends on prior forms of primal oblivion and primal perversion, from some other source leads into the maelstrom of a sort of self-made violence – unless one is content with mythical narrations which only *present* what cannot be *explained*. Besides, there is no reason why practical philosophy should be more anxious to provide explanations than is theoretical physics, which after all has it that the cosmos started with a big bang. To show that the inexplicable is inexplicable does not mean that we veil something we do not want to take notice of; on the contrary, mystification starts with the explanation of the unexplainable. Historians may dismiss these reflections as futile speculations far removed from reality, but they would be wrong. As history shows, exaggerated visions which admit of realisation tend to be exceptionally effective.

If there is something like a fact of violence, then it is not up to us to choose it; there are only various ways of treating it. Even renouncing violence takes place *in and by* speaking and doing, that is, within a field which is already marked by violence. The attempt to think the unthinkable finds its practical resonance in the attempt to do the impossible – im-possible insofar as it surpasses the range of given possibilities and existing rules, and in the attempt to do it again and again and not once for all. Let me finish with a text passage, taken from Jorge Semprun's novel *Quel beau dimanche!* (translated into English as *What a Beautiful Sunday!*). The Spanish author, himself a burnt child who dreads the fire, burnt not only by violence, but also by ideologies of violence, quotes Merleau-Ponty and Malraux: 'There are just wars, but no just armies', and himself continues: 'There are just wars, but no innocent armies'. However we select and distribute the adjectives one thing seems to be sure: any (definitive) solution of the question of violence would itself be a violent solution.

Endnotes

* First published under the title 'Aporien der Gewalt' in M. Dabag, A. Kapust, B. Waldenfels (eds): *Gewalt. Strukturen, Formen, Repräsentationen* (Munich: Fink, 2000), pp. 9–24. I thank Donald Goodwin for his assistance with the English version.

1 Arendt, H.: *On Violence* (London: Allen Lane, 1970), p. 6.

2 These are indeed strong presuppositions. They belong to a response-orientated and pathos-based sort of phenomenology which I have largely developed else-where. See *Antwortregister* (Frankfurt: Suhrkamp, 1994), translated as *Responsive Register*, trans. by D. F. Goodwin, (Evanston, Ill.: Northwestern University Press, forthcoming) and *Bruchlinien der Erfahrung* (Frankfurt: Suhrkamp, 2002).

3 Cf. Röttgers, K.: *Spuren der Macht* (Freiburg: K. Alber, 1990).

4 Cf. Merleau-Ponty, M.: *Merleau-Ponty à la Sorbonne. Résumés de cours 1949–1952* (Grenoble: Cynara, 1988), p. 85.

5 Concerning the following reflections see my earlier article 'Grenzen der Legitimierung und die Frage nach der Gewalt', which places the emphasis on the issue of the violation of others' claims, referring to such authors as H. Arendt, M. Foucault, M. Merleau-Ponty, E. Levinas and M. Weber. The article has been published in German in: *Der Stachel des Fremden* (Frankfurt a. M.: Suhrkamp, 1990) pp. 103–119 and in English as 'Limits of Legitimation and the Question of Violence' in J. B. Bradly and N. Garver (eds): *Justice, Law and Violence* (Philadelphia: Temple University Press, 1991).

6 See Bühler, K.: *Theory of Language* (Amsterdam/Philadelphia: J. Benjamin, 1990), § 15 and my own reflections on the dialogical dimensions of action in: *Antwortregister*, op. cit., p. 452–457.

7 The 'before' of the pre-legal or pre-moral claim must not be understood in terms of events located on a temporal line, but rather in terms of a certain precedence (*Vorgängigkeit*) which corresponds to the inner lateness (*Nachträglichkeit*) of our response, including legal and moral sorts of responding. Responding means being not completely up to date. Most theories of practice and discourse miss this point because the specific time of speaking and acting is permanently overshadowed by questions of meaning, goals and rules.

8 Concerning the relation between claim (*Anspruch*) and right (*Anrecht*) see *Antwortregister*, op. cit., part III, ch. 12.

9 Locke, J.: *Second Treatise of Government*, (Cambridge, MA: Hackett Publishing Co, Inc, 1980), III, 16

10 I have extensively explored this deep dimension of experience in my last book, *Bruchlinien der Erfahrung,* op. cit..

11 In this way one may distinguish between different types of collective violence in Bolshevism and Nazism as certain historians do.

12   Ladd, J.: 'The Idea of Collective Violence' in Brady, J. B. and Garver, N. (eds): *Justice, Law and Violence*, op. cit., p. 19.

13   Ibid., p. 23.

14   The concept of the collective is ambiguous because it comprehends both the organisation of a group (which may be in accordance with private interests) and the symbolical regulations of group membership. The fact that the distinction between private and public itself has historical roots may be passed over in this context.

15   Merleau-Ponty, M.: *Phenomenology of Perception*, trans. by C. Smith (London: Routledge & Kegan Paul, 1962), pp. xii, 428; Merleau-Ponty, M.: *Phénoménologie de la perception* (Paris: Gallimard, 1945), pp. vii, 489.

16   More about this in *Antwortregister,* op. cit., part III, ch. 8: 'Ineinander von Eigenem und Fremdem' and *Topographie des Fremden* (Frankfurt a. M.: Suhrkamp, 1997), ch. 3: 'Verschränkung von Heimwelt und Fremdwelt'.

17   See the discussion of politics and morals in Semprun's novel *What a Beautiful Sunday!* trans. by Alan Sheridan (London: Harcourt Brace Jonanovich, 1982), pp. 228–236.

18   Aristotle, who so strongly emphasises the goal direction of action and the weighing up of practical motives, already introduces a class of 'mixed actions' which are located between voluntary and involuntary. These hybrid actions are subject to natural or social constraints (such as sea storm or extortion) so that we do what we do not want to do (*Nicomachean. Ethics*. III, 1). In the case of voluntary acts, Aristotle takes into account the reaching of a state (for example drunkenness) and the formation of habits which considerably restrict the range of action. (*ibid.*, III, 7). Cf. also Merleau-Ponty's critique of Sartre for confronting individuals with direct actions without considering the refraction of practical projects by collective symbols, cf. *Adventures of the Dialectic*, trans. by J. Bien (Evanston: Northwestern University Press, 1973), ch. 5; *Les aventures de la dialectique*, (Paris: Gallimard, 1967), ch. V.

19   The proverbial *De mortuis nil nisi bene* should be extended to a stronger *De victimis nil nisi bene*. The two maxims should not be understood as calls for posthumous justification or historical glossing; they only mean that those who have survived should not abuse the defencelessness of the dead by speaking the last word about them.

20   Arendt, H.: *Eichmann in Jerusalem. A Report concerning the Banality of Evil* (New York: Penguin Books, 1994), pp. 287f.

21   Cf. on this point Merleau-Ponty's lucid and and careful rapprochement of phenomenology and structuralism in his article 'From Mauss to Levi-Strauss' in *Signs*' translated by Richard C. McCleary (Evanston, [Ill.]: Northwestern University Press, 1964), pp. 114–125.

22   See in this context Leonardo's remark in Goethe's *Wilhelm Meisters Wanderjahre* (book 1, ch. 11), which refers to the first meeting with the 'nut-brown girl': 'A vivid impression is like another wound; one does not feel it when it is

suffered. It is only later that it begins to hurt and to fester.' Note that in this context Goethe is speaking of an injury *inflicted on the other* which hurts the person *who inflicts* it. This shows a remarkable intertwining of one's own affects and those of the other.

23   Levinas, E.: *Otherwise Than Being, or Beyond Essence*, trans. by A. Lingis (Pittsburgh: Duquesne University Press, 1998), p. 127; *Autrement qu'être ou au-delà de l'essence* (The Hague: M. Nijhoff, 1974), p. 202.

24   Hegel, G.: *Phenomenology of Spirit,* trans. by A. V. Millar (Oxford: Oxford University Press, 1977), p. 407; *Phänomenologie des Geistes*, (Hamburg: Meiner, 1952), p. 470.

25   See my chapter on Levinas: 'Singularität im Plural', in: *Deutsch-Französische Gedankengänge* (Frankfurt a. M.: Suhrkamp, 1995).

26   Cf. Levinas' dedication of *Otherwise than being or beyond essence:* 'In the memory of...'

27   *Ultima ratio* need not only translated as 'last resort' but also as 'reason at the end'. Concerning 'Gewaltsamkeit' as a specific instrument of politics see Max Weber: *Economy and Society* Vol. 1 (Chicago: University of Chicago Press, 1978), pp. 54f.; *Wirtschaft und Gesellschaft*, (Tübingen: J. C. B. Mohr (P. Siebeck), 1976), p. 29.

28   The concept of counter-violence (*Gegengewalt*) is already found in Kant, though with a negative accent (see *Über den Gemeinpruch...*, Werke vol. VI, ed. Weischedel, [Frankfurt: Suhrkamp, 1968] p. 156).

29   See my extensive discussion of order in *Order in the Twilight* (Ohio University Press 1996); *Ordnung im Zwielicht Ordnung im Zwielicht* (Frankfurt a. M.: Suhrkamp, 1987).

30   When Derrida refers to a 'transcendental violence' in his famous article 'Violence and Metaphysics', in *Writing and Difference* (Chicago: University of Chicago Press, 1978), pp. 79–153 this can only mean that violence *takes part* in the foundation of sense.

Vittorio Bufacchi

Violence by Omission

When thinking about violence, most people conjure up the picture of a distinctive act being performed by the perpetrator of violence, with destructive or harmful consequences for the victim. For example, when reading the following passage from Jonathan Glover's account of one of the many genocidal massacres in Rwanda in 1994, what comes to mind is probably the act of dismembering a fellow human being by machete blows:

> A massacre at Kibeho was seen by a schoolgirl, Yvette. She saw many brutal killings, including a baby killed with a machete and thrown down the toilet. Yvette received two blows which nearly killed her. Later she was interrogated, beaten, raped and made pregnant.[1]

It is beyond doubt that murdering someone by machete blows constitutes an act of violence. And yet, while this is a paradigm case of violence, it would be wrong to assume that all acts of violence follow a similar configuration. Above all, apart from direct acts of destructive or harmful conduct, an act of violence can also be done through an omission. Violence by omission is an aspect of the act of violence that often gets overlooked. It is precisely this hidden type of violence that will be explored in this paper. In what follows, it will be argued that in terms of doing violence, there is no difference between a direct action and an omission, even though violence by direct action and violence by omission may not always carry the same moral weight.

1.   How Violence is Done

'Doing something' usually entails the performance of a direct action with certain consequences: 'doing the dishes' involves the physical action of scrubbing a plate with a sponge; 'doing homework' implies the physical action of writing in a notebook; etc. Yet we can also do something by not performing an action, for example when we burn the toast by not switching off the grill before the slice of bread is incinerated. In the latter case, which will be referred to by the generic term of 'omissions', we do something by doing nothing.[2]

'Doing violence' is not different from doing anything else. In all paradigm cases of violence, when an act of violence occurs, the perpetrator performs a direct action (punching, kicking, dispensing machete blows, etc.) that has the effect of inflicting injury or suffering on a victim. Not surprisingly, most definitions of violence suggest that an act of violence necessarily entails a direct physical act that causes harm or destruction. Thus Ted Honderich defines violence as 'a use of physical force that injures, damages, violates or destroys people or things'.[3] John Keane describes an act of violence in terms of

> the unwanted physical interference by groups and/or individuals with the bodies of others, which are consequentially made to suffer a series of effects ranging from shock, bruises, scratches, swelling or headaches to broken bones, heart attack, loss of limbs or even death.[4]

Norman Geras suggests that violence can be defined simply as 'the exercise of physical force so as to kill or injure, inflict direct harm or pain on, human beings'.[5]

The above definitions capture our basic intuitions about violence, and they certainly cover the majority of cases of violence. Yet there are other instances of violence that cannot be accounted for by these definitions. For example, the most extreme cases of neglect are also a form of violence, even if neglect means not doing something. The tragic death of eight-years old Anna Climbie in 1997, murdered by her great aunt and her boyfriend, is a case in point. Anna was the victim of many aspects of violence. She was found bound hand and foot, naked, in a bathtub in a tiny flat in London in the middle of winter. The 128 marks found on her body are a clear indication of direct acts of physical violence. Anna was beaten with a variety of weapons including belt buckles, bicycle chains, coat hangers and shoes. Razor blades were taken to her fingers and a hammer to her toes. But apart from these direct acts of violence, Anna also suffered from certain intentional non-acts of violence, or violence by omissions. Anna was not loved or cared for. She was not fed properly, or even given adequate clothing; she was stuck in a black binbag which caught her excrement and trapped acids that burned her body. The state pathologist confirmed that the underlying cause of her death was severe neglect and malnutrition. These intentional omissions are as much a form of violence as the more obvious direct acts of abuse. Had Anna Climbie been subjected only to the omissions and not to the direct physical abuses, she would still be the victim of violence.[6]

The death of Anna Climbie suggests that violence is done by either doing something (a direct action) or by not doing something (an omission). The fact that violence can be done via an omission adds a new dimension to the meaning of violence.

2. Omissions

Defining an omission in terms of 'not doing something' has the drawback of there being more than one way of not doing something. It is useful therefore to make three sets of distinctions regarding the nature of omissions: the first between an omitted action and an omitting action; the second between negative causation and negative action; the third between bilateral and trilateral omissions.

Ted Honderich deserves credit for introducing the first distinction. An omitted action describes a mere nothing, or what Honderich calls 'an unrealised possibility', whereas an omitting action is an action done instead of another action. Honderich explains this point by way of the example of omitting to turn off the radio at 12 noon:

How did I not turn off the radio at noon? As it happened, I did not turn off the radio at noon by *staying my hand*, be performing that little action after having made a first move towards turning off the radio. My staying my hand *was* or *was identical with* my not turning off the radio at noon'.[7]

In this example, not turning off the radio was an act performed by the omitting action of staying my hand.

There are two types of omitting actions, negative causation or as negative action. This distinction was first introduced by Harris:[8]

Negative causation – A's failure to do X caused Y where A could have done X and X would have prevented Y.

Negative action – A's failure to do X with the result Y will make the doing of Y a negative action of A's only where A's doing X would have prevented Y and A knew, or ought reasonably to have known this, and where A could have done X and knew, or ought reasonably to have known, this.

The difference between negative causation and negative action is particularly important in terms of allocating moral responsibility for one's omitting actions. According to negative causation, one is responsible for everything and anything one failed to do. If I meet a friend on Saturday at 3 p.m. for a game of tennis, I am responsible for causing the death of a stranger in my local hospital who could have been saved had I been donating blood at 3 p.m. on Saturday rather than playing tennis. On the other hand, according to negative action I am responsible for the death of the stranger in the hospital if and only if I knew that he could have been saved by my donation of blood, or that his death was foreseeable if I failed to donate blood, but nevertheless I proceeded to play tennis on Saturday at 3 p.m.

There is also a third type of distinction that deserves to be discussed, between bilateral and trilateral omissions. In a bilateral re-lationship, Perpetrator (P) does violence to Victim (V) through an omitting action. For example, if an elderly father has a heart attack, in the presence of his son, who withholds the medications necessary to keep his father alive (perhaps because he will inherit a massive fortune when his father dies), the son is committing an act of violence through omission. In a trilateral relationship, a third party is involved, Witness (W), who by not intervening allows (P) to do violence to (V).

If apart from the father dying of a heart attack and his son withholding the medications to save his life, there is also a daughter present at the scene, who fails to intervene either by trying to get the medications from his brother or by calling for help, she is also doing violence by omission. In this case both (P) and (W) are doing violence to (V), in the case of (P) for his omitting action of not giving his father the medications, and in the case of (W) for allowing (P)'s negative action to take effect.

The concept of 'allowing' something to happen is crucial here. As Philippa Foot points out, *allowing* here means forbearing to prevent: 'For this we need a sequence thought of as somehow already in train, and something that an agent could do to intervene. (The agent must be able to intervene, but does not do so)'. [9] Being a witness to an act of violence, W is doing violence to V when W is aware of P's act of violence, is in a position to intervene, but does nothing to stop P or to rescue V. The condition of being 'aware' of what P is doing to V is crucial here, especially in terms of the distinction we encountered before between Negative Causation and Negative Action. In the case of Negative Action, unlike merely Negative Causation, W's action X would have prevented P from doing violence to V, and W knows, or ought reasonably to have known, that doing X will prevent P from doing violence to V.

The three sets of distinctions regarding violence by omission are represented graphically in figure 1 on the next page:

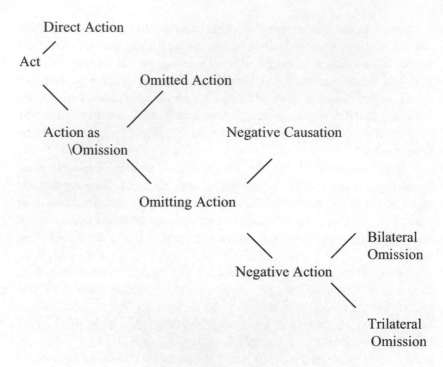

Figure 1: Acts and Omissions

3. The Equivalence Thesis

So far it has been suggested that there is more to an act of violence than a direct action with harmful consequences; violence can also be done through an omission. In the remaining parts of this paper the moral status of an act of violence by omission will be considered. It will be argued that while in most cases there is no difference from a moral point of view between violence by direct action and violence by omission (the Equivalence Thesis), this is not always the case. This is where the distinction between bilateral and trilateral omissions becomes crucial; there are times when violence by omission in a trilateral relationship carries less moral weight than violence by omission in a bilateral relationship, or indeed less than violence by direct action.

In recent years the debate whether there is a moral difference between an act and an omission has evolved in response to Philippa Foot's claim that there is a moral distinction to be made between acts and omissions, for example the act of sending poisoned food to underdeveloped countries, and the omission of allowing people in the underdeveloped world to die of starvation. Foot is not saying that allowing people to die of starvation is not morally problematic, especially since at some level all of us living in the West contribute to their misery; nevertheless argues that from a moral point of view there is a distinction between what one does or causes and what one merely allows:

> Most of us allow people to die of starvation in India and Africa, and there is surely something wrong with us that we do; it would be nonsense, however, to pretend that it is only in law that we make the distinction between allowing people in the underdeveloped countries to die of starvation and sending them poisoned food.[10]

According to Foot, even though our omissions carry some moral weight, an omission is morally speaking less serious than the act.[11] Unfortunately, Foot's argument is based on certain moral intuitions which are never fully explained or justified.[12] In what follows an attempt will be made to justify Foot's moral intuitions, by providing an argument based on the distinction between bilateral and trilateral omissions.

Foot's position is captured by Jonathan Glover as follows: 'in certain circumstances, failure to perform an act, with certain foreseen bad consequences of that failure, is morally less bad than to perform a different act which has the identical foreseen bad consequences'.[13] Glover rejects Foot's position, which he refers to as 'the act and omission doctrine', on the grounds that the reasons usually presented in its defence are found lacking. Of course Glover is prepared to accept that many acts are worse than their (apparently) corresponding omissions, to the extent that the bad consequences of the act may be worse or more inevitable than the bad consequences of the omission; there may be various side-effects that stem uniquely from certain actions but not from omissions, and more inevitable because the consequences of an actions are more direct than the consequences of an omission. This suggests that in most cases the consequences of a direct act tend to be worse than the consequences of an omission, although the mere fact that a particular consequence results from an omission rather than an act is of no moral significance.

Glover considers the case where a government official fails to provide an adequate allowance for old age pensioners in his yearly budget when doing so is known to provide a greater number of deaths among the elderly. Glover admits that there are at least two reasons why it would be morally worse if this official went into a retirement home and shot the same number of people as would have died as a result of his policy on pensions. First, there may be various negative side effects that stem uniquely from shooting the pensioners. For example, the other residents might be terrified and experience psychological harm or at least have their sense of security undermined, not to mention the effect on the loved ones of the deceased. Secondly, the direct action of shooting the pensioners ensures their deaths to a far greater degree, while the omission (in terms of the policy) still leaves open the possibility that the people who would be affected might be assisted and saved by others. Yet this case suggests that the moral difference between an act and an omission exists only because the consequences of the act tend to be more severe than the consequences of the omission. The fact remains that there is no moral significance whether similar consequences result from an omission rather than an act.

Glover is not alone in his negative assessment of Foot's act and omission doctrine, with Harris and Honderich being two other authoritative, like-minded exponents of the same view. Harris argues that 'there can be no moral difference between positive and negative actions with the same consequences'[14], while Honderich endorses the belief that 'by our ordinary omissions we do as wrong as we might by certain awful acts'.[15] I suggest we refer to the position defended by Glover, Harris and Honderich as the Equivalence Thesis. The issue here is not simply whether omissions qualify as acts of violence, since clearly they do. It is not even whether omissions carry moral weight, again clearly they do. Instead, the issue is whether acts and omissions are equally wrong, or wrong to the same degree. The Equivalence Thesis takes an uncompromising position on this issue, recommending that we measure the moral weight of our omissions on the same scale as the moral weight of certain acts.

It is this position that is defended by Glover, Harris and Honderich. When Glover says that our omissions are not 'morally less bad' than certain acts, he is saying that omissions are at least as morally bad as certain acts. When Harris says that there is 'no moral difference' between omissions and acts, he is saying that from a moral point of view certain omissions cannot be distinguished from certain acts. When Honderich says that 'by our ordinary omissions we do as wrong as we might by certain awful acts', he is saying that on moral grounds omissions are on a par with certain acts.

It seems to me that in order for the Equivalence Thesis to hold, two conditions must be met: foreseeability and alternativity (that is to say, the possibility of alternative action). The condition of foreseeability is straightforward; the agent in question must be in a position to be able to predict the harmful consequence of their omitting action. The condition of alternativity is more complex, being constituted by two different components: first, it must be *possible* to act in a different way (the choice-set must hold more than one option); second, it must be *viable* to act in a different way (the different options within the choice-set must be more or less comparable in terms of facility of access).[16]

There are cases when both conditions are met, and the Equivalence Thesis holds. Consider the following example:

The Inheritance Case. A man will inherit a fortune when his father dies. With this in mind, when the father has a heart attack, the man omits to give his father medicine necessary for keeping him alive.

In the Inheritance Case, introduced by Glover,[17] the foreseeability condition is met, to the extent that the man knows, or ought reasonably to have known, that his actions would result in the death of his father. The alternativity condition is also met, to the extent that the alternative to the omitting action, namely to give the father the necessary medicine, was not only a possible option, but it was also viable. Because all the conditions are met, in the Inheritance Case we can agree with Glover, Harris and Honderich that there is no moral difference between the omitting action of withholding the medicine and the act of killing the father.

While the Equivalence Thesis holds in the Inheritance Case, this is not always the case. In fact, in the vast majority of cases of omitting actions the Equivalence Thesis does not hold, to the extent that the conditions of foreseeability and alternativity are either not met, or they apply only to a lesser degree. Consider the following example:

The Oxfam Case. Take my action today of paying $1,200 for the air fares to Venice, giving my credit card number on the phone to the travel agent. That was an ordinary action with an ordinary effect, getting the seats. In doing the thing, I omitted to contribute $1,200 to Oxfam. If I had done that instead, some lives would have been saved.

In the Oxfam Case, discussed in great detail by Honderich,[18] the foreseeability condition is met, to the extent that no one could plead ignorance to the gross inequalities in the world today, or to the existence of charities such as Oxfam that are the only reason preventing the statistics on global starvation from making even more depressing reading. Of course one has only a vague idea of who will be suffering for one's omitting action, or who exactly will benefit from one's charity, unlike in the Inheritance Case, but that is irrelevant. From a moral point of view everyone has the same moral standing, whether at home or abroad, no matter the race, gender or nationality, therefore it could be argued that we have a duty to take equal account of the interests of everyone, whoever they are and wherever they happen to be.

As for the alternativity condition, it is a different story. It cannot be denied that technically speaking it is *possible* to forego a trip to Venice in order to make a donation to Oxfam, but there is more to alternativity than merely the possibility of performing an alternative action. Apart from being possible, the alternative must also be *viable*. In the Oxfam Case, strange as it may sound, it may not always be viable to expect a person to forego a trip to Venice. In order to see why an alternative action is not always viable, it may help to rewrite the Oxfam Case without any reference to Venice or $1,200, as follows:

The Oxfam Case (2). Take X's action today of paying Y for the air fares to Z. That was an ordinary action with an ordinary effect, getting the seats. In doing the thing, X omitted to contribute Y to Oxfam. If X had done that instead, some lives would have been saved.

Z, the desired holiday destination, does not have to be Venice, and Y, the cost of the holiday, does not have to be $1200. Does the Equivalence Thesis still hold if Y is $200 rather than $1200 and Z is, say, Blackpool[19] rather than Venice? Let's assume that instead of spending $1,200 on Venice, X spends $200 on a holiday in Blackpool, would X be off the moral hook? According to my understanding of the Equivalence Thesis the answer would have to be 'no', since X could have sent Oxfam the $200 if only X had the decency to spend his holiday at home, doing gardening and reading a novel, rather than going to Blackpool. Clearly it is *possible* to donate money to Oxfam anytime one thinks of going on holiday, but I would argue it is not *viable* to expect that to be always the case.

There are times when donating money to Oxfam rather than going on holiday is not viable. Refusing to take my wife on holiday, because I feel under a moral obligation to donate all the money I would have spent on the holiday to Oxfam, is problematic not so much because I would be depriving my wife of experiencing the beauty of Venice, but because in doing so I am not performing the action of a loving husband, which is a crucial aspect of the person I want to be.[20] In this example, and contrary to what may seem at first, what is viable is not determined by the subjective preferences one happens to have. Instead, what is viable is defined impartially in terms of what all suitably qualified impartial rational persons would agree on. Bernard Gert defends this impartial approach in his account of justifying violations to the moral rule:

> Justifying violations of the moral rules is similar to justifying the moral rules themselves. It consists in showing that all suitably qualified impartial rational persons can or would publicly allow this kind of violation of the moral rules. [...] [A]ll rational persons agree on the procedure by which a violation can be justified. This procedure must be such that it can be part of a public system that applies to all rational persons, which means that it must be understandable to all rational persons and not irrational for them to use it in making decisions about how to act and judgments on the actions of others.[21]

Leaving aside the well-known controversy over rationality and irrationality, Gert's account of morality as impartiality causes problems for the Equivalence Thesis, since all suitably qualified impartial rational persons would agree that it is not always viable to expect people to forego their holiday in exchange for a donation to Oxfam. In other words, while the Equivalence Thesis holds that there is no moral difference between the act of sending poisoned food to Africa and the omission of not donating money to Oxfam, I am suggesting that there is a difference, and the difference is captured by the alternativity condition. If my grandmother dies of hypothermia in a cold flat in London while I'm on holiday in Venice with my wife, then the Equivalence Thesis would hold, as all suitably qualified impartial rational persons would agree that there is no moral difference between the positive action of killing my grandmother and the omitting action of going on holiday with the same consequences. But by the same token it is not always viable to expect people never to go on holiday on the grounds that the money could have been spend differently, with more beneficial consequences for someone on the other side of the world. The alternativity condition (in terms of what is viable) is much weaker in the Oxfam Case compared to the Inheritance Case.

The conclusion to be drawn from the above analysis is that, contrary to the arguments put forward by Glover, Harris and Honderich, sometimes omissions and actions carry different moral weight. There are degrees of moral wrongness, and while to some extent we all share the burden for the starvation occurring today in certain parts of the world, and we all could (and should) do a lot more to prevent it, it does not follow that an omission always carries the same moral weight as an action which has the same consequences.[22] Honderich says that the omitting action of not giving $1200 to Oxfam 'has the effect of some lives being lost, *the same effect as* the possible action of ordering your armed forces to stop the food convoys getting through for a while'.[23] Even if an omission and an action have the same effect of some lives being lost, it does not follow that there is no difference between certain omissions and certain acts. The difference is determined by the fact that the foreseeability and/or alternativity conditions may not be fully met.

4. Moral Absolutism and Moral Dilemmas

Underpinning the Equivalence Thesis there appears to be a commitment to what can be labelled 'moral absolutism'; namely, the view that the value of an action, unless it is morally neutral, is either morally good or evil. The alternative to moral absolutism is the kind of 'moral gradualism' embraced by Foot, whereby certain actions and omissions carry different moral weight, hence in certain cases an action can be morally worse than an omission.

Of the authors we have discussed so far who champion the Equivalence Thesis, Honderich is the one who most clearly embraces moral absolutism. In a recent paper, Honderich makes the following point:

> There are degrees of moral responsibility, and shares of moral responsibility for things, and degrees of humanity or decency in a whole life. But there are not degrees of being right or degrees of being wrong. The question of which action is right is a question to which the only relevant response is a verdict. You do not have three possible answers.[24]

It is precisely this assumption of moral absolutism that is most problematic about the Equivalence Thesis.

The limits of moral absolutism, or extreme universal moral realism,[25] can be exposed by what in the literature is called a 'moral dilemma'. Following Walter Sinnott-Armstrong[26] we can define moral dilemmas as 'situations where there is a moral requirement for an agent to adopt each of incompatible alternatives, but where neither moral requirement is overridden in any way that is both morally relevant and realistic'. The term 'realistic' has a specific meaning here, referring to a moral requirement that is so strong that anyone who violates it does what is morally wrong. Paradoxically the example Honderich uses to defend the Equivalence Thesis, the Oxfam Case, is a perfect example of a moral dilemma.

The problem with moral absolutism or extreme universal moral realism can be exposed by working through certain moral dilemmas, like the Oxfam case, where different agents can still personally favour different alternatives, and their personal rankings or choices will determine what they ought to do. As Sinnott-Armstrong points out, 'since [extreme universal] moral realists deny that any moral judgements depend on such mental factors as moral beliefs or choices, extreme universal moral realism is false'.[27] Elaborating on the Oxfam case, suppose that I have to choose between paying $1200 for the airfare to Venice, a surprise gift for my wife's 40th birthday, and not taking my wife to Venice but instead donating the same amount to Oxfam. The conflicting moral requirements might be described as equal, since on one side there is the omission to help Oxfam, and on the other side there is the omission not to take my wife to Venice on her 40th birthday. Both omissions carry moral weight. The choice between omissions reflects what Sinnott-Armstrong calls 'a way of life':

> this notion is vague, but what is important here is that a way of life includes a tendency to rank one kind of value above another and to choose accordingly. Such rankings are moral beliefs, and such ways of life can be chosen [...] such ways of life *do* affect what agents ought to do in some moral dilemmas.[28]

The point about 'a way of life' is that this is what makes our life meaningful. The choice I make not only reflects the person that I am, but also the person I want to be. This, in part, is the moral significance of choice. Thomas Scanlon refers to this as the 'demonstrative value' of choice:

> On our anniversary, I want not only to have a present for my wife but also to have chosen that present myself. This is not because I think this process is the one best calculated to produce a present she will like (for that, it would be better to let her choose the present herself). The reason rather, is that the gift will have a special meaning if I choose it – if it reflects my feelings about her and my thoughts about the occasion.[29]

If Sinnott-Armstrong and Scanlon are right, then there is a fundamental problem with the type of moral absolutism, or extreme universal moral realism, which is assumed as valid by the Equivalence Thesis.

The shortcomings of the Equivalence Thesis become even more evident if we examine the historical failure to rescue Jews during the Nazi occupation of Europe.

5. The Case of the Rescuers

The rescue of Jews in Nazi Europe, and in particular the moral standing of bystanders, is one of the most complex and controversial moral issues coming out of the Holocaust. The issue of bystanders is particularly interesting for our account of violence and omissions because, by virtue of allowing the violence to continue, or by not rescuing the Jews, the bystanders are themselves doing violence to the victims.

While all bystanders carry some blame for the death of many Jews, it will be argued that there is a moral difference between the omitting actions of at least some bystanders and the direct actions of the perpetrators of the Holocaust. The difference will be highlighted not by comparing bystanders to perpetrators, an issue that has attracted a great deal of attention in the literature on the Holocaust, but by comparing two different sets of bystanders. It is therefore not my intention to review the extensive literature on the bystanders during the Holocaust;[30] instead I will focus on one specific empirical fact about the rescue operation that has only recently come to surface. In their important article 'The Importance of Being Asked: The Rescue of Jews in Nazi Europe', Varese and Yaish analyse the most extensive data set on rescuers,[31] and conclude that *being asked* is a significant predictor of helping behaviour. Two-thirds of the rescuers were asked to help, and only one third initiated their action. Moreover nearly all (96%) of those who were asked to help Jews did so. The statistical analysis provided by Varese and Yaish is much more sophisticated than I can give it credit for here, taking into account a number of variables such as religion, gender, economic conditions, geography, identity of asker, etc. But for our purposes we can focus on one simple basic fact: the vast majority of rescuers needed an extra reason to stimulate their helping behaviour, and 'being asked' seemed to work as a trigger mechanism.[32]

Let's now consider the following two hypothetical scenarios: Anton and Beatrice are both living in France under Nazi occupation in the 1940s, and although they are both opposed to the Nazi regime, and appalled by the mistreatment of the Jews, yet neither Anton nor Beatrice become rescuers. Notwithstanding the fact that they are both non-rescuers, there is an important difference between Anton and Beatrice; namely, Anton does not become a rescuer even after being asked to do so (he belongs to the minority 4% who did not become rescuers even after being asked according to the statistical analysis provided by Varese and Yaish), whereas Beatrice was never asked to rescue anyone, not by a friend, or stranger, or by a Jewish family looking for shelter. Is there a moral difference between their omissions? In both cases the omission has the same effect; some Jewish people lost their lives when they could have been saved. Yet, I would argue that being asked rather than not being asked to become a rescuer makes a difference in terms of the moral weigh of their omissions. The difference is that the alternativity condition is much weaker in Beatrice's case than in Anton's case.

As previously argued, there are two parts to the alternativity condition: first, the alternative action (to become a rescuer) must be a possible alternative. That condition clearly holds for both Anton and Beatrice, since becoming a rescuer was an option (admittedly not an easy one) for all non-Jews living in Europe at the time. Secondly, the alternative action must be viable. This condition holds for Anton more so than for Beatrice. In the context of life under German occupation in France, even if we do not anticipate someone to spontaneously look for Jews in need of rescuing, we would expect them to assist the vulnerable when directly asked for help. To become a rescuer was a more viable alternative in the case of Anton than in the case of Beatrice. The fact that Anton was asked to become a rescuer suggests that the opportunity to become a rescuer presented itself as a viable option,[33] unlike in the case of Beatrice, who was never asked, hence in her case becoming a rescuer was a more difficult option compared to Anton.

The reason for distinguishing between Anton and Beatrice is not to suggest that Anton was morally responsible for his omissions whereas Beatrice was not. Anton and Beatrice, like all bystanders, must shoulder some of the responsibility for what happened. Having said that, to paint all non-rescuers with the same moral brush is inaccurate, and perhaps even unfair on some bystanders in comparison to other bystanders. There are moral differences between non-rescuers that must be acknowledged, and even though all bystanders carry some blame for the plight of the Jews, from a moral point of view they are not all the same. The fact that there is a moral difference between bystanders suggests that there must also be a moral difference between bystanders and perpetrators, and if that is the case, the Equivalence Thesis does not always hold.

6. Conclusion

The aim of this paper was to highlight a hidden feature of what constitutes an act of violence, namely, the fact that violence can be done through an omission. Assuming the validity of this claim, the paper went on to tackle the question whether there is a difference, from a moral point of view, between an omission and a direct action, when both have the same consequence. It was argued that while in many cases there is no difference between a direct action and an omission, and therefore an omission can be as bad or as wrong as a direct action, there are times when an action and an omission carry different moral weight. This is not to deny that an omission can be as much an act of violence as a direct action, or that violence by omission often carries the same moral weight as violence by direct action. At the same time, depending on the circumstances dictated by the conditions of foreseeability and alternativity, certain omissions carry less moral weight than certain direct actions, even if they have the same consequences.

Endnotes

1   Glover, J.: *Humanity: A Moral History of the Twentieth Century*, (New Haven, CT: Yale University Press, 2001), p. 120.

2   Occasionally it is even possible for the same act, such as doing a musical performance, to be done either by performing a certain action – hitting the keys on the piano keyboard – or by not performing a certain action – sitting perfectly still in front of the keyboard without generating any sounds from the piano, as suggested by John Cage's famous piece for piano, 4'33".

3   Honderich, T.: *After the Terror* (Edinburgh: Edinburgh University Press, 2002), p. 91 and '*After the Terror*: A Book and Further Thoughts', *The Journal of Ethics* 7.2 (2003), p. 15.

4   Keane, J.: *Reflections on Violence* (London: Verso, 1996), pp. 66–67.

5   Geras, N.: *The Contract of Moral Indifference* (London: Verso, 1990), p. 22

6   *The Guardian*, Saturday 13 January, 2001.

7   Honderich, T.: *Violence for Equality* (London: Routledge, 1993), p. 68.

8   Harris, J.: *Violence and Responsibility* (London: Routledge & Kegan Paul, 1980), p. 45.

9   Foot, P.: 'The Problem of Abortion and the Doctrine of the Double Effect', in *Virtues and Vices* (Oxford: Blackwell, 1978), p. 26.

10   Ibid., pp. 26–27.

11   Foot's thesis is about moral weight rather than moral responsibility. The question of moral responsibility raises a number of other issues, fundamentally about determinism and free–will, which will not be addressed in this paper. For those interested in issues of moral responsibility, an argument roughly along the same lines as Foot's has been defended by Fischer and Ravizza in Fischer, J. and Ravizza, M. (eds.): *Perspectives on Moral Responsibility* (Ithaca, NY: Cornell University Press, 1993).

12   Foot makes an attempt at providing a theoretical basis for treating some omissions as morally different from certain acts when she introduces the distinction between positive and negative duties. Negative duties describe our obligations not to intentionally harm others, while positive duties refer to our obligation to positively benefit someone. Foot holds that we are generally more stringently bound by a negative duty than we are by a positive duty, and that violating a negative duty is worse than violating a positive duty, even if not violating a negative duty has the consequence of harming a greater number of people.

13   Glover, J.: *Causing Death and Saving Lives* (Harmondsworth: Penguin,1977), p. 92.

14   Harris, J., op. cit., p. 9.

15   Honderich, T.: *Violence for Equality* (London: Routledge, 1989), p. 100.

16   I am grateful to Brian Burgess for a very helpful discussion about these two conditions.

17   Glover, J., op. cit., p. 95.

18   Honderich, T.: *After the Terror* (Edinburgh: Edinburgh University Press, 2002), p. 74.

19   Blackpool, in the north-west of England, is a small seaside resort famous for its shoddy hotels, cheap food and tacky entertainment. In the 1950s and 1960s it used to be the destination of many working class families who could not afford to go abroad.

20   The significance of this choice will be explained in Part 5 below.

21   Gert, B.: *Morality: Its Nature and Justification* (New York: Oxford University Press, 1998), p. 222.

22   It may be the case that advocates of the Equivalence Thesis mistakenly regard praise and blame as opposites, thus while it is praiseworthy to donate money to Oxfam, there may not be any blame in not donating the money. As Gert argues: 'The usual way of talking about praise and blame have obscured the distinction between moral standards and responsibility standards. Praise is not the opposite of blame, but of condemnation, and is related to moral standards. Blame and its opposite, credit, are related to responsibility standards.' (op. cit, p. 323)

23   Honderich, T.: *After the Terror* (Edinburgh: Edinburgh University Press, 2002), p. 75 (emphasis added).

24   Honderich, T.: '*After the Terror*: A Book and Further Thoughts', *op. cit*, p. 180.

25   Extreme universal moral realism is the view that moral judgments are true if and only if certain conditions hold which are independent of the actual and ideal moral beliefs and choices of the judger and the judged. The condition of 'actual and ideal' is what distinguishes this extreme version of moral realism from a weaker or moderate moral realism, which claims independence from actual, but not ideal, mental states. An ideal mental state is captured by a fully informed, rational, impartial spectator.

26   Sinnott-Armstrong, W.: 'Moral Realisms and Moral Dilemmas', *The Journal of Philosophy*, 84.5 (1987), p. 266.

27   Ibid., p. 267.

28   Ibid., pp. 270–271.

29   Scanlon, T.: 'The Significance of Choice', in *The Tanner Lectures on Human Values, Vol. 8* (Salt Lake City: University of Utah Press, 1988) p. 179.

30   For an excellent analysis by a political philosopher of the many issues regarding bystanders, see Geras, N., op. cit. See also Glover: *Humanity: A Moral History of the Twentieth Century*, op. cit., ch. 40, pp. 379–393.

31   Varese, F. and Yaish, M.: 'The Importance of Being Asked: The Rescue of Jews in Nazi Europe', *Rationality and Society*, 12.3 (1987). The data collected by the Altruistic Personality and Prosocial Behaviour Institute (APPBI), which contains a sample of 346 identified Jewish rescuers and 164 non–rescuers. This

data was used by Oliner, S. P. and Oliner, P.M.: *The Altruistic Personality* (New York: The Free Press, 1988).

32   In a more recent paper, Varese and Yaish explore the interaction between pre-existing dispositions (a pro-social personality) and situational factors (direct request for help). They reach three important conclusions: First, rescuers were more likely to help the more pro-social their personality was. Second, being directly asked for help increased the likelihood that a person with a pro-social personality would help. Third, the stronger a given pro-social disposition is, the more likely it is that a situational factor activates that existing inclination. Cf. 'Resolute Heroes: The Rescue of Jews During The Nazi Occupation of Europe', *Archives Européennes de Sociologie*, Vol.XLVI, No.1.

33   As Gross points out, in some cases the asking party was someone from the resistance movement, who may even have offered economic incentives to the rescuers. Cf. Gross, M. L.: *Ethics and Activism* (Cambridge: Cambridge University Press, 1997).

Eve Garrard

Violence, Cruelty and Evil

What is the relationship between violence and evil? Many people think that violence is in some way central to evil; thinking perhaps that evil acts are always violent, or perhaps making the stronger claim that violent acts are always evil. Others think that even if violence can sometimes be justified, nonetheless it is always at least *prima facie* evil. But on further investigation it is not clear that even this weaker claim is true, so some more complex account of the relationship may be needed. Of course, on the way to answering this question we will have to consider just what violence and evil are. Whatever the problems of getting a satisfactory account of violence are, there are far greater problems with providing a satisfactory account of evil, so I hope to use this investigation to cast some light on what such an account should be like. But before I address the question of what we take violence to be, let me first say a little about what I'm *not* going to take evil to be.

We use the concept of evil in several different ways. Firstly, we sometimes use it to cover everything in the world that's in some way bad, as when we talk of moral evils such as brutality, for example, *and* natural evils such as earthquakes. Here it is a term that picks out everything to which we give a markedly negative evaluation. It is this usage which we find in the traditional problem of evil, which involves the (alleged) incompatibility between God's omniscience, His omnipotence, His benevolence, and the presence of evil (in this broad sense) in the world. Sometimes, however, we use evil in a more restricted way, to apply only to matters involving agency. In this usage, evil amounts to all the bad or wrongful actions performed by human agents (or supernatural ones, for those whose metaphysics leaves room for the supernatural). This is 'the evil that men do', and in this sense of evil, *moral* evil, it is the subject of a huge amount of moral theory, since it really just amounts to the whole of immorality. In this paper I am not going to address the overall subject of immorality, except in passing. Nor am I going to say anything at all about the theological problem of evil, for two reasons: firstly, the account of evil I'm interested in is a purely secular one, since it is a notable feature of secular moral discourse that appeals to the idea of evil are quite often made – think of the so-called 'empire of evil' or 'axis of evil', or the journalistic treatment of Myra Hindley and of Dr Harold Shipman.[1] It would be nice to get a clearer idea of just what we are attributing to a person or action when we call it evil in a *secular* context. And the other reason I'm going to say nothing about the theological problem of evil is that it isn't directly involved with a third, quite distinctive, way in which we use the term evil. In this third usage, it picks out a subgroup of the acts which we regard as morally evil (in the second sense given above – i.e. morally wrong), a subgroup which evokes from us a particular kind of horror. Think of the contrast we sometimes draw when we say of an action: 'That wasn't just wrong, it was *evil'*, or of a person: 'He wasn't just a thug, he was a truly evil person.' The journalistic references to Hindley, particularly after her death, can only be fully understood in terms of this third usage, and we also find it in some of the political judgements we make about the great catastrophes which so disfigured the last century, and may well disfigure this one. We do not merely say of the Holocaust that it was wrong, or bad – these terms don't seem to capture the depth of horror that contemplation of that event rightly induces in us. It's this third sense of evil that I'm interested in – what secular meaning can we give to it? What does it amount to, in a secular context? And it's evil in this third sense that I hope to illuminate, even if just by a little, by investigating the connection between it and violence.

1. Violence and Evil

So in considering the relationship between violence and evil in this third sense, what account of violence should we be deploying? The most significant issue here for our purposes is whether or not our account of violence should be a fully evaluative one (as in, for example, the definition of violence as the illegitimate use of force, or alternatively as the presence of harmful social injustice), or whether the account should be neutral on the moral status of acts of violence. There are many problems with the evaluative definitions sketched out here, but the real and conclusive difficulty is that they make it impossible to raise the question of whether violence can ever be justified, since the (negative) answer is built into the definition itself. On these accounts of violence, as C. A. J. Coady says: 'all violence will be morally illegitimate by explicit definition, which represents the serious fudging of a central question.'[2]

For that reason, I'm going to settle for a definition of violence which does not beg that question, since it's going to be so important for the issue of how violence is connected with evil. Coady provides just such a definition, namely: *the exercise of physical or psychological force so as to inflict injury on or damage to persons or property.*[3] This definition isn't entirely non-normative, since it deploys the concepts of injury and damage, which are normative concepts, but at least it doesn't presuppose that violence must be unjustified.

So now we can raise just that question: can violence ever be justified? The answer seems to me to be uncontrovertibly yes, since an innocent agent who, purely in self-defence, injures an attacker, seems to me to be both violent and justified in his action. This intuition isn't entirely uncontentious, since some people are hostile to any form of violence, thinking that it's always wrong. But a further implication of their position is that it would be wrong to defend a helpless child from attack by others if doing so involved violence, and this is so counter-intuitive that sorting out the issue at the depth required would take more space than is available here.[4] So I'm just going to take it that violence is at least sometimes morally justified.

What does that show us about the relationship between violence and evil? The first thing it demonstrates is that violence isn't sufficient for evil, because violence is sometimes justified, whereas evil actions are *never* justified. (That is, so long as we are using 'evil' in its third, most restrictive sense.) All evil actions are at least wrong, whereas some violent actions are permissible, and may even be obligatory. Perhaps more contentiously, it can plausibly be argued that violence isn't necessary for evil either. An evil programme of corruption of the innocent may successfully be carried out without resort to violence on the part of the evil-doer – think of Iago's treatment of Othello here. So violence is neither necessary nor sufficient for evil.

However, it doesn't follow just from that that violence plays no role in what our account of evil should be like. Two different reasons for claiming this may be offered: firstly, it might be thought that the provision of necessary and sufficient conditions for evil is a project doomed to failure, since we have so signally failed to find such conditions where we have tried the hardest to do so, most notoriously in the case of knowledge. We no longer try to provide such definitions in philosophy, it may be argued, and look instead to such procedures as examining paradigm cases to help us give an account of the concepts we are interested in. And the great paradigm cases of evil, it may plausibly be claimed, are all cases involving violence.

This, I think, is true: both at the individual and at the political level, evil has paradigmatically involved violence, as in the cases of Brady and Hindley, the Wests, Rwanda, Cambodia, the Holocaust. But such cases have also involved cruelty, deception, betrayal, torture, psychopathy – so it's not yet clear what the involvement of violence amounts to. What have we got when we have a paradigm case? Standardly, we have a sufficiency claim: if anything is evil, then this is evil. But we have already established that violence isn't sufficient for evil. So what the paradigm cases show us is, at best, a claim about a cluster of properties: the cluster presented in the actions of, for example, Frederick West, are sufficient for evil to be appropriately applied to those actions. But this gives us no guarantee about any individual member of the cluster; that member may appear in other clusters of properties without the action bearing those properties being evil. Furthermore, other cases of evil may not display all the properties in the cluster: it would be surprising if there were no features in common between different cases of evil, but we needn't suppose that the common features appear in all cases of evil. More likely we have here a family resemblance between the various cases.[5]

So far, we have found no very privileged role to be played by violence in the construction of evil, other than that it appears, along with many other properties, in the paradigm cases. However it could be argued that this results from too crude an understanding of the relationship between non-evaluative properties such as violence, and fully evaluative properties such as evil. We have dismissed violence from playing any very special role because evil acts aren't always violent, and violent acts aren't always evil, indeed they're sometimes justified. But this is just to suppose that unless there is a (true) principle in play claiming that violent acts are always (or never) evil, then there's no further structured relationship to be found between the two properties. However although violence isn't always evil, or even wrong, it can plausibly be suggested that it's always *prima facie* wrong, and maybe *prima facie* evil. This is the suggestion that the property of being violent carries a certain moral loading with it, into whatever context it appears. In the case of violence that loading is negative, but it may sometimes be outweighed by the positive moral loading of other properties in the context, such as defending the innocent from threat. Nonetheless, that negative loading is always present in cases of violence, even where it is outweighed. Effectively, this is to claim that violence is always wrong-*making*, that it always pushes an action in the direction of being wrong, and maybe it's evil-making also, even if it doesn't always succeed in making the actions possessing it evil.

As a general point about the structure of moral claims, this is of course correct. Properties such as courage or benevolence can quite persuasively be claimed to be *prima facie* right, to be right-making for any action which possesses them, even if they can be outweighed by other wrong-making properties which the action also possesses, hence failing to make the action overall right. But the claim is less persuasive in the case of violence. Consider the case of a major perpetrator of horrific evil – a Pol Pot, perhaps, or an Auschwitz guard – a torturer with his hands dyed in his victims' blood. If such a person, secure in his overwhelming power, is finally prevented from continuing his deadly activities, some violence in his overthrow may be a *right-making* feature of his defeat. Is it not a good thing for him to have some taste of what he has inflicted on victims who, unlike him, were innocent? This is not an argument in favour of giving him what he deserves, since what this torturer deserves may be something that no civilised person or state should contemplate delivering even to the worst of perpetrators. (And even if we did contemplate giving evil-doers their just deserts, there is also a set of issues about the morality of forgiveness that would have to be seriously addressed. There are several reasons why it isn't always right to give people what they do truly deserve.) However, assuming the constraints of civilised behaviour to be in place, perhaps even as far as ruling out capital punishment, it nonetheless might be morally preferable – more fitting, and also maybe better for him, not to mention better for his victims – that the perpetrator experience *some* violence at the hands of his conquerors.

If this is so, then violence isn't even *prima facie* wrong. And if it isn't *prima facie* wrong, then it isn't *prima facie* evil. This shouldn't entirely surprise us: the relationship between the thin moral properties such as right and wrong, and the non-evaluative properties in virtue of which they are present, is too complex to be captured in the Rossian net of *prima facie* relationships. The *prima facie* right features mentioned above – courage, benevolence, honesty – are neither non-normative, nor non-evaluative: on the contrary, they are all examples of thick moral concepts (that is, concepts which have both a descriptive and an evaluative component). So perhaps we should be looking primarily at the thick properties to fill out our account of evil. However, this doesn't mean that no significant role is to be found for violence – it may be that violence has a distinctive relationship with one of the thick moral concepts which in turn is significantly connected with evil.

2. Cruelty

One such concept is that of cruelty. It is quite hard to find an adequate definition of cruelty which doesn't generate deeply counter-intuitive cases. Hallie offers this definition: 'Cruelty is the activity of hurting sentient beings'.[6] This is clearly unsatisfactory; since by this definition much medical practice would count as cruel. Bernard Williams glosses cruelty as the desire to cause suffering,[7] which again seems too wide, since many occasions in which an agent desires to cause suffering won't be cases of cruelty (e.g., cases of justified punishment). Judith Shklar's definition of cruelty in *Ordinary Vices* is: 'Cruelty is the wilful inflicting of physical pain on a weaker being in order to cause fear and anguish'.[8] This has the advantage of introducing the agent's purposes into the definition, though the precise purposes offered are not entirely convincing – an agent's purpose in performing a cruel act need not be to induce fear or anguish; it could be to disable the victim, or to prevent her acting in some undesired way. But it restricts cruelty to the infliction of *physical* pain, and rules out the possibility of psychological cruelty, a reality all too evident in the world around us. She does, later in the book, refer to *moral* cruelty, which she glosses as 'deliberate and persistent humiliation, so that the victim can eventually trust neither himself nor anyone else',[9] and this recognises the role of psychological suffering in a way that becomes explicit in the definition she gives in a later paper, according to which cruelty is 'the deliberate infliction of physical, and secondarily emotional, pain upon a weaker person or group by stronger ones, in order to achieve some end, tangible or intangible, of the latter'.[10]

However, this definition is still highly problematic. It ensures that retributive punishment is always cruel, and that so (perhaps less contentiously) are sports such as boxing.[11] Many of our child-rearing practices, such as expressing strong disapproval of undesired behaviour as a way of altering it, and also much of our medical (and some social science) research, will similarly have to be classified as cruel. Considerations such as these (and others) have led John Kekes to formulate a definition which introduces two further factors:

according to Kekes, a cruel act is one in which the agent takes delight in or is indifferent to the serious and unjustified suffering which the action causes to the victim.[12] The two further factors here introduced are the agent's state-of-mind, and the excessive or unjustified nature of the suffering involved in cruelty. Kekes thinks that reference to the agent's state-of-mind is necessary if we are to rule out punishment, and painful therapy, from being cruel.[13] But this is a mistake: the inclusion of the requirement that cruel acts be unjustified is sufficient to exclude punishment and painful therapy from the class of cruel actions. It's quite plausible to say that unjustified punishment is indeed cruel: we do think that hanging as a punishment for sheep-stealing is cruel because it's an excessive punishment, and hence unjustified. And though a surgeon who took delight in the suffering he caused to his patients might count as a cruel person, his actual surgical practices, so long as they were justified (i.e., in the patient's interests and with her consent), would not amount to cruel treatment.

However, Kekes is right in thinking that the definition of cruelty must contain some reference to the agent's state of mind. This is because such reference is needed to rule out (culpable) *mistakes*: without some distinguishing state of mind, medical negligence (which leads to inappropriate treatment and hence to unjustified suffering), or culpably erroneous punishments where the wrong person has been convicted of a crime, would have to be seen as cruel actions.[14] Now the negligence is of course wrong. But that isn't enough to show that it's *cruel*. Someone who negligently provides the wrong diagnosis, or carelessly misinterprets the evidence in court, has certainly done something blameworthy. But that doesn't seem sufficient reason to stretch the concept of cruelty to cover such cases, thereby weakening it – too many things now fall under the concept – and hence undermining its evaluative force (we standardly think that cruelty is worse than negligence). The distinction between wrongful infliction of suffering which is careless or negligent, and wrongful infliction of suffering which is cruel, is exactly captured by reference to the agent's state of mind – the negligent agent won't take delight in the suffering his acts lead to, nor will he be indifferent to it, since he won't have been aiming at the suffering at all.

Cruelty as we have now defined it is a thick moral concept: its evaluative loading is built into the definition by way of the requirement that cruel acts always involve unjustified suffering. So cruel acts are always at least *prima facie* wrong – that is, such acts always have a wrong-making feature. Can we make the stronger claim, that cruel acts are always wrong, simpliciter? At first sight it seems as if we can. The reference to *unjustified* suffering appears to ensure that if an act is right, it can't be cruel, since any suffering it involves won't be unjustified. But this is too quickly dismissive of the problem. Torture has a reasonable claim to being always cruel – that's why so many people think it's so very wrong. But even those who abhor torture might think it justified in really extreme cases – to save the lives of millions, say.[15] In such a case, would the torture cease to be cruel? I'm inclined to think that it wouldn't, so long as all the other elements cited in the definition were present – the taking of delight in the suffering, in particular.[16]

Now we seem to have two unattractive alternatives: either cruel acts are always wrong, so torture isn't always cruel; or cruel acts are sometimes right, hence they don't always involve unjustified suffering. But as we saw earlier, we need the requirement that the suffering be unjustified in cases of cruelty, to rule out punishment and painful therapy from being cruel. This problem arises because an act being justified or unjustified is a global matter, it's a judgement about how the various reasons for and against doing the act pan out overall. And if we build this requirement into the definition of cruelty, it's always going to exclude justified actions. So perhaps we need a way of saying what's wrong with the suffering involved in the cruel act without making this global judgement about it. We could say it's *undeserved* suffering. That would capture what we want without including punishment in the ambit of cruelty. Unfortunately it doesn't help us with the case of painful therapy, since standardly people don't *deserve* the suffering which illness and its treatments bring. However, we can regard a medical condition as *meriting* a particular kind of treatment, and perhaps the idea of meriting will capture both the things we want to exclude from being cruel. So we can revise the definition of cruelty to read: *an action is cruel if the agent takes delight in, or is indifferent to, the serious and unmerited suffering which he causes to the victim.*

Punishment isn't cruel, since the suffering it causes is merited (at least in principle); painful therapy isn't cruel, since the suffering it causes is also merited, by the ravages of the disease being treated. On this definition, torture will still turn out to be cruel, even if it's overall justified. So cruelty isn't always wrong (though of course it usually will be). But unlike violence, it is always a wrong-*making* feature of an action, since inflicting serious and unmerited suffering always tells against the moral status of an act which involves it.

3.   Evil

Are cruel acts always evil? Not always – there are some acts, such as bullying or beating, which though undoubtedly cruel just don't seem horrific enough to warrant being called evil (in the sense with which I'm here concerned). Indeed as we have just seen, some cruel acts may be justified, but no evil acts are justified. So cruelty isn't sufficient for evil. Are evil acts always cruel? This seems a much more plausible claim. The great paradigm cases of evil are certainly cases of terrible cruelty, though as we saw with violence, that may not be enough to reveal a distinctive relationship between cruelty and evil, and it certainly isn't enough to show that cruelty is necessary for evil. And in fact it isn't: the case of corruption mentioned earlier on might not involve any suffering; if the corruption was sufficiently complete, the corrupted one might feel no pain or regret about her condition – corruption is like that. But someone who set out to completely corrupt an innocent agent might well count as an evil-doer. So cruelty isn't a necessary condition of evil. But if cruelty is neither necessary nor sufficient for evil, why should we think it any more closely connected to evil than violence is?

     At this point we need to look more closely at the nature of evil itself. Various accounts have been given of evil (in the restricted sense on which I'm focussing in this paper); here I will canvass two fairly representative ones. Firstly, some people think that evil acts are ones which produce huge amounts of suffering – the greater the suffering, the more likely the action is to be evil. The initial plausibility of this view evaporates, however, when we consider war. *All* wars produce great amounts of suffering, but not all wars are unjustified,[17] whereas all evil acts are wrong, and hence all evil acts are unjustified. The Allies who waged and ultimately won the Second World War caused enormous amounts of suffering, perhaps more than if the Nazis had been entirely unopposed from start to finish.[18] But World War II is generally regarded as a just war (which is not, of course, to say that every act done in pursuit of Allied victory was justified). So the production of huge amounts of suffering isn't sufficient for actions to be evil. Nor is it necessary. Think of the child (or adult) who gleefully, with relish, tortures a helpless dog. Think of torturers and killers like Frederick West. Neither of these produce as much suffering as even a small military battle, yet they are quite plausible candidates for evil-doing. So the account of evil in terms of the production of huge amounts of suffering isn't convincing.

A quite different account focuses on the evil-doer's motives: an evil-doer, it is claimed, is one who embraces evil, who acts *in order* to do evil. Perhaps there are such agents (Milton's Satan is often taken to be an example: 'Evil, be thou my good.'). But this motivation can't be plausibly attributed to the great paradigm cases of evil-doing. There is absolutely no reason to believe that Eichmann, or Pol Pot, or the killers in the Rwandan genocide, acted in order to do evil. Many didn't even think that they *were* doing evil. This account of evil just isn't going to capture the core cases, the ones where we're sure that if there is such a thing as evil, this is where it is to be found.

The project of identifying the non-evaluative features in virtue of which acts are evil is very hard to carry out, and it may be that no such identification is possible, since it may be that the considerations in virtue of which an act is evil do not form a closed set, because the properties in question vary according to context in their evil-making power. But this is not to say that no general account can be given of what evil is. We can distinguish between what makes an act evil, and what it is for an act to be evil; just as we can distinguish between what makes an act right, and what it is for an act to be right. In the case of rightness, questions about what makes an act right are handled by normative moral theories such as utilitarianism and deontology. Candidate answers will cite features such as maximising happiness (for the utilitarians), or conforming to agent-relative as well as agent-neutral duties (for the deontologists). But the question of what it is for an act to be right is a meta-ethical question, drawing on matters to do with objectivity, anthropocentrism, and so forth. One candidate answer is that right actions are ones which evoke merited responses of approval; clearly this answer is compatible with a range of different answers to the normative-theoretical question.

Similarly, in the case of evil, the answer to the question about *what it is* for an act to be evil will cite quite different features from answers to the question about *what makes* this or that act evil. Here is a possible answer to the former question: what it is for an act to be evil is for it to have a very distinctive motivation which involves a kind of moral blindness. The agent who performs an evil act is impervious to the very serious moral reasons against acting in that way.

I won't attempt a full defence of this view here, having tried to give one elsewhere.[19] But I do want to focus on a notable feature of this account of what it is for an act to be evil, namely that it's a very formal account, and is neutral between quite a wide range of different substantive moral views. Depending on what we take to count as very weighty moral reasons, we will come up with quite different lists of evil acts. And this seems to be exactly what we find in debates about which acts are evil – when Ronald Reagan was laughed at for calling the Soviet Union the evil empire, it was because those who laughed didn't think that the policy-makers of the Soviet Union actually were so very impervious to the most weighty moral reasons, or at least not any more impervious than those of the USA itself. The disagreement wasn't about what it is for an act to be evil, but rather about the moral state-of-play in the particular case. Another point in favour of this account of evil is that it explains our very distinctive response to evil – our chilled horror not only at what is done, but at what the evil-doer has become. Someone who is impervious to the most serious moral considerations is suffering from a deformation in his practical reason, something which is at the heart of our concept of a person. This concept is so central to our moral responses and practices that distortions and deformities of the characteristics in virtue of which we are persons evoke something of the same response, only with far more justification, that facial deformities often quite wrongly produce.

4 Conclusion: Cruelty, Evil and Violence

How does this conception of evil connect with the account of cruelty which we have been examining? Evil acts, on this conception of evil, are ones in which the agent has a distinctive motivational pattern: he is impervious to the weightiest reasons against acting as he does. (This is, of course, compatible with him acting on a variety of different kinds of reasons: the evil derives from the reasons he doesn't see, rather than from those he does.) That is, an essential feature of evil actions is the state of mind of the agent. Cruelty, on the account given above, also makes essential reference to the state of mind of the agent: the agent acting cruelly is taking pleasure in, or being indifferent to, the serious and unmerited suffering of the victim. There is an isomorphism here which makes cruelty structurally apt to play the role of evil-making property. If we regard the production of serious and unmerited suffering as one of the weightiest reasons there can be against action, then it will not be surprising if cruel actions are evil, since one who takes delight in, or is wholly indifferent to, producing such suffering is likely to be impervious to its reason-giving power. The cruel agent need not, of course, be impervious to the fact that he is producing so much suffering – indeed, in the case of one who takes delight in it, he is bound to know of its existence. What he is impervious to is the reason-giving power of that suffering: he just doesn't see it as a reason to desist, let alone one of the weightiest reasons there can be.

Judith Shklar (and others) have argued that it is distinctive of liberalism to rate cruelty as the worst of vices, and cruel acts to be avoided above all else. This is not an entirely convincing claim, since even liberals might endorse a cruel action if it were the only way to avoid some very great catastrophe, and furthermore, non-liberals may abhor cruelty quite as much as liberals do.[20] But certainly liberal societies do seem to find cruelty particularly repellent, and even if it isn't regarded as the *summum malum*, it still figures largely in our understanding of viciousness; in general the production of serious and unmerited suffering is regarded as a very weighty reason against performing certain actions. Insofar as suffering counts strongly with us, to that extent imperviousness to it as a reason for action will strike us as abhorrent, as a major deformity in moral understanding, of the kind which we attribute to evil-doers. Hence cruelty is likely to have a close connection with evil, since it involves states of mind which imply the kind of imperviousness to moral reasons which, it has been suggested, is essential to evil.

As we saw above, cruelty isn't necessary for an action to be evil. That is because it isn't the *summum malum*; as Kekes and others have persuasively argued, there is no *summum malum*, no master vice or kind of action whose negative moral loading outweighs all others in all circumstances. There are other ways of being evil than cruelty: a silent and painless genocide (were such a thing to be possible) would still be evil even though it involved no suffering. On a more individual scale, some people regard Harold Shipman as a truly evil agent, but it is quite possible that his many victims suffered very little. Nonetheless evildoing normally involves suffering, since the weighty reasons to which it is impervious standardly (though by no means invariably) involve the production of suffering. Of course, a society which didn't rate suffering so highly as we do, which regarded it as a less serious matter, would be much less likely to think of cruel acts as evil ones. One advantage of the account given above of what it is for an act to be evil is that it is neutral between different sets of values, and is neutral between different construals of the status of these values. A moral realist will suppose there is a truth of the matter about which values are the most important ones, and hence a truth of the matter about which acts are evil. A non-cognitivist, or a relativist, will have a different story to tell about the status of the relevant judgements. All the same, the non-cognitivist can still use this account of what it is for an act to be evil, and if cruelty is outstandingly important in her moral code, she can endorse this treatment of its relation to evil. This neutrality is, I think, a strength of the view I'm proposing: we don't want to determine our moral metaphysics by our commitments in the theory of evil.

Where then does violence figure in this story? It is not a thick moral concept, and the state of mind of the agent plays no distinctive role in our understanding of what it is, so its connection with evil is not a very direct one. However, it is not accidental that violence seems to many people to point in the direction of evil. Cruelty, which *is* closely connected with evil, need not involve violence – a person who gloatingly withholds information about her son's survival from a mother who fears that he has been killed acts with cruelty, but not with violence. However, given our natural propensity to resist attempts to inflict pain on us, cruelty will often need to resort to violence. Insofar as cruelty is implicated in evil, it is likely that violence will be involved in evil also. It is only likely, not inevitable. But it is enough to account for some of our deep and justified suspicions about the ready resort to violence. Violence is often (though not always) wrong. And insofar as it connected with cruelty, it is apt to share its implication in evil.

Endnotes

1   See also Hitchens, Christopher: 'Fighting Words: Evil', *Slate*, 31 December 2002, *http://www.slate.com/id/2076195/*; Gunnell, Barbara: 'Take Cover: Evil is Back', *New Statesman* 11 February 2002.
2   Coady, C. A. J.: 'Violence', *Routledge Encyclopaedia of Philosophy* (London: Routledge, 1998), accessed 23 November 2005, from http://www.rep.routledge.com/article/S065SECT3
3   Coady, op. cit.
4   A pacifist response might involve the claim that the intuition I'm trading on here results from social conditioning that perpetuates the cycle of violence. But this involves empirical claims about the source of human violence which are highly contentious. I'm grateful to Steve de Wijze for discussion of this point.
5   See Gaut, Berys: '"Art" as a Cluster Concept', in Carroll, Noël (ed.): *Theories of Art* (Madison: University of Wisconsin Press, 2000), pp. 25–44 for a development of this kind of account of concepts.

6   Hallie, Phillip: 'Cruelty' in Becker, L. C. and Becker, C. B. (eds): *Encyclopedia of Ethics* vol. 1 (London: St James Press, 1992), pp. 231–232.

7   See Williams, Bernhard: 'Virtues and vices' in Craig, E. (ed.): *Routledge Encyclopedia of Philosophy*, op. cit., from website: http://www.rep. routledge.com/article/L112SECT4, retrieved February 11, 2006.

8   Shklar, Judith: *Ordinary Vices* (Cambridge, MA: Harvard University Press, 1984), p. 8.

9   Ibid, p. 31.

10   Shklar, Judith: 'Liberalism of Fear' in Rosenbaum, N.L. (ed): *Liberalism and the Moral Life* (Cambridge, Mass: Harvard University Press, 1989), p. 30.

11   This raises an interesting issue about the effect of the victim's consent to otherwise cruel acts: it seems to make a difference to the moral status of the act, but it's unclear whether it removes the cruelty, or removes its wrong-making powers.

12   See Kekes, John: 'Cruelty and Liberalism', *Ethics* 106.4 (1996), pp. 837–838.

13   Ibid, p. 840.

14   It's not clear whether reference to the agent's state of mind is also needed to deal with cases of non-culpable error, because it's not clear whether such errors lead to *unjustified* suffering. Just as we can have justified false beliefs, perhaps we can inflict justified though needless suffering. But this is too extensive a topic to deal with here.

15   This question touches on the issue of 'dirty hands' – a topic too large to cover here. See e.g., Rynard, P. and Shugarman, D. (eds): *Cruelty and Deception: the controversy over dirty hands in politics* (Peterborough, Ont.: Broadview, 1999).

16   It might be argued that an act which inflicts great suffering, but is performed purely to save the lives of millions, won't be the same kind of act as one in which the agent enjoys the suffering, and hence won't count as a case of torture at all, thus undermining the conclusion that some cruel acts are justified. But this view, in which the nature of the act is determined by the reasons for performing it, doesn't leave room for the possibility of doing the right act for the wrong reasons (and vice versa). This seems to me to be too high a price to pay for insulating right acts from bad motivations. I'm grateful to David McNaughton for discussion of this point.

17   This claim is, of course, contentious. I am just assuming here that pacifism isn't a tenable position, since there isn't space to argue for that view here.

18   Here I'm relying on the fact that wars always produce more suffering overall than the alternative to them. But only those who endorse a very simple form of utilitarianism will think that this settles the matter of whether war is ever justified.

19   See Garrard, Eve: 'The Nature of Evil', *Philosophical Explorations* 1.1 (1998).

20   See John Kekes, op. cit., for argument to this effect.

Burkhard Liebsch

Freedom *versus* Responsibility?
Between Ethical Indifference and Ethical Violence[1]

1. Preliminary remarks: violence and violation, freedom and responsibility

Either directly or indirectly (for example as readers or as distant spectators) we are confronted in our daily life with a broad spectrum of diverse forms of violence. This spectrum extends from obvious and spectacular forms of violence to very subtle phenomena which are not easy to discover *as* forms *of violence*. What finally culminates in mass murder, genocide, expulsion and ethnic 'cleansing' often begins with less obvious forms of violation such as social discrimination, the constant refusal to let others participate in social and political life, sheer ignorance and demeaning indifference. Doesn't violence indeed 'begin' here, that is when we behave vis-à-vis others as if we were alone? asks Levinas. (If this proves to be true even silence and concealment may be regarded as forms of violence.)

What do the aforementioned forms of violence – the extreme and obvious ones on the one hand and the subtler ones on the other hand – have in common? What justifies regarding all of them as forms of violence? Do they have a lowest common denominator? Would not the possibility to explicate such a denominator presuppose a complete line-up of the diverse forms of violence and, what is more, in each case an adequate description of the specific phenomenon?[2] A phenomenology of violence encompassing the whole spectrum of forms of violence is, however, not available. Nevertheless, I advocate at least as a provisional proposal to understand violence in any of its diverse forms as a phenomenon of violation. What (and who) is violated, in which form and by which means depends on the specific case in point.

Since things cannot suffer from violence they may be destroyed, deformed or otherwise mutilated but not violated. Violation of something, thus, refers at least indirectly to the violation of others – that is of their sensibility, their integrity, their sense of who they are, their sense of belonging to others, to a social, political and judicial world of living-together. Violence presupposes vulnerability and *depends* on the vulnerability of the other. Only when someone 'offers' himself as a vulnerable object of violence, can violation take place. Violence is violation of others; and violence cannot happen when nobody offers himself or is exposed to violation. To be exposed to violation means to be exposed in one's vulnerability. As vulnerable subjects we wish to hide or to protect ourselves – in spite of knowing very well, that, in the end, nothing can safeguard us in an absolute sense. As long as we exist as corporeal beings we cannot avoid being exposed to the other's freedom, which proves, in Hobbesian eyes, to be a freedom to do violence, that is, to violate others in their vulnerability. Seen that way, freedom and vulnerability must be regarded as co-constituents of human coexistence. And any phenomenon of violation provokes *to ask*: who was responsible, and why did it take place? To be sure, there are phenomena of violation which cannot (directly) be attributed to somebody's free will. Structural violence violates in spite of our inability to blame somebody for what violates anonymously. Nevertheless, it is widely acknowledged that violation must, in the last instance, be rooted in the freedom of human subjects who can be blamed for their responsibility. Whenever somebody acts freely and proves to be accountable the *question* of responsibility comes into play when the deed results in violation of others. The experience of responsibility is, however, not restricted to our factual freedom. What is more: the experience of responsibility can even *contradict* our notion of freedom: If we are in a certain sense responsible (in a sense, to be sure, which remains to be clarified) in situations where we do or did not seem to have an alternative aren't we, then, condemned to be responsible in a way that renders the idea of a radical freedom non-sensical?[3] Mustn't the idea of a radical freedom which would be *free from responsibility* be regarded, then, as misleading? On the other hand: if we stick to the idea of radical freedom, can responsibility then rightly be attributed to our 'being', which apparently is not to the disposition of our freedom? Can we *be* responsible and *be* free at the same time?

In the following considerations, I will put the understanding of freedom and responsibility into question – insofar as it docs not take into account a radicalisation of freedom which finally may release freedom from any connection with responsibility. Freedom in that sense would enable us to violate others without being responsible and without recognising the other's vulnerability as something ethically significant. While that may *prima facie* seem to be a rather strange notion of freedom, it can be argued that it is in fact deeply rooted in our western tradition of ethical and political thinking; and, what is more, that certain historical phenomena could be interpreted as a confirmation of such a notion of radical freedom.[4] I take it as a yet open question whether or not recent philosophy has given an adequate answer to the challenge of these phenomena. Rather, I present in the following some considerations concerning what appears to me as an intimate relation between freedom and responsibility, which can be described as a *chiasm*, i.e., a cross-over of responsibility and freedom. I will begin with some rather general remarks with respect to a highly influential notion of freedom, which suggests that *the sense of freedom is essentially unrelated to responsibility* and *that responsibility affects freedom only afterwards, belatedly*. This notion implies, moreover, that radical freedom cannot be regarded as an inevitably 'responsible' freedom. The 'radicality' of freedom would in this perspective preclude a responsibility inevitably 'given' to us which in turn would preclude to get radically rid of responsibility. The guiding thread of my considerations will be the question how a 'responsible freedom' is possible, which cannot be regarded as being absolutely free *from* responsibility. My attempt to clarify the relation between freedom and responsibility opposes a notion of freedom as entirely unrelated to responsibility. My final remarks will go a step further in addressing the question whether an 'absolute', irrevocable responsibility (as it is advocated by Levinas), which rules out ethical indifference, must be involved in forms of *ethical violence*.

2.   Negative freedom and situated responsibility

The *Encyclopaedia of Philosophy* tells us that 'it is best to start from a conception of freedom that has been central in the tradition of European individualism and liberalism'. According to this conception, freedom 'refers primarily to a condition characterised by the absence of coercion or constraint' imposed by others.[5] This definition tells us nothing about how to *use* one's freedom – e.g., as an owner of oneself who has – if we take Hobbes and Locke seriously – the 'natural right' to take anything that does not already belong to another as his property.[6] Freedom in the purely negative sense seems to be reduced to a 'state of being', as it were, which runs the risk of being lost at the very moment when it ventures to become practically effective. It has often been noted that such an 'abstract' notion of freedom does not do justice to the challenges of freedom as *praxis* and that it fails to recognise how closely negative and positive aspects of freedom turn out in practice to be intertwined. Whatever we project into the future must depend on circumstances, opportunities, temporal constraints etc. in order to bring about something new. The topography of our practical life – its 'field of freedom' (Husserl)[7] which allows the new to emerge – can never be completely calculated beforehand. Only afterwards do significant contours of its practical 'landscape' come to the fore, which enable us to realise something new – contours previously hidden behind the proximate field of our attention. A purely negative conception of freedom makes us believe that the negativity of human freedom in principle owes nothing to antecedent conditions. Within the framework of this conception these conditions are generally taken as a threat to submerge our freedom by way of their protracted determining force.

In contrast to this position it can be argued, that it is a certain ideology of negative freedom as emancipation from any heteronomous determination which hinders most the unfolding of freedom's positive potentials. Even (indeed, especially) to those who allegedly got rid of their past as the temporal background (*'Gewesenheit'*) of their actual being, positive freedom may turn out to be an unbearable burden.[8]

A seemingly annihilated past that could no longer inscribe itself into our present would leave us nothing to project into the future.[9] Someone who believes in the pure negativity of his freedom may enthusiastically herald his liberation from genealogical ties and promise to begin a new life in order not to discover but to create an authentic self which leaves the constraints of his past behind. He will, however, most likely come to the painful realisation that such a self cannot be the product of a pure construction. Someone who in an excess of negative freedom wishes to deracinate himself in order to reinvent his identity risks betraying himself with respect to the familial past in which he remains deeply steeped. The repercussions of the past's determinations may affect us unconsciously. They form nevertheless our present being and our having-been-somebody, which alone can serve as the starting place for any attempt to become another. Seen in this way, the radicalisation of negative freedom amounts to the liquidation of the possibilities of positive freedom.

Sartre's famous dictum, 'we are condemned to be free', should, thus, be reinterpreted so as to indicate that it is up to us to capture the sense of our freedom in a way that does not undermine the possibilities the given situation offers to us. In this perspective, our conceptions of freedom are to be regarded as more or less (in)sufficient, (in)adequate, truthful or deceptive *realisations* of freedom which in turn shape its practical reality. It is only here, in the midst of adversity and hardship, that we can put our understanding of freedom to a test in order to realise its situatedness, which itself will always include some degree of coercion and constraint.

In reality not only do coercion and constraint take many different forms – sometimes concealed forms not easily discernible as such; there is also no clear-cut demarcation line between coercion, constraint and sheer interference with others. One must not only put up with such interference but also take into account and recognise it as the medium of the exercise of one's freedom. An individual's life must 'interfere', to say the least, with lives of others in order to allow him to be free in a 'positive' sense, which means here: to be enabled to do this or that in a meaningful way.

Regarding the aforementioned notion of negative freedom it is only the *character* of interference that can be at stake. If I do not want to have my life to 'interfere' with the lives of others, I doom myself to isolation in which any freedom (in its positive meaning) fades away. Whatever *negative freedom* refers to – e.g. freedom from the burden of one's past, from the entanglement in personal loyalties, from the powerful influences of others that may threaten to suppress us etc. – it makes sense only as freedom *within* our relations to others. Obviously, a notion of *negative freedom in the abstract sense of 'immunity from coercion or interference by others'*[10] does not adequately pay tribute to the challenges of the exercise of freedom. Negative freedom is not enough when we not only desire to be or to feel free but, rather, when practical abilities, competencies and resources of behaving and acting are at stake. It may well be that very different meanings of freedom come into play here and that freedom will finally turn out as a hetero-geneous notion comprising irreducibly different aspects, modes and subjective, social and political dimensions of freedom, i.e., freedom of speech, of association, of movement, of disposal of one's property and so on. Nevertheless, freedom has often been considered to be a unitary concept insofar as it depends on our *self-determination.*[11]

According to this notion, the freedom to behave and act freely is ascribed to someone under the premise that his actions and deeds were (or should be) determined by himself – i.e., that what he does can be attributed to his *free will* or, to put it yet in another way, that it rests on his *agency*. Agency presupposes negative freedom at least in the sense of *insufficient determination* by 'external' conditions; to this negative aspect of freedom the notion of agency adds the idea that self-deter-mination amounts to the determination *of something,* which shall be brought about by the self: the *project* or the *pragma.*[12]

Put this way, the idea of freedom as self-determination suggests that responsibility is only a secondary attribute of our freedom which owes nothing to responsibility, at least with respect to its original con-stitution. Philosophers have indeed 'often supposed that the concept of 'freedom' can be fixed independently of responsibility and that only after the meaning of 'freedom' is specified we can determine whether, and under what conditions, a person is responsible.'[13] This supposition is, however, evidently at odds with our experience. Whereas a certain notion of responsibility (if not responsibility in general) may *logically presuppose* freedom in our experience, primarily it is in our *being responsible* that we *realise* our freedom. Enmeshed in concrete 'forms of life,' (Wittgenstein) we find ourselves as always already being responsible.[14] Freedom does not emerge as an 'existential' concern in the position of a detached subject, not situated in the world in which his self-determination would prove to be effective. On the contrary, freedom takes shape as a problem of our embeddedness in the lives of others, as a tension between connectedness with others and distanciation, between relatedness and dissociation. It is in concrete orders of coexistence (*Mitsein, Being-with* to speak with Heidegger) – where we first respond to the needs of others and experience them responding to us as finite beings – that we realise what freedom means: to respond or not to respond, to meet other's needs or to refuse to do so. What this amounts to is living up to one's – often conflicting – duties and responsibilities in regard to the other or to fail or to reject them as incommensurable with our own life etc. To be sure, these experiences – tragic as they may turn out – entail only fragments of freedom *within* given orders of coexistence. A freedom which strives to transcend the parochialism of limited forms of social life must undergo, on the other hand, thoroughgoing revisions of what it means to be a self as a subject of self-determination no longer accepting local loyalties as ultimate measures of his freedom.

However, even with respect to a *disembedded* self that refuses identification with his belonging to social life in order to take refuge in his legal membership in a political community, freedom and responsibility cannot fall apart completely. On the contrary, both notions *prima facie* remain closely related to each other – albeit the character of their relation must change under such conditions. Whereas we first discover our freedom as situated selves whose responsibility turns out to be a *responsive* responsibility with its responsiveness to others as its prime virtue, under conditions of detached living in political societies responsibility in terms of accountability prevails. In societies where almost everybody is a nobody in his relations to others we don't rely on responsiveness but, instead, on objective responsibility, imputability and liability, which are open to judicial judgement.

In this 'objective' sense responsibility turns out to be a rather impoverished concept. The entire responsiveness of responsibility is in danger of falling into oblivion if we confine its meaning to imputability and liability. We are used to presupposing not only that we may be responsible for anything that depends on our freedom but also that freedom is an implication of our responsibility. We are free at least *in principle* to act *otherwise* than we did in the past, presently act or intend to act in the future. It is our knowledge of scopes of behaving or acting otherwise that motivates us to attribute freedom to those we hold or make responsible for something. Often enough, however, this 'otherwise' appears to be nothing but a retrograde supposition, which is hardly justifiable in practice. In many cases being responsible or being subject to the attribution of responsibility by others does *not* correspond to our subjective experience when we feel that we actually had no alternative to behave or act otherwise. Nevertheless, we cannot get rid of our retrograde accountability. In its temporality, our responsibility has to take into account an *anticipated retrograde accountability*. After a certain delay I must eventually accept that I have done something different from what I intended to do. Accepting my accountability, I must admit that the future can pervert the inner sense of my deeds and even of the project(s) of my life through which I may hope to discover who I am. The belatedness (*Nachträglichkeit*) of that which may retrospectively affect the facticity and sense (*noema* or *pragma*) of what I have done submits me to the perspective of the other as a *judge* who is (under certain conditions) entitled to hold me responsible and to charge me with my 'objective' guilt, whatever my intentions may have been. In this case we have to realise a surplus of responsibility which surpasses the experience of subjective freedom. To the other as judge of my deeds which provoke his approval or reprobation, the question of whether I might have acted differently than I did may in fact be quite irrelevant. Following Dewey, we could very well argue that theories of responsibility go wrong when they focus on a state of mind that precedes deeds for which person are held liable. In contrast to this, Dewey maintains that one 'is held responsible in order to *become* responsible, that is, responsive to the needs and claims of others'.[15]

So called neo-Aristotelians want us to believe that only concrete fellow-beings who belong to our own forms of life are relevant in this respect. And they claim that we have to resort to the communal conditions of situated selves in order to rediscover how deeply a responsibility – that cannot be reduced to accountability, liability or imputability – affects our social life as fellow beings. Thus, authors as diverse as Sandel, Etzioni, MacIntyre and Taylor maintain that an impoverished notion of responsibility in terms of a judicial perspective, which depends on the bequest of modern acquisitive individualism cannot take into account the virtue of responsibility as a mode of concern for others.[16] Furthermore they argue that without such a virtue no legal-political system can survive. Here, responsibility is not taken as that which allows blaming others for their misdirected freedom but, rather, as a virtue *par excellence* that should guide the exercise of positive freedom in the name of the common good. In the following, I will refer to these neo-Aristotelian conceptions only in passing in order to draw attention to a radicalisation of the idea of responsibility, which *cannot* be confined to 'fellow beings'. I shall argue that this radicalisation amounts to a most provocative confrontation with the modern idea of a freedom, which in its negative as well as in its positive meaning seems – at least from the perspective of modern individualism – to be primarily one's own property and in its constitution owes nothing to the other. In the remainder of my considerations I will give at least some hints as to how the different dimensions of responsibility we have touched upon so far relate to each other.

In the context of my present considerations the label 'neo-Aristotelian' might well appear out of place insofar Aristotle neither developed a full-fledged philosophy of freedom nor a coherent idea of responsibility. To be sure, in an Aristotelian perspective philosophy in itself can be understood as the praxis of responsibility *par excellence* devoted to universal justification (*logon didonai*). However, the Aristotelian notion of responsibility (if there is one at all), is only related to a *situated freedom* limited to deliberation on means within a given ethical order of political coexistence. Aristotle describes the freedom of deliberation as being embedded in ethical and political forms of life which cannot be transcended by freedom. Freedom is the realisation of our life as being directed towards a given end, which is the good. The good is not at our disposal. In the Aristotelian perspective, the good which is to be realised as the *telos* of our common existence must be regarded as being pre-formed in our nature, or, to be more exact: in the nature of those individuals who always already coexisted politically, that is, of those men who deserve to participate in public life as legitimate members. As is well known, Aristotle drew from this the normative conclusion that women, slaves and barbarians who do not belong to a particular political order are to be excluded from legitimate membership. Thus, Aristotle's famous notion of the human as *zoon politikon* must not be regarded as a universal anthropological concept but, rather, as a restrictive junction of membership and nature. One must be a fellow-citizen in order to deserve to be called a human being in the full sense. Coexisting in the name of the realisation of the common good pertains only to the nature of those who belong to the respective political order. The others whose legitimate membership in the political community can be contested with regard to their 'alien' nature do not share the same teleological orientation towards the good which serves as the ultimate sense of freedom.

On the other hand, those who coexist in order to realise the good through their freedom should be evaluated in terms of the virtues. In this sense the members of the political community should strive to be judged to be good characters in terms of the virtues. The ethical notions of character, virtue, vice and the good make sense only with reference to the particular forms and modes of coexistence, the practices and settings which render them intelligible as teleologically oriented towards the realisation of the good. Aside from this pre-given frame of reference talking about responsibility would make no sense.

The same holds true for freedom. In an Aristotelian perspective, the notion of freedom becomes ethically and politically unintelligible if it gets dislodged from the concrete scopes of deliberation where the realisation of the finality of the good should take place. In this respect, the good is once and for all the *sense* of freedom. In terms of the good, freedom makes sense only within an order of ethical and political coexistence which is oriented towards the realisation of the good, that is, of what the members of the concrete form of coexistence could be if they realised their potential. Outside of this context the political does not exist; and neither does freedom insofar as its deliberate use must be understood as being teleologically directed towards the political realisation of the ethical good. *Ethnos* and *demos* seem to limit the boundaries of the political, of the ethical and of freedom as well. What puzzles us and is 'likely to affront us – and rightly – is Aristotle's writing off of non-Greeks, barbarians and slaves [not to speak about women], as not merely not possessing political relationships, but as incapable of them.'[17] No less must we be astonished about the fact that freedom in its political and ethical sense can only emerge inside the particular order of coexistence where the good seems to be taken for granted or incontestable.[18]

That an explicit notion of freedom is missing in Aristotle can at least to a certain extent be explained by the fact that he never took into account the radical contingency of the order of ethical and political coexistence. Rather, he confined himself to descriptions of the limited fields of deliberation in the midst of finite situations where freedom never bears on ends or on the ethical or political meaningfulness of deliberate action.[19] A radical freedom that would put into question this meaningfulness *as such,* cannot even arise if it is taken for granted that man is free and has 'concrete responsibilities, concrete virtues only when he is capable of situating himself within historical communities in which he recognises the meaning of his own existence'. Today some communitarians seem to go even a step further in claiming that freedom and responsibility are 'real' only as features of a situated self, which 'ontologically' belongs to concrete forms of life and coexistence with others. Their critics, on the other hand, maintain that the conditions of the free coexistence of 'modern' or 'post-modern' beings are at odds with such neo-Aristotelian premises.

Since under (post-)modern conditions many, if not most individuals no longer seem to be irrevocably rooted in given forms of life it is up to them to find out what is good for them and for their fellow beings. Their respective beliefs have emerged as being irreducibly heterogeneous. Conflicts concerning what we regard to be the good for some or all of us have appeared to be unsettleable. We all have too many disparate and rival political and ethical concepts and the *mélange* of our fragmented cultural inheritance leaves us no way of settling the issue between them through rational discourse.[20] Possibly too quickly this heterogeneity is attributed to conflicts – or *différend* – between different forms of life – suggesting, as it often happens, that it is ultimately their ethnic, incommensurable 'substance' that causes recurrent, tragic conflicts about the right and the good.[21]

I don't think that such a position will prove tenable. The recently popular revitalisation of 'substantial' ethnicity appears as a spectre of genealogical myths that make us believe that our belonging to collective life – and in that sense our identity – is not at all a matter of choice and options but, rather, a question of fate. Doesn't such a belief run the risk of naturalising the heritage of the forms of life so that their conflicts seem to be predestined by their 'substantial' incompatibility? The modern idea of freedom was established precisely against the *fatalisation* of the forms of coexistence in which we find ourselves enmeshed.

The radicalisation of this idea (which we owe to Nietzsche), however is incompatible with an *ethical substance* in the sense of *Sittlichkeit,* which Hegel had tried to synthesise with modern freedom. Since the emergence of the modern individual self, which Nietzsche sought to liberate from anything given or binding and from any demanding authority, the burden of freedom rests seemingly solely on the individual, on the private arbitrariness of its choices. Even neo-Aristotelians cannot avoid paying tribute to this development.

> If the life of the virtues is [at least under modern conditions] continuously fractured by choices in which one allegiance entails the apparently arbitrary renunciation of another, it may seem that the goods internal to practices [or to forms of life] do after all derive their authority from our individual choices; for when different goods summon in different and in incompatible directions, 'I' have to choose between their rival claims. The modern self with its criterion-less choices apparently reappears in the alien context of what was claimed to be an Aristotelian world.[22]

This not only concerns modern *reinterpretations* of the ancient world but also attempts to *revitalise* it.

MacIntyre, on the one hand, sought to rehabilitate the virtues suggesting that only 'a *telos* which transcends the limited goods of practices by constituting the good of a whole human life' can avert the decline of ethical life altogether. On the other hand, he is ready to admit that nevertheless 'a certain subversive arbitrariness' inevitably invades our ethical life.[23] This arbitrariness is, however, not limited to the choice between different goods; it radically affects, seemingly at least, the 'existence' of the good. No good that surpasses the multiplicity of goods which inform practices is available any longer *as a telos* which could be attributed to a given order of our coexistence. Which is not to say that the notion of the good is obsolete. Rather, it follows that the good cannot be regarded as being *given* as the teleological sense of the different, radically contingent social or political orders which we continuously try to stabilise against the constant threats of their totalisation, sclerosis, degeneration and violent destruction. Neither the so-called global village nor any other all-encompassing cosmopolitan order will ever promise to re-establish an incontestable meta-good.

In this sense we all are the heirs to the Hobbesian destruction of the Aristotelian legacy. With Aristotle, we should say that human beings that belong together as being directed towards the good are politically *related* to each other and that they are – in contrast to strangers – only *as such* fully human beings. With Hobbes we would have instead to accept that we are strangers from the start. In the Aristotelian world 'there is no "outside" except that of the stranger', says MacIntyre.[24] Either one is part of the given ethical world or one exists detached from it in an ethical desert without any neighbour to whom one could be related in terms of the good. 'A man who tried to withdraw himself from his given position [in the Aristotelian world] would be engaged in the enterprise to make himself disappear.'[25] In the Hobbesian perspective the new-born must be regarded as *being always already 'disappeared'* in this sense. Its mother, we read in *De homine*, has to treat her child as if it could become her later enemy. From the start, we all prove to be 'unrelated', that is, *ethically alien* with respect to each other. Seen in this way, it makes good sense to say that modern society is indeed – and not only in its 'surface appearance' – 'nothing but a collection of strangers'[26] externally related in a political system which owes its *raison d'être* in the last instance to nothing else but to its members' fear of the other as one's potential murderer. This fear evidently functions in Hobbes' writings as the counterpart of an ethically indifferent freedom which is free to commit any form of violence against any other if only one's self-preservation is substantially in danger.

3   Traces of ethical violence

Levinas has tried to give an appropriate answer to this challenge – not by recurring to a substantial good or by way of an anachronistic idealisation of an out-dated form of life but, rather, by taking Hobbes seriously. For Levinas, the ideal of a good which represents the entire sense of a particular or universal order of human coexistence cannot be maintained. Not only do we find ourselves enmeshed in a plurality of contingent orders interfering with, and contradicting, each other, but we must also take into account the 'strangeness' of the other, of any other, of the species as well as of our breed. Levinas does this much more consistently, however, than Hobbes tried to do. With Hobbes, Levinas takes the modern destruction of teleological pre-deliniations of the sense of human coexistence for granted. He refuses, however, to draw the conclusion that the other must consequently shrink to an ethically indifferent entity.

The other, any other, says Levinas, confronts us with an *alterity* which resists any attempt to understand, to imagine or to *re-present* it. The other is not a 'phenomenon'. He „appears' in the orders of our present only in so far as to leave the trace of his retreat into the irrevocable absence of his alterity. Wherever experience allows the other to appear, it will be under the conditions of the present, that is, under the conditions of *re-presenting* time. Levinas, however, maintains that the alterity of the other, on the one hand, and the other-as-remembered, the other-as-presented and the other-as-anticipated, on the other hand, are radically incommensurable. The other as radically other, whose epiphany surpasses all phenomena, cannot at least be *reduced* to what appears in the order of experience. In the 'appearance' of the other any phenomenology will find only the wake of the effacement of his trace.[27]

Levinas claims that the otherness of the other cannot be reduced to *ethical indifference* as Hobbes would have it. He tries to convince us that the other's strangeness and our non-indifference vis-à-vis the other are two sides of the same coin and as such indissoluble. This indissolubility is proven, Levinas maintains, by the experience of responsibility, that is, the experience of non-indifference vis-à-vis the other as stranger. In other words: a phenomenology of the experience of responsibility should be able to demonstrate that a freedom alleged to be originally unlimited finds its master in the gift of a responsibility which the other-as-stranger has always already given to us. To this responsibility we have to give the answer of our own responsibility; we *cannot avoid* giving it and we *have to* give it if the otherness of the other *demands* an answer. We cannot avoid giving an answer – if only the answer of rejecting the responsibility which has been given to us. The conviction that *even such a negative answer cannot liquidate the gift of responsibility* – as the ultimate demarcation line which our freedom cannot transgress – is the kernel of Levinas' ethics. Levinas does not intend to deny the freedom to answer responsibly or otherwise. The gift of responsibility invokes a responding other who accepts it and takes care of it. If the responding other refuses to do so, that is, if he refrains from 'bearing' his responsibility he can nevertheless not annihilate *his being invoked* as a responsible other.

In the following, I'll try to explicate this thought in order to clarify the internal relation between freedom and responsibility that emerges here. The other exposes us to the imperative to take responsibility for him which allows no exception or substitution of ourselves as responsible beings. It is 'me' who is demanded to recognise and to acknowledge my responsibility – whatever that will mean in different concrete situations. (Not to let him die alone, to care for him, to share [...]) It is an

> unlimited responsibility [...] even if the responsibility amounts to nothing more than a responding 'here I am,' in the impotent confrontation with the Other's death, or in the shame of surviving, to ponder the memory of one's faults.[28]

Under the other's eyes – anterior to any deliberation – we are subjected to his claim to (*Anspruch auf*) something and his appeal to (*Anspruch an*) someone. This 'someone' is me. No other human being can figure as my substitute in the position as the original responding other who always already finds himself being exposed to the other's demand, which *subjectivises* me as ethical subject. To put it paradoxically: my freedom as an ethical subject begins with the other. My freedom, thus, turns out to be a responsive freedom,[29] which in its responsiveness precludes any possibility not to answer to the other at all. If I refuse to give an answer, I keep a silence which is *significant* insofar as the demanded answer *fails to appear*. My refusal cannot annihilate that which makes it intelligible *as* a refusal. If my answer fails to appear, it is exactly this failing which does appear. In this case my failing refers back to that which called for an answer. *What* we answer is our contribution; *to what* we answer and *that* we must answer is not.

This does not render our freedom superfluous. On the contrary. It comes into play even more significantly insofar as *how* we answer counts. If the demand of the other is originally unlimited, even excessive, as Levinas, Derrida and others maintain, I can never do justice to it. Any answer which I can give will be limited and restricted. Only through a restricted answer can I realise my concrete responsibility. This will never be enough; even less so if, in the face of the other, the Third regards us, and with him all of mankind, as we read in *Totality and Infinity*. I cannot do justice to an excessive responsibility which exceeds – in a violent manner – any concrete possibility of responding. Unlimited responsibility calls for restricted responsibility in order not to collapse in irresponsibility. The practice of a restricted responsibility, however, must inevitably be irresponsible *insofar* as it can never sufficiently do justice to an unlimited responsibility. To cling to an unlimited responsibility, on the other hand, would amount to denying to any other the answer of our concrete responsibility which we owe him. Thus, unlimited responsibility entices us into an absolute irresponsibility, that is, into the worst form of an ethical betrayal. What we owe the other and the other others is to take care of our concrete responsibility, which cannot help but realise only a fraction of what we should give them by way of our responsive responsibility. Giving them less is better than trying to give them all that would be their due – which would amount to giving them practically nothing.

On the other hand, we cannot withdraw from the excessive demands of responsibility in order to keep us within a given order of our liability with respect to certain others. Such a restriction of responsibility to responsibility for certain others would violate the otherness of the other in its entirety – whether he belongs to the respective order or not. At least in Levinas' perspective this must be the case. His radical ethics ventures to prove that the otherness of the other inevitably remains an ethical, that is, non-indifferent 'reality' which renders us responsible even if we are strangers to him. The attempt to seek refuge in a *reservatio moralis* always comes too late. In this sense, the ethical transgresses and exceeds any limited order of responsibility which tends to strip the other of his alienness or alterity in order to reduce him to his role, function or legal status in terms of membership in an 'Aristotelian world' etc. If we could reduce responsibility to different orders of responsibility allowing us to measure, to calculate and distribute it, then, indeed, the dream of 'every good conscience' could become true, namely the dream that we can say: it's enough, we have done enough, we are 'quits' with responsibility and with the others who unremittingly beset us with their claims and appeals.

This way out is blocked if we cannot ignore the excessive demand of responsibility, of different responsibilities in the face of the other and the other others. Our responsibility is an *excessive responsibility*. Paradoxically such responsibility requires belated restriction in order not to result in an irresponsibility, which prevails where we fail to give concrete answers in our being called into question by the other's demands. The forcible restriction of responsibility *in the name of its realisation* is the task of our freedom. The 'primary', excessive responsibility for the other, which originates, and is given to us, in the other's presence, precedes any free initiative, even any understanding, contract and consent, as Levinas claims. Instead of being rendered superfluous, however, it is up to our freedom to save responsibility from its break-down in the irresponsibility of its own excessive demanding. Seen in this way, we have to assume *responsibility for responsibility* in our responding to the gift of responsibility. Only if we assume this responsibility, can responsibility really become 'real'.

Instead of having the relation of responsibility and freedom result in a pure dualism of 'responsibility beyond freedom' vs. 'freedom without responsibility' we should reconsider the relation in terms of a *chiasm*: our responsibility for the other and the other others needs our freedom in order to allow us to give a concrete, responsive answer to the other's gift of responsibility.[30] Otherwise, our responsibility would be reduced to an effect of a cause, that is, to irresponsibility.

Conversely, our freedom must be considered as the *answer* to the other's demand or appeal. Otherwise, our freedom would have to be regarded as a sheer manifestation of a self-sufficient, self-determining subject responsible only to himself. If we shy away from both positions, which share irresponsibility vis-à-vis the other *as other* as their common denominator, it is because we begin to realise that responsibility and freedom must testify to each other, if the other is not to be reduced to an ethical nothing.

Responsiveness which mediates between freedom and responsibility contradicts a notion of negative freedom as 'immunity from interference with others'; it tells us nothing, however, about how to use our freedom. The responsiveness of our freedom doesn't even preclude us from refusing to give *any concrete* answer to the other's appeal or demand. In order to prevent the possibility that freedom is given absolutely free reign, Levinas comes close to the affirmation of an ethical determination and *violence* which makes us 'hostages' of the other's injunction in order not to let us escape into irresponsibility. To the irresponsibility of freedom he, thus, opposes a primary responsibility as obedience to the other without alternative. Consequently, what I have to answer vis-à-vis the other seems to

> dawn in the ego as a commandment understood by the ego in its very obedience, as if obedience were its very accession to hearing the prescripttion, as if the ego obeyed before having understood, and as if the intrigue of alterity were knotted prior to knowledge.'[31]

This primary *obéissance* would, however, liquidate my self-responsibility and dissolve it into the ethical violence of heteronomy if the *inevitability* of my answer to the other's demand could prescribe *what* I have to do for him. Levinas not only seems to downplay this difference, he also doesn't sufficiently pay tribute to the scopes of answering *within* relations to others and to our various possibilities of distanciation *from* different forms of belonging to more or less 'significant' others. As members of social communities and political societies we are not doomed to stick to the 'embeddedness' of our self that emerges in primary relations with fellow beings. On the other hand, Levinas is right in claiming that our responsibility is not *a priori* limited to 'close' relations. He fails, however, to outline the relations of radical responsibility, which he advocates so vigorously, to our conflicting social and political responsibilities and to the wish to live with and for others in institutions, which ought to be just and fair.[32] Levinas clearly realised that it is the task of social and political freedom, i.e., of praxis in its fullest sense, to guarantee the durable existence of such institutions. His radicalisation of ethics, however, provokes the open question whether the social and political orders of human coexistence must necessarily and forcibly 'forget' the radical otherness of the other as the ultimate source of our responsibility. Is there an ethical oblivion beneath the ethnic, cultural and historical ground of our life-forms?

To be sure, what I said so far does not exhaust in the slightest the problems of ethical violence. Whereas Levinas is right in criticising the abstract opposition between freedom and responsibility seemingly deeply steeped in the western philosophical tradition, he only insufficiently realises the unexpected forms of violence, which happen to emerge in the midst of the ethical sense of freedom he advocates so emphatically. An excessive demand of the other can only be answered by way of a forcible restriction, which seems to be doomed to do violence to the unlimited appeal of the other. This must be even more the case if *others* are at stake whose appeals force us to compare them as claims, to balance and to offset them against each other, that is, to establish an economy of justice which cannot do justice to the uniqueness of any other's, originally unlimited appeal. Far from getting rid of violence once and for all through the chiasm of freedom and responsibility, it is the ethical violence of restriction of unlimited demands, which only promises to help realise the *minimum* of violence.

Without referring to a teleological sense of human coexistence in political forms of life, Levinas takes it for granted that paying tribute to the demand of the other as appealing to our responsibility should amount to the minimum of violence. Not the slightest degree of violence which proves to be avoidable would be acceptable in this perspective. Levinas suggests the establishment of an absolute standard, namely to do justice to the idea of an unconditional and originally unlimited responsibility vis-à-vis the other. Moreover, his philosophy draws our attention to ethical forms of violation which result from the absolute impossibility to do justice to conflicting demands of the other and other others at the same time.[33] Compared with well-known, often scandalous phenomena of violence referred to at the beginning of my considerations, these forms of violence are less obvious. Nevertheless, they should not go unnoticed because they challenge any ethical attempt to come to terms with violence. In explicating this, I come back to Hobbes once again.

In a Hobbesian perspective, we are born as strangers who are predestined by our very nature to preserve and protect our entirely unrelated – that means for Levinas: *ethically indifferent* – life against any deadly threat. Born to be free without being in any respect responsible to any other admits excessive violations precluded only by the power of a sovereign state, which is thought in Hobbes' philosophy as guarantee of collective security based on social contract. Anything is allowed when the state does not serve this purpose insofar an individual's self-preservation is in real danger. In this case no living individual – whose freedom will, in the last instance, not renounce its own sovereignty – would be hindered by any restriction – not even by an old-fashioned law prescribing: you shall not kill [...] The only 'natural law' is – ethically indifferent – self-preservation. Against this dissolution of freedom and responsibility, Levinas directed his notion of *non-indifference as the sense of freedom,* which appears to be 'always already' responsible vis-à-vis the other. To be sure, Levinas never intended to outline a comprehendsive theory of society or a political philosophy, which could tell us how to minimise violence *practically* and how to *secure this aim as a common good* when we can no longer rely on an Aristotelian teleology. In my view, he confined himself, rather, to rehabilitate under the anti-Hobbesian heading 'non-indifference' a notion of responsibility which allows us to identify *violence as violation*, that is, as violation of the other's demand or appeal to our responsibility. Levinas attempts to show what is lacking in Hobbes (if not to refute Hobbes) in this respect in demonstrating that this responsibility is inevitably given to us. Instead of nourishing thereby the utopian hope to come to terms with violence some time he makes us sensitive to subtle forms of violence *within* the ethical itself.[34] Far from strictly resisting any form of violation, the responsibility of freedom harbours violence in its own sense.

Endnotes

1   Charity Scribner, Christian Grüny and Ian Kaplow have brought this paper into readable English. I am grateful for their support and for Felix Ó Murchadha's careful editorial work.

2   Cf. Liebsch, B., Mensink, D. (eds): *Gewalt Verstehen* (Berlin: Akademie Verlag, 2003).

3   On the other hand, we all know of an experience of freedom that does not seem, at least at first glance, to be inherently related to the issue of responsibility. Imagine the freedom to create, to dream or to project something which does not affect other's life or well–being. Nevertheless, even in these cases the supposed relatedness of freedom and responsibility does not completely fade away. For it is only in the future's horizons that we can discover whether or not our freedom interferes with an other's life.

4   Extensive discussion of this line of reasoning can be found in: Liebsch, B.: *Geschichte als Antwort und Versprechen* (Freiburg i. Br.: Velbrücke Wissen-schaft, 1999); *Zerbrechliche Lebensformen. Widerstreit – Differenz – Gewalt* (Berlin: Akademie Verlag, 2001).

5   Partridge, P. H.: 'Freedom', in: Edwards, P. (ed.): *Encyclopedia of Philosophy*, vol. 3, (New York: MacMillan, 1967), pp. 221–224.

6   Cf. Steinvorth, U.: *Freiheitstheorien in der Philosophie der Neuzeit* (Darmstadt: Wissenschaftliche Buchgesellschaft, 1987), pp. 77, 97.

7   Cf. Merleau-Ponty, M.: *Phenomenology of Perception*, trans. by Colin Smith (London: Routledge & Kegan Paul, 1962), p. 454.

8   If we take it for granted, with Nietzsche and Rorty, however, that what I am depends entirely on my will and that the past is without reserve subject to my reinterpretation then, indeed, no once and for all fixed value or yardstick can exist which could serve as an objective measure of my freedom.

9   Cf. Ricœur, P.: 'New Developments in Phenomenology in France: The phe-nomenology of language', in *Social Research* 43.1 (1967), pp. 1–30, esp. p. 9; 'L'humanité de l'homme', in: *Studium Generale* 15 (1962), p. 320.

10 Partridge, P.H.: 'Freedom', op. cit., p. 223.

11 Cf. Ricœur, P.: *The Self as Another*, trans. by Kathleen Blamey (Chicago: University of Chicago Press, 1992), ch. 4, 1.

12 Only in passing I wish to point to the ambiguity of the term self-determination which refers either to determination by the self or to determination of the self. Cf. Steinvorth, op. cit., p. 145. In each concrete case a person's intentions, voluntariness and deliberation etc. may be questionable. But to be a person implies one's liability. For practical purposes we often make no distinction between responsibility and liability. In truth, however, these notions cannot be regarded simply as synonymous. Whereas liability can be limited to a judicial perspective (which presupposes personal responsibility as a necessary condition

of the justice of a person's receiving what he deserves), responsibility emerges also in situations where nobody could accuse us of having failed our duties and obligations.

13   Cf. Kaufman, A. S.: 'Responsibility, Moral and Legal', in: Edwards, P.: (ed.): *Encyclopedia of Philosophy,* op. cit., pp. 183–188,

14   For Nietzsche, the mastery and domination of will consists precisely in its seemingly unlimited ability to alter not only its means but also its values and ends. The autonomy of the will, thus, turns out to be altogether incommensurable with the idea of responsibility *as given,* as resting on an objective, unchangeable order. Nothing given can, at least in this perspective, resist the domination of my free will – not even the past, which may be recreated or reinvented.

15   Dewey, J.: *Theory of the Moral Life* (New York: Inwington, 1980), p. 170. Here we should distinguish responsibility and reponsiveness. Cf. Waldenfels, B.: 'Response and Responsibility in Levinas', in Peperzak, A. T. (ed.): *Ethics as First Philosophy* (London: Routledge, 1995), pp. 39–52.

16   Cf. Sandel, M.: *Liberalism and the Limits of Justice* (Cambridge: Cambridge University Press, 1982); MacIntyre, A.: *After Virtue,* (Notre Dame: University of Notre Dame Press, 1984); C. Taylor, *Philosophical Arguments* (Cambridge: Cambridge University Press, 1995); Etzioni, A.: *The Golden New Rule. Community and Morality in a Democratic Society* (New York : Basic Books, 1996).

17   MacIntyre, A., op. cit., p. 159.

18   Cf. Steinvorth, *op. cit.,* p. 16.

19   Ricœur, *Oneself as Another*, pp. 89–96.

20   Cf. MacIntyre, A., op. cit., pp.. 52 ff., 58, 65, 117.

21   Cf. Liebsch, B.: *Gastlichkeit und Freiheit. Polemische Konturen europäischer Kultur*, (Freiburg i. Br.: Velbrücke Wissenschaft, 2005).

22   MacIntyre, op. cit., p. 202.

23   Ibid., p. 203.

24   Ibid., p. 126.

25   Ibid.

26   Ibid., pp. 250f.

27   Cf. Derrida, J., 'At this very moment in this work here I am', in Bernasconi, R. & Critchley, S. (eds): *Re–Reading Levinas* (Bloomington: Indiana University Press, 1991), p. 37.

28   Cf. Levinas, E.: 'Diachrony and representation' in *Time and the Other (and additional essays),* trans. by R. A. Cohen (Pittsburgh: Duquesne University Press, 1987), p. 110.

29   Ibid., p. 105.

30   The metaphorical notion of 'chiasm' refers here to a crossing over of responsibility and freedom which is to say that both notions should be regarded as *inherently related* to each other without being *reducible* to each other.

31   Ibid., p. 106.

32   Cf. Ricœur, P.: *The Just* (Chicago: University of Chicago Press, 2000); *Le Juste* (Paris: Seuil, 1995).
33   One must go ever farther and take into account corresponding conflicts *within* single demands. This would lead us finally to acknowledge irresponsibility *within* responsibility. Cf. the author's parallel discussion of injustice *within* justice: 'Sinn für Ungerechtigkeit und Probleme institutionalisierter Gerechtigkeit im "globalen" Horizont', in *Archiv für Rechts- und Sozialphilosophie* 4 (2003), pp. 497–519.
34   In more elaborated form I tried to develop these considerations in Liebsch, B.: 'Der Sinn der Gerechtigkeit im Zeichen des Sinns für Ungerechtigkeit', in Kaplow, I, Lienkamp, C. (eds): *Sinn für Ungerechtigkeit. Ethische Argumentationen im globalen Kontext* (Baden–Baden: Nomos, 2005), pp. 11–39.

Diane Enns

At the Limit:
Violence, Belonging and Self-Determination*

Ten years after becoming the victim of a brutal sexual assault and attempted murder, Susan Brison asks about the possibility of survival: 'How can one go on with a shattered self', she asks, 'with no guarantee of recovery, believing that one will always "stay tortured" and never "feel at home in the world"?'[1] Her reference to the victim's loss of certainty in a 'profoundly disorienting' world provides a startling contrast to the Italian philosopher Giorgio Agamben's injunction to think the political survival of the world in terms of the refugee. He writes:

> Only in a world in which the spaces of states have been [...] perforated and topologically deformed and in which the citizen has been able to recognise the refugee that he or she is – only in such a world is the political survival of human-kind today thinkable.[2]

Brison's body, quite literally 'perforated' and 'topologically deformed' and her experience of homelessness in the world, of being without belonging – whether it is to the world or to her own self – appear as obstacles to overcome in the attempt to survive. To recognise oneself as a refugee in a perforated state, perhaps like a shattered body, appears to be a suspect route to survival for the victim of violence. In these passages we encounter on the one hand a question regarding the possibility of human survival in a fractured, homeless condition, and on the other, the insistence that political survival is possible *only* in such a condition.

In the following discussion, I want to explore this intriguing disjunction to investigate what narratives describing the experience of being a victim of violence can contribute to current discourses concerning the relationships among violence, self-determination, and belonging. My point of departure is a philosophical discourse on violence that bears the monumental weight of the twentieth century's totalitarian regimes and the Nazi Holocaust. Philosophically, this discourse alludes to an economy of violence in language, to the violence of thought itself, of thematisation and naming.[3] Politically, it is concerned with the violence carried out in the name of identity and self-determination. Whether manifest in a preoccupation with the violence of thought or with the violence of political identifications – of gathering and belonging in the name of identity – an unambiguous association between violence and totality is assumed. The antidote appears self-evident: disrupt the totality, whether it is the teleological project of a philosophical system, a nation-state, collective or individual. Welcome the other, Levinas urges. Do not speak of the category woman, Butler warns. Free political action from all unifying and totalising paranoia, Foucault demands.

How do we listen then, to Jean Améry, survivor of Auschwitz, who states unequivocally: 'That one's fellow man was experienced as the antiman remains in the tortured person as accumulated horror'?[4] What do we make of the fact that from the perspective of the victim, both the expelling of the other and the re-making of a shattered self are essential for survival, if only to dull the effects of what victims describe as an occupation of the body by the trauma? That telling one's story is, as Cathy Caruth puts it, 'to engage in the process of re-finding one's own proper name, one's signature'?[5] In spite of vast historical and individual variations, this process can be seen to operate in the struggle to survive numerous instances of human violation, from the insidious erosion of daily life for a colonised people, the trauma of sexual and physical assaults experienced by rape and torture victims, to the total subjugation of the concentration camp prisoner, barely existing on the border of the living and the dead.

We are confronted with two paradoxical notions of violence then. A violence of totalisation, unification, gathering, naming, identifying, delineating borders, against a violence understood as shattering, fragmenting, dehumanising, un-naming.[6] One point of demarcation is the condition of belonging. We gather ourselves together under the rubric of an identity in the name of belonging, which sometimes turns into fierce attachment. Fragmented borders are perceived as the loss of a sense of belonging. Conversely, perhaps nowhere else is belonging experienced as complete as in a totality. How would violence appear, how would it be re-written, if the condition of belonging were undermined? Can we appropriate belonging itself, as Agamben ventures, yet reject all identity and every *condition* of belonging, and to what end? What effect would such a thought experiment have, if any, on the violent excesses of political engagement?[7]

Today, as we face unprecedented global violence, some of which is carried out in the drive for national self-determination in the face of imperial powers eager for war, and some of which occurs in the name of peace and freedom, we need to acknowledge the effects of pain and trauma on the individual and collective body. For pain, in one sense, is about attachment and belonging. Philosophically, we need to tread carefully between these violences, probe our assumptions regarding the violence of imperialism and the violence of resistance. Are these distinct? Is there violence *in-itself*? Is violence inherent in acts of self-determination, as Samuel Weber and Hent de Vries suggest?[8] The following discussion is motivated by such questions, and by a desire for the fresh political vision necessary to emerge from a global politics dancing the deadly tango of violence and counter-violence. I will argue here that Brison and Agamben point us in one possible direction.

1. Identity and the longing to belong

In the etymology of the verb 'belong' we discover an association between yearning and belonging. From the old English 'langian', which perhaps derives from the German '*bilangen*', meaning to reach or to yearn,[9] belonging evokes an element of desire that resonates with the wealth of narratives bequeathed to us by the twentieth century describing a life without belonging; a life under conditions of colonisation, apartheid, or other forms of state repression in which citizenship, rights, land and dignity are withheld. The longing to belong emanates from these narratives as palpably as the desire for justice, retribution or freedom. Indeed, belonging, whether to a national or ethnic identity, to native land or to the human species, is assumed to be the very condition of freedom. It is in the name of this desire to belong that violent acts of resistance – some of extreme cruelty, we can't forget – are carried out in the world today.

Reflecting on the semantic difference between *Gewalt* and the English equivalent, violence, the second more or less implicitly referring to identity, Samuel Weber states:

> In English 'violence' suggests an incursion upon a sphere of self-containment or at least a sphere in which the self relates to itself. In German, *Gewalt* can entail such an incursion but it need not: it can designate quite the opposite, the self or institution maintaining itself, imposing its order upon others or against obstacles.[10]

Yet in both cases, Weber concludes, a relationship of conflict between self and other, identical and nonidentical, is implied. This leads him to ask, 'Just what is the relationship of violence to the self and its functions, above all, self-determination?'[11]

Frantz Fanon provides us with the most famous response to this question, when he describes the violent 'dehumanisation' of the native Algerian by the French settler. In 'Concerning Violence' we read that the coloniser considers the native an animal; he speaks of 'the yellow man's reptilian motions', 'the stink of the native quarter', and of 'breeding swarms' and 'foulness'.[12] With this dehumanising gaze the settler brings the native into existence, Fanon reminds us throughout the text. Indeed, if decolonisation is 'always a violent phenomenon' – 'a meeting of two forces, opposed to each other by their very nature' – it is because the settler has created the violent, Manichean world responsible for objectifying the native.[13] Thus the violence that erupts from just beneath the skin of the native originates in the settler, and '*that same violence* will be claimed and taken over by the native' at the moment when he decides to embody history in his own person.[14] In his well-known preface to this work, Sartre concurs, asking whether the European cannot 'recognise his own cruelty turned against himself [...] his own settler's savagery, which they [the colonised] have absorbed through every pore and for which there is no cure'.[15]

If Fanon captures the spirit of revolutionary fervor, of a powerful desire for justice and freedom among the world's oppressed populations, he also disturbs readers with his moral justification of a retributive counter-violence. Sartre's eager endorsement of the 'mad fury', the 'bitterness and spleen' of the colonised and its role in the 'recreation of man', is the logical extension of an antagonistic relationship between the self and its other. Fanon assumes this existentialist premise, and although he stresses that the settler is responsible for this Manichean world-view, he too claims that it is 'precisely at the moment [the colonised] realises his humanity that he begins to sharpen the weapons with which he will secure its victory.'[16] The struggle for self-determination is here considered a violent one *necessarily*.

The question of when, precisely, the self – or the nation, the people – is determined and the violence required to secure it quelled, is not often broached. The history of anti-colonial movements has shown that self-determination is not enough to bring about the promises of revolutionaries for freedom, particularly freedom from violence and the abuse of power. Violence and counter-violence can spiral into a vicious cycle that leaves no one unaffected in a newly-independent society. The antagonism of a bipolar relationship between self and other is often simply mapped onto new configurations of the friend/enemy distinction. Certainly, problems arise even before the desired resolution, as is clear in the frequent forgetfulness on the part of anti-colonialists regarding their own colonisation of woman. There is no coming to terms with the settler, Fanon tells us, for what the colonised demand is not the settler's status, but the settler's *place*.[17] 'The look that the native turns on the settler's town', he states, 'is a look of lust, a look of envy; it expresses his dreams of possession – all manner of possession: to sit at the settler's table, to sleep in the settler's bed, with his wife if possible.'[18]

In these brief remarks we discover the key to subsequent critiques of emancipatory movements that fundamentally assume this *displacement* and the necessity of a counter-violence –'*that same violence*' – to achieve the desired place. Such a determination of the self reveals itself to be a determination of the *other*.[19] Violence is not then only the violation of the other against the self, against which this self must struggle to exist, but arises from the creation of new others in the process; others who are excluded from the dream of possession, rendered unknown, invisible, and ultimately, *without place*. What questions does this raise regarding the intimate relationship between violence and belonging; belonging to place, to humanity, to the self? What dangers accompany such desires; dangers of possession, exclusion, and ultimately, destruction?

The identity politics debates of the past two decades have reflected on these questions and articulated the problematic of 'totalising' identities. Feminist theorists such as Judith Butler and Gayatri Spivak, as well as critical race theorists, suggest both that acts of 'self-totalisation' in the name of political agency, and the totalising practices of ethnic and religious identity struggles are extremely contentious and require an urgent investigation into 'non-totalising' identity formations.[20] There is an acceptance in these debates that some claims in the name of identity are necessary, while others have simply gone too far, based on the presence or absence, or perhaps the degree, of violent acts of exclusion.

This explains Seyla Benhabib's distinction between an identity politics based on the belief that identity is secured by *eliminating* difference and one premised on the *negotiation* of difference.[21] As such, she exemplifies the problem that feminists have long struggled with: how to maintain the 'good' and necessary aspects of identifications (namely, political agency or empowerment) while rooting out the 'bad' elements (violent, exclusionary practices). Yet Benhabib here assigns the 'good' (or at least better) politics to North American resistance movements, and the 'bad' (or worse) practices to North African or Middle Eastern politics, essentially glossing over a number of historical differences in the economic and socio-political conditions of life in these respective places. Most importantly for my purposes here, these distinctions demonstrate a surprising silence on the *experience* of violence and State power, while implicitly assuming that it is insurrectionary or revolutionary violence which renders a politics of identity either an elimination or a negotiation of difference. Overlooked as well, is the desire to belong, manifested more fiercely the more severe the dispossession, the homelessness, the disenfranchisement, the 'dehumanisation'.

The assumption of a synthetic relation between violence and totality should be problematised on the basis of this desire and the ethical distinction that must be acknowledged between the violence of domination and that of resistance.[22] Surely, the fact that some violences are worse than others would have a critical impact on the method of response, and the degree to which the gathering of identity matters in such a response. Fanon is important here because he isolates the effect of colonial violence on the body and psyche of the colonised; he describes the *experience* of violence as fundamentally a violation of what is human about being human, and what makes life what it is. He stresses that the basic requirements for human life are dignity, respect, and reciprocity. It is for this reason that an ethical distinction must be considered between an originary violence and a counter-violence, but for this same reason, we must stop short of accepting the claim that violence is a *necessary* response to violence. In accounting for the pain of violation, as a category of analysis that is too often ignored in debates on violence and self-determination, and the temporal aspect of the survival process, we might begin to formulate an alternative direction for political resistance.

2.   Violence and the remaking of a self

Brison gives us a moving emotional and philosophical account of her recovery process after being raped, strangled, beaten, and left for dead on a sunny afternoon in the south of France, in a work entitled: *Aftermath: Violence and the Remaking of a Self*. She opens with a description of how violence shatters the self and our 'fundamental assumptions about the world, including beliefs about our ability to control what happens to us'.[23] In the months following the attack, the world no longer made any sense, Brison explains, for it had become 'profoundly disorienting', 'utterly strange and paradoxical'.[24] Philosophy could not provide meaning or help her to 'feel at home in the world' because there was no explanation for the attack. 'I had ventured outside the human community', she writes, 'landed beyond the moral universe, beyond the realm of predictable events and comprehensible actions, and I didn't know how to get back.'[25]

In terms that may resonate for the refugee, Brison expresses the pain of displacement, of exile from the body, the human community and the world, even from philosophy. She evokes a longing to belong to these 'places' that is reminiscent of anti-colonial narratives. The 'getting back in', recovering the loss of this home in the body and the world, is perceived as crucial for survival. As Fanon describes a process of dehumanisation, Brison describes the 'undoing' or 'disintegration' of the self that alludes to the same antagonistic relation between self and other. When the trauma is inflicted intentionally, she states, it not only shatters one's fundamental assumptions about the world and one's safety in it, but it also severs the sustaining connection between the self and the rest of humanity. Victims of human-inflicted trauma are reduced to mere objects by their tormentors: their subjectivity is rendered useless and viewed as worthless.[26]

Brison frequently refers to parallels between her own trauma and that of Holocaust survivors; a brave effort to expose the pernicious effects of silence on the political nature of rape as well as on the sheer frequency of its occurrence. Clearly, the parallels are significant. In Améry's narration of his experience of torture by the Gestapo at Fort Breendonk, a 'reception camp' during the German occupation of Belgium, he speaks of the 'self-negation' of a complete transformation into flesh: 'Frail in the face of violence, yelling out in pain, awaiting no help, capable of no resistance, the tortured person is only a body, and nothing else beside that.'[27] Pain, whether from physical and sexual assaults or psychological torment, has a similar effect here: the stripping of what makes human life what it is. Brison writes that for the first few months after her attack she led 'a spectral existence' not sure whether she had died and the world continued without her, or whether she was alive 'but in a totally alien world'.[28] Who or what is it that dies here? In a chapter curiously entitled 'Outliving Oneself' she cites Charlotte Delbo's simple but enigmatic declaration: 'I died in Auschwitz, but no one knows it.' Brison points to a similar kind of death of her own. When asked whether she has recovered, she replies not, if this means she is back to where she was before the attack: 'I am not the same person who set off, singing, on that sunny Fourth of July in the French countryside. I left her in a rocky creek bed at the bottom of a ravine. I had to in order to survive.'[29]

Brison articulates a self that always-already assumes the respect of the other. The wounding, the victimisation, occurs in the threat posed to this fundamental assumption. It is not then, strictly a violation of the boundaries of an enclosed autonomous self but a violation of human reciprocity. Améry attests to this when he attributes a similar kind of 'death' to the fact that the expectation of help as well as a minimal prospect of resistance in the struggle for survival, are 'constitutional psychic elements,' without which, he tells us, 'a part of our life ends and it can never again be revived.'[30] This occurs at the very first blow from a policeman's fist; a blow in which the other 'forces his own corporeality on me [...]. He is on me and thereby destroys me. It is like a rape [...].'[31] It is only when attacked that the other becomes an anti-man, in Améry's words. Our trust in the world is contingent on the unwritten social contract that 'the other person will spare me'.[32] For rape victims in particular, this violation is repeated every time the account is not believed, a denial Brison claims is 'an almost universal response to rape'.[33] Each time someone failed to respond to her attempts to talk about the assault, she states, 'I felt as though I were alone again in the ravine, dying, screaming. And still no one could hear me. Or, worse, they heard me, but refused to help.'[34] The importance of testimony is therefore explained by the fact that the self is 'created and sustained by others'.

Aftermath is intriguing for what might be read as ambivalence towards the fundamental premise of the narrative, exemplified in the book's subtitle: *Violence and the Remaking of a Self*. In the earlier parts of the account, which Brison tells us were written in the two years following her assault, we encounter frequent allusions to the shattered self and its losses: security, a unified sense of the body, as well as self-esteem, love, and work.[35] We are informed: '[I]n order to recover, a trauma survivor needs to be able to control herself, control her environment (within reasonable limits), and be reconnected with humanity.'[36] This control, particularly of the fear of future attacks – of walking alone, for example – and of the symptoms of post-traumatic stress syndrome, leads to the return of a sense of autonomy, which Brison claims is the most apparent transformation in survivors of trauma. She stresses however, that this control or autonomy is 'fundamentally relational' for it is the necessity of speaking to others about her attack that profoundly demonstrates the vulnerability of one's life in relation to another.[37] If the self is created and sustained by others, Brison warns, it can also be destroyed by them.[38]

In the final chapter of the book, this early emphasis is tempered. Brison admits that while her initial discussion of the effects of trauma stressed the loss of control and the disintegration of a formerly coherent self, she believes now that trauma 'introduces a "surd" – a nonsensical entry – into the series of events in one's life, making it seem impossible to carry on with the series'.[39] Trauma shattered her assumption of life as a discernible pattern: 'I thought I had made a certain sense of things until the moment I was assaulted [...]. I thought I knew how [...] to project myself [...] into an imagined future [...]'.[40] She concludes that survival is facilitated by narrative not because it reestablishes 'the illusions of a coherence of the past, control over the present, and predictability of the future', but because it opens up a future, 'making it possible to carry on without these illusions'. This future appears to remain open because of an 'uneasy paralysis' that leaves one with only a present; a present that has no pre-determined meaning.

Only the hope for a 'bearable future' then makes it possible to go on with a shattered self, without guarantee of recovery, in a state of homelessness in the world. Given that since the victim of an 'unpredictable' violence loses faith in the use of 'inferences from the past' to predict a future, Brison claims,

> [T]here's no more reason to think that tomorrow will bring agony than to think that it won't [...] so one makes a wager, in which nothing is certain and the odds change daily, and sets about willing to believe that life, for all its unfathomable horror, still holds some undiscovered pleasures.[41]

In short, the experience of trauma, while necessitating the struggle for remaking a self, enables Brison to acknowledge and accept the almost unbearable unpredictability of life, and of a self which can never construct a complete narrative.

I find this an enigmatic reflection on the possibility of survival for a traumatised individual. It provides a stark contrast to a passage from Améry's work on suicide, completed shortly before he took his own life, in which he explains what it means to belong to oneself: it is 'not actually a seizing of myself, but an aggression against the outside world, which in any case is hostile, which I have to hold far from me in order to exist, to endure'.[42] Who is to say why one person survives and another does not? Who can understand the permanent mark on the body of the traumatised? If there is no arrival point at which one has recovered, it is because the victim's memories remain in the body 'in each of the senses,' as Brison puts it, 'in the heart that races and skin that crawls whenever something resurrects the only slightly buried terror'.[43] In Améry's words: 'It still is not over. Twenty-two years later I am still dangling over the ground by dislocated arms, panting, and accusing myself.'[44]

These phantoms that haunt the victim of violence do not remain private affairs, but are carried into civil society, passed on to succeeding generations in the guise of hatred, vengeance, memory or perhaps hope.

While we should be wary of an uncritical embrace of the victim's testimony as unmediated truth, we need to take this haunting into account, to 'read' it as we would any other text. That the history of violence is inscribed on the body, and that the body attempts to heal by constructing whole narratives, even if this wholeness turns out to be illusory in the end, must be recognised in all forms of self-determination.

What might this suggest about political strategies to avoid violent conflict in the name of self-determination? What is the most appropriate way to respond to a violence that inhabits the body in such a manner? What do our current political solutions miss? Evidently, it is not enough to accomplish decolonisation, remove dictators, or impose foreign occupation and the alleged Western values of freedom and democracy. There must be an acknowledgement and understanding of what it means to survive trauma, both on an individual level and for a nation or people. I would argue that personal accounts of what it means to survive an act of violation can be useful in understanding the process of collective survival during and after political acts of violent aggression, of which we have a tragic number of examples. A people who are born into violence, witness the brutal killing of their loved ones, experience daily harrassment by an occupying ruler, imprisonment, torture or rape, no doubt are individually and collectively inhabited – perhaps irrevocably – by the trauma of their violation. Is it any wonder that hatred and violence continue after a revolution, after the desired liberation from an occupying power or authoritarian regime?

3.   Violence and the condition of belonging

In light of the association I have traced between trauma, pain and a violated, fractured self whose recovery is contingent on re-establishing a sense of belonging, it seems incongruous to claim that we must, as citizens, recognise ourselves as the refugees that we are, for the sake of political survival. Yet Brison has already pointed towards an understanding of the fragility of the trauma survivor's re-created self and the necessity of carrying on without the illusion of certainty and predictability. Her narrative therefore shares something of Agamben's radical attempt to disrupt the condition of belonging – whether to nation, identity or even the human species – a preoccupation that saturates his work.

The passage referred to in my introductory paragraph forms Agamben's conclusion to a discussion of Hannah Arendt's essay 'We Refugees'. He is intrigued by her assertion that refugees, 'driven from country to country', interested in a lucid contemplation of their nationless condition, rather than assimilation to a new national identity, 'represent the vanguard of their peoples'.[45] It is possible that today, Agamben suggests, given the unstoppable decline of the nation state, the refugee could be the 'only thinkable figure' for the people of our time and we will have to abandon our familiar representations of political subjects – Man, the Citizen and its rights, the sovereign people – 'and build our political philosophy anew starting from the one and only figure of the refugee'.[46]

The refugee thus operates as a limit figure for Agamben, a 'disquieting element' in the order of the nation-state because it breaks the identity between the human and the citizen and between nativity and nationality.[47] What is new in our time, he argues, is that this figure is no longer an exception to the rule. Growing populations of humankind, described by Agamben as 'a permanently resident mass of noncitizens who *do not want to be* and cannot be either naturalised or repatriated', are no longer representable inside the nation-state. It is the refugee as a limit-concept therefore, that throws sovereignty and the nation-state into radical crisis.[48]

It is the '*do not want to be*' here that is crucial, yet Agamben does not remark on the significance of this fact for an analysis of the refugee. He speaks of refugees as noncitizens who may have nationalities of origin, but prefer not to benefit from their own states' protection.[49] The 'We' in the title of Arendt's essay then refers to her own condition as a refugee who appears to reject assimilation or to be returned to her country of birth, not the refugees she spends most of the essay describing, or the countless refugees we could think of today who wait in unbearable conditions to return home. Why doesn't Agamben acknowledge, as Arendt does, the *desire* to belong? Why does he only include the refugees *who do not want to be* naturalised or repatriated?

Agamben asserts that all the categories of our political tradition must be rethought in light of the relation between sovereign power and what he calls naked or bare life [*la nuda vita*].[50] This concept is derived from the Greeks' use of two terms to signify what we usually mean by life: *zoē*, which expressed the simple fact of living common to all living beings, and *bios* which indicated the form or way of living proper to an individual or a group (being human, being animal). Bare life recalls Aristotle's distinction between mere life and the good life. Such a distinction is the basis of the division between public and private life, which the Western political tradition has upheld, being preoccupied only with the former. The *polis* is where justice arises from the human community's capacity to reflect on what is best and necessary for the common good. Bare life, like *zoē*, designates 'that naked presupposed common element that it is always possible to isolate in each of the numerous forms of life.'[51]

Politics has encroached onto this naked element of human life, Agamben claims, a politics in which it is no longer the sovereign's right over the subject to make die and let live, but the right to make live and let die. Unless we analyse this 'interlacing' of politics and life – become so tight it is difficult to unravel – we will not succeed in illuminating the opacity at the center of the political nature of bare life, he warns; an essential task if we are to understand the coming politics.[52]

This explains his exemplary use of the refugee, for the refugee demonstrates the inclusion of bare life into politics. The facticity of birth is what becomes at stake in the question of rights. Without citizenship, without the pure fact of birth – the principle of nativity – the refugee is without rights. Birth *becomes* nation. Agamben deduces from this that 'there is no autonomous space in the political order of the nation-state for something like *the pure human in itself*. This is evident in that refugee status has always been considered a temporary condition that should lead either to naturalisation or to repatriation. Therefore, he concludes, 'a stable statute for *the human in itself* is inconceivable in the law of the nation-state'.[53]

What can it mean to posit a 'pure human in itself'? With this concept Agamben approaches the condition that the colonised describe as 'dehumanised,' or that Brison and Améry articulate as a kind of death, an 'outliving of oneself,' a transformation into pure flesh or bare life. A notion of the human in itself not only applies to the bare life of the refugee then, but to that of the colonised or the raped woman's body, also occupied by a foreign power. The intimate experience of violence can be thought here as profoundly public, profoundly political, at the same time. This would address the incomprehensible silence regarding the political nature of the violence of rape. Indeed, the very fact that for Agamben, 'the inclusion of bare life in the political realm constitutes the original – if concealed – nucleus of sovereign power' renders problematic any fixed distinction between public and private acts of violence.[54]

Agamben develops this 'human in itself' as a notion of singularity that is neither the particular nor the universal. In *The Coming Community*, he suggests that the Latin *'quodlibet'* – commonly and correctly translated as an indifferent being, as in 'whatever, it doesn't matter' –really says the opposite in its form: 'being such that it always matters.' The Latin always already contains a reference to the will or desire in *libet*. The 'whatever' being Agamben refers to is singular not in its indifference with respect to a common property – being French or being Muslim, for example – but in being such as it is.[55] It is thus reclaimed from identifying with this or that category, not to be reclaimed for another group, nor for the 'simple generic absence of any belonging,' but for *belonging itself.*[56] Agamben calls this the 'lovable' as love is never directed only to a particular property of a loved one, nor to 'an insipid generality' but towards the loved one with all of its predicates, its being such as it is.[57] Whatever being is simply, lovable.

The political implications of this notion of singularity are drawn out in the final essay of *The Coming Community* in which Agamben refers to the protests of Tiananmen Square as unique in demonstrating the absence of the condition of belonging to an identity. What was most striking about these protests, he points out, was 'the relative absence of determinate contents in their demands.' Beyond a broadly-defined call for freedom and democracy, the protestors did not possess any identity to vindicate nor any bond of belonging for which to seek recognition. He adds:

> *The novelty of the coming politics is that it will no longer be a struggle for the conquest or control of the State, but a struggle between the State and the non-State (humanity), an insurmountable disjunction between whatever singularity and the State organisation.*[58]

Yet the State cannot tolerate a community of singularities without any representable condition of belonging, Agamben argues. In fact this would be the State's principal enemy. 'Wherever these singularities peacefully demonstrate their being in common there will be a Tiananmen, and, sooner or later, the tanks will appear.'[59] The 'coming community' is therefore not a utopian place beyond the reach of violence, but an expression of a politics as a means without end.

It may be difficult to imagine such a community without belonging. Agamben's notion of whatever singularity is not however, a negation of belonging altogether, only of belonging as a *condition*. To clarify he turns to Saint Thomas's writings on the nature of 'limbo.' According to the latter, the 'inhabitants of limbo' are the unbaptised children whose punishment cannot be hell since they die with no other fault than original sin. They can only be given a punishment of privation: the perpetual lack of the vision of God. Agamben argues however that this punishment turns into a natural joy since these inhabitants of limbo do not know that they are deprived of the supreme good. 'They persist without pain in divine abandon', he notes, 'God has not forgotten them, but rather they have always already forgotten God; and in the face of their forgetfulness, God's forgetting is impotent.'[60]

In light of the concerns of this paper, this analogy is provocative. That these inhabitants of limbo live without the pain of knowing they are deprived of God, that they have always-already forgotten God, is the key to understanding what it means to live without the condition of belonging. It means having always-already forgotten our attachment to nation, to the land of our birth, to identity categories of all kinds. We can deduce from this that one cannot however, 'persist without pain in divine abandon,' in the abandonment of belonging, without this forgetfulness. We must ask, what are the conditions of this forgetfulness? How do we consider those who cannot forget, who, unlike Arendt's refugees, long to return? How do we consider the rape victim or the Holocaust survivor who wants only to expel the other and crawl back under the perceived safety of the body's own skin?

4.   At the limit

This remains the nagging question. I would argue that Brison, like
Agamben, deals with a limit-concept. The victim of extreme violence
provides us with an exemplary threshold for exploring questions of self-
determination, for at the moment of violation, when an unspeakable
reduction to flesh or pain occurs, when all that exists for the victim is
bare life and the necessity of survival, it makes no sense to refer to
relationality or non-totalising self-formations. The violated body can
only survive by expelling the other – the rapist, the coloniser, the torturer
– in the most immediate, radical sense possible.

Brison, as a victim and survivor of an act of extreme violence,
enables us to think through the political implications of pain and trauma
and the desire for remaking a shattered self. Although I want to be
cautious about any simple traversal from the individual to the collective
or national, one could argue that her narrative is paradigmatic for national
struggles. For a colonised or occupied people experience trauma on a
massive scale and the desire for self-determination is couched in terms
of dignity, respect, and recognition. When one has to hold the other far
from oneself in order to exist and endure, this process cannot simply be
reversed. This is why the notion of parity in political conflicts where the
power relation is completely out of balance, often prohibits adequate
solutions; we must recognise the ethical distinction between the violence
of resistance and the violence of the perpetrator. We must make judgements even in the muddiest of ethical and political dilemmas.

Brison's narrative is at the limit, however. There is a temporal
nature to the recuperation of a self, as she reveals in her shift towards an
acceptance of the fact that she was never in a 'safe' world to begin with,
and can survive with this knowledge; indeed, must accept this knowledge
in order to survive. Recovery is a non-teleological process – a means
without end, like the coming politics Agamben envisions. Her own desire
to recover the losses that resulted from the experience of rape and assault
becomes tempered by the acknowledgement that life was always-already
contingent and uncertain.

Brison and Agamben can teach us something here about political
survival on an individual and collective level. Fanon's unapologetic

acceptance of the necessity of revolutionary violence, while an understandable response to the originary violence of colonisation, is not appropriate in what is now (for the most part) a post-colonial world. Today we are dealing with an entirely new set of actors, problems and violent practices that urgently require a rethinking of our political categories: of what it means to be a citizen of a nation, of freedom and autonomy, and of victimisation. While we are all affected by these new global events and predicaments, we are not *equally* traumatised or victimised. I want to argue that it is the 'we' of the un-traumatised whose responsibility it is to live in the forgetfulness of all conditions of belonging; the 'we' who are fortunate enough to live without the relentless, daily fear of violence and repression, though we are subject – consciously or not – to the same unpredictability of life as those who are scarred by violence. This is not by any means then, a demand for victims of violence to forget the event of their trauma, but for *we others* to abandon our conditions of belonging – to borders, to strict identities, to whole narratives.

For those of us who are not inhabited by the trauma of past violences, this 'always-already having forgotten' that Agamben articulates may not be difficult to envision. In a cosmopolitan place where identities are welcome distractions from the monotony of sameness, where difference poses no threat, but instead provides art, culture, and friendship, we could argue that the 'punishment of privation' be it a privation of a common heritage, of the land of our birth, or of a sound ethnic, racial or gendered identity, turns into a 'natural joy.'

We are therefore in a position to take on the responsibilities of a coming politics.

What this might mean is alluded to in a brief essay by Agamben, who warns that we currently face the most extreme developments of the paradigm of security in the name of a state of emergency. He writes:

> Maybe the time has come to work towards the prevention of disorder and catastrophe, and not merely towards their control. Today, there are plans for all kinds of emergencies (ecological, medical, military), but there is no politics to prevent them [...]. It is the task of democratic politics to prevent the development of conditions which lead to hatred, terror, and destruction – and not to reduce itself to attempts to control them once they occur.[61]

Brison, for her part, leaves us with the thought that 'none of us is *supposed* to be alive.' We are all here by chance and for a short time only. Life, however, 'profligate, irrepressible – flaunts itself everywhere.'[62]

Endnotes

*   The author would like to thank Antonio Calcagno for his insightful comments on this paper.

1   Brison, Susan J.: *Aftermath: Violence and the Remaking of a Self* (Princeton: Princeton University Press, 2002), p. 66. In this narrative, Brison, a philosopher at Dartmouth College in the United Sates, provides a philosophical exploration of the process of survival – the recreation of a self – after a brutal rape and near murder while visiting the south of France.

2   Agamben, Giorgio: *Means without end: notes on politics,* trans. Vincenzo Binetti and Cesare Casarino (Minneapolis: University of Minnesota Press, 2000), p. 26.

3   I am thinking here of the discussions found in Emmanuel Levinas: *Totality and Infinity: An Essay on Exteriority*, trans. Alphonso Lingis (Pittsburgh: Duquesne University Press, 1969); Jacques Derrida: 'Violence and Metaphysics' in *Writing and Difference* (New York: Routledge, 2001); Walter Benjamin, 'Critique of Violence,' *Reflections: Essays, Aphorisms, Autobiographical Writings*, trans. Edmund Jephcott (New York: Harcourt Brace Jovanovich:, 1978), and less explicitly in the work of Michel Foucault (See for example his preface to Gilles Deleuze and Felix Guattari, *Anti–Oedipus: Capitalism and Schizophrenia* (London: Athlone Press, 1984).

4   Améry, J.: *At the Mind's Limits: Contemplations by a Survivor on Auschwitz and its Realities*, trans. Sidney Rosenfeld and Stella P. Rosenfeld (Bloomington: Indiana University Press, 1980), p. 40.

5   Caruth, Cathy: *Unclaimed Experience: Trauma, Narrative, and History* (Baltimore: Johns Hopkins University Press, 1996), p. 53.

6   It is worth noting that Levinas acknowledges both of these modes of violence in *Totality and Infinity*. The self-same does violence to the other by reducing the other to sameness, but the other does violence (albeit a good violence) to the self by interrupting its sameness.

7   Agamben, Giorgio: *The Coming Community*, trans. Michael Hardt (Minneapolis: University of Minnesota Press, 1993), p. 87.

8   See the introduction to *Violence, Identity and Self-Determination*, eds Hent de Vries and Samuel Weber (Stanford: Stanford University Press, 1997) in which the editors suggest that the ideal of self-determination and the value system of which it has long been the cornerstone can no longer be accepted as self-evident after such

events as the disintegration of the former Soviet Union, the former Yugoslavia and other occurances of civil strife in Eastern Europe. They remark, provocatively, that perhaps violence occurs not in the passage from self to other, or other to self, but 'in the very attempt to delineate borders that separate self from other. If so then 'violence' could no longer be considered simply to 'befall' its victims from without, but rather would be related to what is generally presupposed to be its other: the 'inviolate' self. If this were so, then, the most mystified sort of 'violence' might even turn out, paradoxically perhaps, to be what seeks to eliminate or to delegitimise violence entirely.' (p. 2).

9 Pickett, Joseph P. et. al.: *The American Heritage Dictionary of the English Language*, (Boston: Houghton Mifflin Company, 2000).

10 de Vries and Weber, op. cit., pp. 82–3.

11 Ibid., p. 83.

12 Fanon, Frantz: *The Wretched of the Earth*, trans. Constance Farrington (New York: Grove Press, 1963), p. 42.

13 Ibid., pp. 35–36.

14 Ibid., p. 40, emphasis added.

15 Jean-Paul Sartre, 'Preface', *The Wretched of the Earth*, p. 16.

16 Fanon, op. cit., p. 43.

17 Ibid., p. 60.

18 Ibid., p. 39.

19 de Vries and Weber, op. cit., p. 1.

20 Kwame Anthony Appiah and Henry Louis Gates Jr., 'Editors' Introduction: Multiplying Identities,' *Identities* (Chicago: Chicago University Press, 1995), p. 1.

21 Benhabib, Seyla: 'The Democratic Moment and the Problem of Difference,' in Seyla Benhabib (ed.): *Democracy and Difference: Contesting the Boundaries of the Political*, (Princeton: Princeton University Press, 1996), pp. 4–5.

22 I am claiming this in spite of Fanon's statement that the violence the colonised turns back on the coloniser is the *same violence*; violence that is initiated by the perpetrator and spreads to the native. This raises the question as to whether we can isolate a *violence-in-itself* regardless of how it is exercised. Fanon's point is that the violence of the native has its origin in the racism and hatred of the settler.

23 Brison, op. cit., p. xii.

24 Ibid., p. x.

25 Ibid., pp. ix, x.

26 Ibid., p. 40.

27 Améry, op. cit., p. 33.

28 Brison, op. cit., p. 9.

29 Ibid., p. 21.

30 Améry, op. cit., p. 29.

31 Ibid., p. 28.

32 Ibid.

33 Brison, op. cit., p. 9.

34   Ibid., p. 16.
35   Ibid., p. 20.
36   Ibid., p. 60.
37   Ibid., p. 41.
38   Ibid., p. 62.
39   Ibid., p. 103. 'Surd' is a mathematical term to denote a number containing an irrational root, or simply an irrational number. In phonetics, a 'surd' is a voiceless consonant.
40   Ibid.
41   Ibid., p. 66.
42   Améry, *On Suicide : a discourse on voluntary death* (Bloomington: Indiana University Press, 1999), p. 101.
43   Brison, op. cit., p. 44.
44   Améry, *At the Mind's Limits*, p. 36.
45   Hannah Arendt, 'We Refugees', *The Menorah Journal*, 31. 1, Jan–Mar (1943), p. 77.
46   Agamben, *Means without end*, op. cit., p. 16.
47   Ibid., p. 21.
48   Ibid., p. 22f., emphasis added.
49   Ibid., p. 23.
50   Ibid., p. 2.
51   Ibid., p. 3.
52   Giorgio Agamben, Homo Sacer: *Sovereign Power and Bare Life*, trans. by Daniel Heller-Roazen (Stanford: Stanford University Press, 1998), p. 122.
53   Agamben, *Means without end*, p. 20, emphasis added.
54   Agamben, *Homo Sacer*, p. 9.
55   Giorgio Agamben, *The Coming Community*, trans. Michael Hardt (Minneapolis: University of Minnesota Press, 1993), p. 1.
56   Ibid., pp. 1f..
57   Ibid., p. 2.
58   Ibid. [Italics in original.]
59   Ibid., p. 87.
60   Ibid., pp. 5–6.
61   Giorgio Agamben, 'Security and Terror,' *Theory & Event* 5.4. (2002)
62   Brison, op. cit., pp. 122–23.

Talia Mae Bettcher

Appearance, Reality and Gender Deception: Reflections on Transphobic Violence and the Politics of Pretence*

The point of this paper is to examine the nature of transphobia and transphobic violence. In particular, I will focus on the representations of 'trans' people as gender deceivers, often used as a tactic in justifying or excusing this violence. In discussing this important aspect of transphobia, I hope to illuminate the related notions of 'authenticity', 'deception', 'appearance', and 'reality' and their connection to gender and sex. I also hope to point to the insufficiency of current transgender theory and politics, and to, through this inquiry, open up a new dimension of analysis which goes beyond some of the current presuppositions of the prevailing framework.

1. Preliminaries

The word 'transgender' is difficult to define, due largely to the fact that it doesn't have one settled meaning. 'Transgender' is often used is as a blanket term that pulls together people who 'do not conform to prevailing expectations about gender'. Used as an umbrella term, it groups together several different kinds of people such as trans-sexuals (male to female and female to male), drag queens and kings, some butch lesbians, heterosexual male cross dressers, and other people, too.

However, it is just as hard to define these 'sub-groups'. For example, 'transsexual' used to have much more of a connection to medico-psychiatric discourse, the metaphor 'trapped in the wrong body', and the notion of 'sex change' surgery. Now, it might not be used that way. It could be used to simply indicate people who wish to avail themselves of surgical or hormonal technologies to alter their bodies to conform to their gendered sense of self or it could be used to indicate people who identify and live as the sex opposite to the one assigned to them at birth.

In this paper, I am not going to try to define or pin down these terms. The fact of the matter is that many people who might be called 'transgender' describe themselves in particular ways that are at odds with how the mainstream world might describe them. For example, while a transsexual women may see herself as a *woman*, other people might see her as a man trying to pass himself off as a woman. Very often, I think that 'transgender people' find that others intentionally disregard their self-identities. So I want to be careful not to impose my categories on 'transgender people' as I see this as one of the basic ways to treat such people with disrespect. Indeed, I want to be very careful with the term 'transgender' itself since it is a contested term that is hardly used by everyone who might potentially be described by it. To be sure, the expression arises principally in an Anglo-American context and can carry theoretical and political presuppositions that are culturally specific and potentially colonising.[1]

So for the purposes of this paper I will use the prefix 'trans' to indicate a person who presents a gender that may be construed as at odds with the sex that is assigned to them at birth or who presents gender in ways that may be construed as 'inconsistent' or 'andro-gynous.' I will use 'mtf' to refer to individuals assigned male at birth whose gender presentation may be construed as 'unambiguously' fe-male, and 'ftm' to refer to individuals assigned female at birth whose gender presentation may be construed as 'unambiguously' male. I do not intend for the terms to attribute identity. I use 'transphobia' not to necessarily indicate fear, but any negative attitude directed towards transpeople on the basis of their being trans.

My discussion of transphobic violence should be seen as falling within what can be called 'trans studies'.[2] Contemporary trans studies has involved, among other things, a departure from the historical objecti-fication of transpeople in theory and research such that transpeople themselves have emerged as subjects/authors instead of just the objects. In this way, some of the extreme transphobic aspects of theory and research has been removed (or at least thinned out), and trans studies has taken on a kind of political liberatory dimension.[3] I take it as a starting point of my work that trans lives and identities are legitimate and in need of no particular defence or justification.

However I also wish to acknowledge that the model of trans theory and politics which has come to dominate is itself fairly specific and open to dispute. It evolved simultaneously with (and in relation to) the queer theory and politics of the early nineties. While the relationship between queer theory and transgender theory and politics has certainly witnessed tensions, current transgender theory and politics borrows many of the key themes of queer theory/politics not least of which is an attack on gender/sex binaries, and the view that all gender/sex is socially constructed. In terms of political realities, close political affiliations with Lesbian/Gay politics have been adopted as well as an emphasis on the importance of increasing trans visibility (e.g.,, through 'coming out').[4]

In this paper I want to focus on some of the basic presuppositions of this prevailing model. My goal is to examine a very particular sort of transphobic violence and to point to the ways in which the current model fails to adequately explain it. In identifying the specific concerns that I have about this model, I do not wish to represent this model as without merit or somehow irremediably flawed. On the contrary, it must be underscored that without this model, any advances which have occurred for transpeople in the past fifteen years (at least for *some* transpeople) would not have been possible. However, I wish to suggest that this model needs to be, in the very least, supplemented with an additional theoretical model, or dimension of analysis.

To be clear, I think that the theory matters insofar as it ultimately grounds actual political strategies which get played out in the real world. And this matters in terms of what happens to flesh and blood people. My concern and motivation is grounded in my personal involvement in Los Angeles-based grass roots responses to transphobic violence, my experience moving through sexist, racist, classist, and transphobic society, and my experience as a white, anglo, transsexual woman living in the United States. In this way, the perspective that I offer is both culturally and geographically located in respects that allow for both insight and blindness. What follows should be understood as limited and informed by these considerations.

2. Transphobia and Transphobic Violence

The experience of transphobic violence and verbal abuse appears to be widespread. For example, a GenderPAC study in 1997 found that almost 60% of the participants had either been victims of trans-based violence or harassment, and 47% of the participants reported having been assaulted in some way over the course of their lives.[5] The Los Angeles Transgender Health Study found that 47% of the participants (all mtf) reported having been physically abused because of gender identity/presentation and 80% reported having been verbally abused because of it.[6] And a recent, unpublished study by Lombardi again finds that over 82% of the participants reported incidence of verbal abuse, physical abuse, or threatened physical abuse.[7]

In 2004 over 26 murders of transpeople were reported world-wide (12 in the U.S.) and in 2003, 32 murders of transpeople were reported world-wide (14 in the US).[8] Most of the reported victims of these murders were mtf, most were people of colour, and it is likely that many were sex-workers. And while it is not always easy to determine whether such acts of violence are partially the consequence of transphobia, it seems probable that many of them were. The consistently high degree of both reported verbal abuse and reported physical assault suggests that transphobic murder is of a piece with general societal attitudes toward transpeople. No doubt such overt hostility is embedded within more institutional or systemic discriminations against transpeople (employment, access to health and social services, access to educational services, etc.) as well – only leading to increased vulnerability.

So how does one begin to offer an account of such transphobic violence? It is worth beginning with the recognition that transphobic hostility and discrimination are intersected by issues of race, class privilege, and misogyny. It is therefore actually quite difficult to pull out 'transphobia' from other factors which can contribute to hostility and violence, and I suspect that the very attempt to do so is a problematic one. A good account of transphobia, it seems to me, not only needs to acknowledge these 'other' factors, but to actually reveal their relation to and implication within various forms of transphobic violence.

It is also important to recognise that there are actually a variety of stigmas which can affect transpeople. For example, just as same-sex sexual orientation can be viewed as 'immoral' or 'sinful', so too gender behaviour and presentation can be taken as unacceptable from a moral point of view or 'in the eyes of God.' Independently of religion and morality, however, transpeople may be judged according to prevalent gender norms (men don't cry, etc.). And there are other stigmas as well – such as the view that transpeople are pathological or mentally ill, which can be distinguished from the view that transpeople are 'sick', or 'bizarre'.

My point is that it cannot be assumed in advance that all transphobic stigmas can be reduced to one explanation or cause. Moreover, given the multiplicity concealed by the term 'transgender' the attempt to provide one monolithic account of transphobia and transphobic violence seems unrealistic.[9] Consider, for example, that it is not uncommon for mtfs to be viewed as sexually available and disposable whores – a stereotype simply not similarly applied to ftms (in mainstream or gay male contexts). Sometimes transphobic stigma can be identity-specific.

In transgender theory and politics itself, however, the characterisation of transphobia exclusively in terms of a hostile binary of the categories of 'man' and 'woman' has become all but canonical. In such a model, transpeople are positioned as either a third gender, or as 'outside' gender, or as occupying a complex spectrum that exists 'in between' the traditional binary gender categories. Gender oppression is characterised as the attempt to enforce this all too rigid binary system upon transpeople who do not fit very well within such a system. Importantly connected to this view is the idea that the rigid binary system forces those who do not fit into these camps out of existence or renders them invisible. Thus, the political strategy of resistance which immediately suggests itself is one of *visibility*. In order to oppose this tendency to erase, then, the mode of resistance is to render oneself visible and hence disrupt this binary system.

To be sure, this model has not been without its critics. For certainly there are many transpeople who situate themselves firmly within one of the traditional inartistic categories, view themselves as 'real men' and/or 'real women', and do not wish to be viewed as 'gender radicals'. For example, the Los Angeles Transgender Health Study (2001) found that when required to choose, 56% of the participants identified as 'female or woman' while only 20% identified as transgender and 15% as transsexual. On the face of it, then, it looks as if these people must be seen as 'part of the problem', 'complicit in their own oppression', 'gender conservative', and so forth. Critics such as Henry Rubin worry that there is a serious gap between transgender theory and politics (on the one hand) and how some transpeople identify on the others. Moreover, as Viviane Namaste observes, this theory/politics risks requiring that trans identities be legitimised on the condition that they conform to a particular political vision (i.e., subverting the binary). She goes on to insist that identities and politics need to be kept separate. She writes, for example:

> Accepting transsexuality means accepting that people live and identify as men and women, although they were not born in male or female bodies. And that this needs to be kept separate from political work. Some transsexuals situate themselves on the left, and do their political work from this perspective. Others are moderate, or deeply conservative politically. I want to say that if we accept transsexuality in and of itself, then we don't need to make it conditional on a particular political agenda.[10]

However, it is the thesis of this paper that beyond such concerns, the prevailing model actually fails to adequately capture an important form of transphobia from the outset, and it consequently provides for inadequate political strategies of resistance to this sort of oppression. The issue, therefore, is not merely that the model fails to square with the identifications of some transpeople. The issue is that the model is itself simply inadequate as a theory of oppression and resistance. For those who claim to be real men and women are themselves engaged in a kind of resistance in the face of hostile forces that would invalidate them. At any rate, I think that any transperson who attempts to maintain identity and life against the force of transphobia is *ipso facto* engaged in a form of political resistance.

In what follows, I want to briefly describe the features of this kind of transphobia. And then, I want to show the failure of the prevailing model in explaining it. In particular, I will argue that this kind of transphobia cannot be explained by appeal to a hostile binary and that the notion of promoting visibility as a strategic response to the oppressive forces of invisibility is an inadequate strategy in addressing this transphobia. I will then further my analysis by examining Sandy Stone's pioneering article 'The *Empire* Strikes Back: A Posttranssexual manifesto' – an article which is the fundamental, early articulation of this model. Finally, I will conclude by drawing out some of the political consequences of this position.

3. The Basic Denial of Authenticity

The kind of transphobia which shall concern me in this paper can be called 'the basic denial of authenticity'. For example, an ftm who identifies as a 'trans man' may find himself represented as 'really a woman living as a man'. One obvious feature of this denial of authenticity is that transpeople are identified in ways that are contrary to or even hostile to their own self-identifications. But the second, less frequently discussed feature is that such identifications are generally embedded within discourse about 'appearance' and 'reality'.

In particular, gender presentation is taken as a kind of appearance and sexed body is taken as a deep reality. Consequently, a transperson who presents as a woman but is taken to have the body of man can be characterised as 'really who a man who appears to be a woman'. Quite often it is genital status which is taken to constitute the deep reality (as opposed to, say, chromosomes).[11] And, as a consequence, the expressions 'really a man' or 'really a woman' turn out to be ways of talking about genitalia.

Recognising this is important. For while it is already acknowledged that the identification of sex with genital status is often what overrides the self-identities of transpeople, what is not sufficiently appreciated is how this figures within notions of 'appearance' and 'reality'. In my view, the notion that genitals are the essential determinants of sex is deeply connected to the notion that genitals are a kind of 'concealed truth' about a person's sex – concealed, that is, by clothing which in part (along with other forms of gender presentation) constitutes a gender appearance. Thus the essentiality of genitals as sex-determining is embedded within a context of (gender) appearance/ (sex) reality which has much do with the relationship between the public and the private.

Unsurprisingly, another feature of the denial of authenticity is that this 'misalignment' between appearance and reality, in cases in which the appearance is convincing, can establish a context of possible 'exposure', 'discovery', or 'revelation' and 'self-disclosure'. In cases in which the 'misalignment' is 'exposed' (against the will of the transperson), the transperson may find themselves represented as a 'deceiver' and accused of fraudulence. However in cases in which the transperson declares themselves or in cases in which the appearance is not convincing in the first place and no initial context of discovery is established, the transperson may find themselves represented as somebody pretending to be or dressing as somebody of 'the opposite sex'.

To the extent that it is within the power of a transperson to generate a convincing appearance, then, they will be confronted by the no-win option of trying to pass (and running the risk of being exposed as a fraud) or else revealing themselves (and coming out as a masquerader or deceiver). And to the extent that it is not within the power of a transperson to generate a convincing appearance or, if it is to control the information that is circulated and available about their status, they may still find themselves represented as a pretender. In effect, because gender presentation and sexed body are viewed in this way (namely as correlated appearance and reality), in all possible permutations, they will have their identity relegated to a mere appearance and find themselves either open to charges of wrong-doing or relegated to somebody who plays at make-believe.[12]

To be sure, these representations of deception and fraudulence arc not new or uncommon. Christine Jorgensen, for example, not too soon after finding herself in a media storm, had to confront the trans-formation of headlines such as 'Ex-GI Becomes Blonde Beauty' into exciting accusations about perpetration of hoax (he's really just a castrated man, just a transvestite, it's all been a complete fraud).[13] And all of this is hardly inconsequential in terms of understanding transphobic violence. For example, Gwen Araujo, a seventeen-year-old youth, was slain at a party when it was disclosed that 'she was really a man.' This disclosure was made through 'genital verification' in the bathroom by somebody at the party. Apparently, some of the men who killed Araujo had had sexual relations with Araujo and flew into a rage when 'the truth was revealed'.[14] Chanelle Pickett,[15] Brandon Teena,[16] Debra Forte,[17] Bella Evangelista,[18] and Joel Robles[19] – to name just a few – were all slain within the context of 'discovery of real sex'. Unsurprisingly, accusations of sexual deception play an important role in blaming the victim in such cases of transphobic violence. For example, what has been dubbed the 'trans panic' de-fence was used extensive by the defence in the trials of the killers of Gwen Araujo. Recently, this strategy helped Estanislao Martinez receive only four years for manslaughter after stabbing Joel Robles to death twenty times with a pair of scissors.

Quite often this type of transphobic violence involving 'exposure of the shocking truth' has connections with sexual violence.[20] For example, rape was clearly a method of 'identity enforcement' when it was disclosed that Brandon Teena was 'really a woman'. Moreover, the murders of both Gwen Araujo and Brandon Teena involved forced genital exposure ('sex-verification') in a bathroom amidst accusations of deception and betrayal. Ironically, it is not uncommon for this alleged 'sexual deception' to itself be represented as a kind of sexual violence. For example, Mark Thorman, in his defence of Michael Madgison, ultimately convicted in the slaying of Gwen Araujo, represented Araujo's alleged deception as a violation 'so deep it's almost primal'.[21] Indeed, similar views have been held about lesbian-identified transwomen by feminist writers such as Janice Raymond who writes of mtf transsexual lesbians, 'rape, although it is usually done by force, can also be accomplished by deception'.[22]

4.   Subverting the Binary

The failure of the 'hostile binary' model to accommodate the basic denial of authenticity can be seen by examining the work that this model does at both the higher, cultural levels of gendered behaviour and presentation and the more basic, biological level of sexed body. Consider the latter. It is simply a biological fact that some human beings may not be identified unproblematically as *either* male *or* female (intersexuals). And it is also a cultural fact that considerable medical attention is paid to placing intersexuals into one category or the other through surgical and hormonal interventions. So a decent case can be made the even that discrete biological categories of male and female are socially constructed by *obliterating* intersexuals through non-consensual surgical re-assignment.

Yet these considerations simply do not explain the deceiver/pretender representations of transpeople and the violence that is involved in such representations. One reason for this is that for some transpeople, once genital status is determined, are unproblematically viewed as inhabiting one of the inartistic gender categories. There is no dilemma, no confusion, no 'falling outside' of the existing scheme. On the contrary, victims of transphobic violence, such as Gwen Araujo, are *without hesitation* viewed by perpetrators as 'really male'. From the perspective of the perpetrator, victims of such violence are hardly gender liminal. If they are punished, they are punished as men who have acted like women or women who acted as men.

At the cultural level, however, one can then at least point to ways in which gender conduct is regulated. Men and women are expected to engage in various sorts of gendered behaviour, and a failure to do so results in sanction for flouting prevalent gender norms. Hence, a man who acts 'too much like a woman' might be regarded as a 'sissy' or as 'gay', and consequently punished accordingly. Similarly, a woman who acts 'too much like a man' might be regarded as 'butch', 'masculine', as well as having her overall sexual attractiveness called into question. Recognising the existence of such norms is obviously important, and it has proven useful to point to such norms as a way of making the case that *everybody* is subject to gender control and punishment. It has helped 'pitch the case' of transpeople to a larger audience. In such a view – transpeople are 'gender benders' or 'gender rebels'. In essence, we are individuals who fly in the face of gender-norms, and are sometimes punished for it.

However, this does not account for the basic denial of authenticity. First, it simply doesn't explain why transpeople are viewed as deceivers or pretenders. At the very best, one could cite the following norm as part of the explanation: Men are not supposed to pass themselves off as women, and women are not supposed to pass themselves off as men. Yet such an account fails to explain why transpeople are viewed as deceivers or pretenders in the first place – it simply proceeds with the assumption that they *are* deceivers or pretenders (the rule is simply that they *shouldn't be*).

Indeed, insofar as such an account is predicated upon 'reading' transpeople *at odds with their own self-identification*, one of the most important features is simply ignored. In other words: The issue is not merely that transsexual women are punished for being men who act too much like women, the issue is also that they were unproblematically represented as men to begin with. Here there is a marked difference between transphobia and homophobia. In the latter case, a gay man will probably actually identify as a man, whereas a transsexual woman will probably not. Because of this, the proposed account elides the fundamental transphobic move by which trans identities are disregarded, as the necessary ground for the subsequent deployment of 'homophobic' violence against transgenders in the first place. Furthermore, the account is transphobic itself insofar as it reiterates the denial of self-identifications in its very explanation of the phobic violence. Indeed, the account clearly adopts the perspective of the attacker himself (in opposition to specific trans-identifications) – a despicable strategy in my book.

For example, the representation of Gwen Araujo as a boy who 'bent gender,' a boy who 'flouted prevailing gender norms', while probably accounting for the basis of *some* transphobic hostility, can only do so by representing her *contrary to her own self-identification*. Yet once we accept her own identification, it becomes unclear in what sense she, as a girl, flouted gender norms *at all*. What is fundamental, at any rate, in understanding this type of transphobia, is not the issue of gender norms which govern conduct, but the fact that gender presentation is viewed as a kind of appearance, and sexed body is viewed as a deep reality.

To be clear, the problem of identity-enforcement is actually very broad – overriding not only self-identifications such as 'man' and 'woman' but also ones which do not sit well within such a binary opposition ('third gender', etc). Indeed, this identity-enforcement can apply in cases of self-identified gay, male drag queens, straight, male cross-dressers, butch lesbians, and other as well. For to suppose that somehow expressions such as 'man pretending to be a woman' or 'woman pretending to be a man' accurately represent the partial or full significance of gender presentation and its relationship to gendered self-conception to any of these people is dubious to say the least. My point is *not* that those who position themselves 'beyond the binary' or who are 'gender benders' or 'rebels' are not vulnerable to this kind of reality enforcement. My point is that it cannot be explained by appealing to the binary alone or to gender norms alone.

This non-reducibility is further revealed by the fact that other modalities of resistance can now be illuminated, ones which quite clearly do not necessarily involve departing from the binary so much as contesting the basic denial of authenticity. For it must be emphasised that any attempt by a transperson to claim authenticity and to survive in this world is necessarily subversive (i.e., is necessarily political). The accusation that some transpeople appeal to an egregious 'gender conservatism' or 'sexism' fails to see how even claims such as 'really a woman trapped in a man's body' literally contests the representation 'really a man who lives as a woman.' To be clear on this point: To treat the 'gender conservatism' of a transperson as somehow equivalent to the 'gender conservatism' of a non-transperson is to erase the radical way in which transpeople are always-already constructed as phonies and subsequently subjected to the most horrifying acts of violence. Perversely, precisely the opposite has been the case in selective representations of transpeople as 'gender conservative'.

So here I join Rubin in his concern about a transgender politics which represents transpeople who embrace 'gender essentialism' as retrograde or invalid, and the request for 'a delicate balance between the legitimacy of trans desires for authenticity or realness while acknowledging the constructedness of our bodies and identities'. [23] The balance can be achieved, I believe, by recognising that even if it is true that all gender is socially-constructed, transpeople are systematically constructed as frauds. Far from separating trans identities and politics, however, I would insist that all transpeople who attempt to claim authenticity in a world that constructs us frauds are radically subversive to this extent and for these very reasons.

In saying this, I do not mean to personally celebrate gender conservatism, homophobia, or sexism. However, I *do* mean to suggest that trans claims to authenticity are resistant and that sometimes this resistance can involve tactics that are politically reactionary in other noticeable ways. Indeed, this kind of resistance can often by harmful – to oneself and others. For example, the desire for realness may leave some transwomen vulnerable in domestic violence situations, or it may lead to competition between transwomen over who gets to count as more real. After all, it is simply not the case that resistance to transphobia is of a piece with resistance to other forms of repression such as sexism any more than resistance to sexism automatically makes one an anti-racist or resistance to racism makes one feminist. Coalitions cannot be assumed, they must be built. And it is also important to distinguish between individual tactics of subversion and survival from any broader, explicit political agenda.

5.   Making the Invisible Visible

The characterisation of transphobia strictly in terms of *erasure* and its related characterisation of resistance in terms of making the invisible visible are likewise open to fairly serious difficulties. For such a view fails to take seriously the fact that the issue is not merely one of *being* visible but *how* one is represented when one is visible. There is good press and then there is bad press. And the eye of the beholder plays some considerable role in the interpretation of the words, actions, and bodies of transpeople. If I am correct about the basic denial of authenticity, then there is a way in which many transpeople may find themselves in no-win situations in which they are either out as pretenders or at risk of being exposed as deceivers. However, a call for trans visibility fails to appreciate the double-binded way in which we are systematically denied claims to authenticity by already being constructed as phonies in the first place. By ignoring the 'pretender' representation, one takes it for granted that 'being read' as 'trans' has an inherently de-stabilising power to prevailing, mainstream conceptions of gender. Yet far from de-stabilising anything at all, mtfs are simply read as 'men who dress up like women' and ftms read as 'women who dress up like men'.[24]

The point does not merely concern how one's body, one's actions, and one's life are liable to be interpreted upon 'coming out', but, also, even how specific terms are themselves interpreted. To be clear: By coming out as a trans woman, for example, one has absolutely no guarantee how the relevant terms will be interpreted. They may easily be understood as 'a man who dresses up like a woman', 'a man who lives as a woman', or even (and this is hardly an improvement) 'a biological male who lives as a woman'.

Many transpeople will be able to attest to the experience of trying to explain our identities only to discover that no amount of explanation ever suffices. The experience is one of 'speaking a different language' and the problem is one of 'translation' and 'comprehension'. Such concerns are surely grave in light of the role of mainstream media (especially as trans visibility increases) in promoting the view that transpeople are, for example, 'men who live as women', and 'really women, appearances notwithstanding'. More deeply, such representations can themselves literally *plead* for the acceptance of transpeople as 'gender-benders' or 'rebels' while effectively *reinscribing* the very mechanism which is fundamental to transphobic violence.[25]

Obviously this has deep consequences in terms of strategies of resistance. For there is inherent in the preceding account a naïve optimism that through one's sheer existence – by simply showing up, if you will – one will engage in a kind of opposition to prevailing schemes of categorisation. Yet, once one recognises that no matter what one says, one will be viewed as inauthentic (either a deceiver or a pretender), the very notion of 'coming out' or 'telling the truth about oneself' becomes an impossibility. For given the gender appearance – sexed body reality contrast, one is always already viewed as a liar.

Surely the very notion of 'honesty is the best policy' needs to be re-thought once we recognise that truth-telling is impossible.[26] To what extent does the tactic of self-revelation, when represented as unproblematically valuable, require of transpeople an oppressively impossible honesty? Surely secrecy, duplicity, and deception ought to be recognised as important tactics in not only personal survival, but in resistant politics more generally. Indeed one might also argue that given the options, successfully passing in the category of one's preference as 'nontrans' is actually the only available strategy in which, if one can successfully pull it off, one can actually claim authenticity in a word that denies it to us. By contrast, 'coming out' and 'self-revelation' appear to play right into the problematic context of 'discovery of the hidden reality' itself connected to accusation of deception. It is little wonder, therefore, that this account is in danger of re-inscribing the very transphobia it fails to explain.

Since 'authenticity' in this model is understood in terms of 'coming out' and truth-telling about one's non-normative status, a transperson who insists upon passing (as non trans) would have to be viewed as acting inauthentically – both to themselves and to others. Consequently, a new appearance/reality distinction is instated (really a trans person, passing herself off as non trans). What does one then say about transpeople who have been living in 'stealth' are exposed as 'really a so-and-so'? At its crudest, this account would simply have to agree with the verdict, although in a different way. Rather than the accusation of pretending to be a woman (when in reality a man), one would see the accusation of pretending to be nontrans (when in reality trans).

In addition to this, it seems to me that the representation of invisibility as *the* problem and visibility as *the* solution presents a one-sided picture of the issues. Such a picture tends to *elide* differences among transpeople. For example, it elides the fact that invisibility and erasure may be especially concerns of *ftms in particular,* while also eliding the fact that *sexualised visibility* may be a distinct concern of mtfs. These latter concerns, however, are not understandable in terms of a politics of visibility alone.

Consider the coercive (racialised) economic conditions which place some mtfs such as trans sex-workers in a situation of being 'already out' in identifiably trans-specific public space. Given the fact that such conditions promote *forced exposure and visibility in dangerous contexts*, we need to ask whether the issue to be address isn't so much one of *invisibility* as it is *enforced, dangerous visibility*. Obviously, a call for visibility makes virtually no sense in this context. Rather than 'coming out as visible', the issue is one of increased safety on the streets and an end to the economic conditions which coerce a visibility when it is not desired. The point, at any rate, is that strategies ought to be specific to the issues and when invisibility is postulated as *the* problem, there is the danger that not all the issues will be addressed.

6.   Sandy Stone and the Empire

The basis of the prevailing model is defended in Sandy Stone's groundbreaking article 'The *Empire* Strikes Back: A Posttranssexual Manifesto'. Since this article is a kind of cornerstone upon which the transgender movement rests and since the central themes (especially the politics of visibility) are developed so well, it is worth examining more closely.[27] In raising my concerns, I wish to acknowledge the significance of Stone's work to trans politics. Indeed, I also wish to point out that the criticisms I raise are anachronistic to the extent that they could not have been raised were it not for Stone's ground-breaking article. I raise these concerns, however, because I am worried about the adequacy of the prevailing model. And I raise them against Stone, because hers is among the best formulations of it.

Stone's article is itself a response to radical feminist critiques of transsexuality (on the one hand) and a critique of medical/psychiatric constructions of transpeople (on the other). Her strategy consists in to some extent *agreeing* with feminist critiques of transsexuality that some mtfs adopt the 'gender reactionary' and 'sexist' views (pointing out the danger of 'totalising' such claims) while charging the medical/psychiatric constructions of transsexuality (and transsexual complicity in this construction) as promoting such a sexist reality.

'Passing' for Stone, flows from medical views which require that transsexuals blend into the main-stream by constructing plausible 'non trans' histories. Her pioneering work involves the demand that transsexuals become 'posttranssexuals' by refusing to disappear into the mainstream and by developing counter-discourses which oppose this oppressive medical model. She insists that transsexuals forgo 'passing', and begin to write ourselves into the discourse by which we have been written.[28] She rightfully insists that 'we need a deeper analytic language for transsexual theory, one which allows for the sorts of ambiguities and polyvocalities which have already so pro-ductively informed and enriched feminist theory.'[29] And she suggests that instead of viewing transsexuality as third gender, it ought to be viewed as a genre, '[…] as a set of embodied texts whose potential for productive disruption […] has yet to be explored'. [30] In light of this, one of the greatest values of Stone's position is her envisioning of not some *unitary* counter-discourse, but rather a *plurality* of such 'disruptions.' Indeed, she sees the discourse of medicalised trans-sexuality as producing erasures precisely through its unitary nature.[31]

To be sure, in enjoining trans folk to become visible, Stone does not insist that we always come out to everybody on all occasions. She writes, in an interview with Davina Ann Gabriel, 'No, I think that would be suicidal. Everyone must choose – because the world is a big place – how much and to whom they reveal themselves.'[32] Nonetheless, she also clearly endorses a politics of visibility, while touting the importance of 'self-revelation'. She writes, '[...] the genre of visible transsexuals must grow by recruiting members from the class of invisible ones, from those who have disappeared into their 'plausible histories'.[33] And, 'I mean that the quality of life improves with self-revelation – mutual, caring self-unveiling as it feels appropriate and graceful'.[34] More deeply, Stone has faith in the power of discourse and self-revelation to effect change, situating the authority to control the meaning of the discourse and self-revelation within the author herself, while failing to discuss the role of the interpreter in assigning meaning to the words and the bodies of those who would self-disclose. Perhaps most troublesome, is that in adopting an exclusive politics of visibility, Stone opens the door to new accusations of deception and pretence. Stone comes close to making such an accusation herself when she writes:

> Transsexuals who pass seem able to ignore the fact that by creating totalised, monistic identities, forgoing physical and subjective intertextuality, they have foreclosed the possibility of authentic relationships. Under the principle of passing, denying the destabilising power of being 'read,' relationships begin as lies [...][35]

Obviously any reinscription of accusations of fraudulence is wildly unintentional. Yet it seems to me that the question must be raised whether the view that Stone unwittingly accomplishes precisely this reinscription. For Stone's remarks clearly place the responsibility for authentic relationships upon the transsubject themselves, rather than upon the person with whom they would interact. She presupposes that the choice for authentic relationships rests fundamentally within the hands of the transsubject, and she identifies authenticity with self-disclosure. Yet how many have found themselves represented by loved ones as not quite authentic? How many times have transpeople, as openly trans, found themselves in 'authentic' relationships with life-partners only to have marriages subsequently annulled on the grounds of 'fraudulence'? To be clear, the transphobic violence stemming from the 'shocking exposure' often concerns precisely this intimacy.

Let me also remark that for Stone there is an important connection between 'passing' and anti-inartistic gender-variance. She sees passing as tantamount to 'the denial of mixture'[36] which she latter explains means 'that we cannot present ourselves as partly male, partly female, or partly anything else. [...] What passing means to me is denying parts of yourself in order to pass yourself off as the person that you want to be.'[37] According to this view, 'denial of mixture' is effectively understood as the denial of a gender complexity, fluidity, or 'in-between-ness' that Stone sees as erased with a traditional inartistic model of sex/gender. She explicitly connects this notion of gender mixture with what she sees as the problematic relationship of transsubjects to traditional (inartistic) gender categories and suggests that this problematic relation be utilised as a place of resistance.[38]

However, I worry whether in identifying gender mixture with the 'problematic' relation of transpeople to inartistic gender categories, Stone effectively *accepts as a basic starting point* the view that transpeople (in the 'best case scenario') count as the gender of their choice 'only with qualification' or 'problematically'. To what degree is the starting point an unacceptable acquiescence to gender invalidation? For whether something counts as a mixture depends a lot upon the specific items which it is taken to mix and how those items are interpreted. For example, whether one's emergence from (say) a boyhood into an adult transgender womanhood is viewed as a mixture will depend upon which life-courses one accepts as standard. Viewed in one way, this life course may not so much constitute a mix of gender categories at all, so much as a relatively standard life-course of a transgender woman.

Moreover, in focusing upon medical constructions of trans-sexuality, it seems to me that Stone does not acknowledge the realities of transphobia which operate well beyond medical discourse, which provide good reasons for 'wanting to pass' and 'deny mixture' in Stone's sense – reasons which consequently require implicating oneself in the day-to-day negotiations of a sexist society. For by glossing 'passing' as a kind of *complicity* or *bad faith*, the resistant agency of trans people in claiming authenticity in a world that systematically denies it to us is simply obliterated.

And there are also other sorts of important mixtures besides ones involving the categories 'man' and 'woman'. One example involves the 'in between' of 'deceiving' those who do not acknowledge one's actual identity, while simultaneously 'being true to oneself' through this very act of 'deception'. Another blend is the complex *ephemerality* that some transpeople experience in being constructed as pretend on the one hand, while seeing themselves as substantial and real on the other. However by emphasising *visibility* over *invisibility*, Stone cannot accommodate gender oppression which concerns the liminality found in between the appearance/reality divide, the public/private divide, and the visible and invisible divide.

6. Conclusion

I believe that what is needed is an appreciation of the double-binded way in which transpeople are always already constructed as 'deceiver/pretenders'. Insofar as trans politics aimed at resisting the construction, it would have to be viewed as a politics of *authenticity*. No doubt, such a view will be anathema to post-modern conceptions of the self, conceptions that selves are nothing more than socially-constructed 'role playing'. Nonetheless, the position is actually *compatible* with such a position. For even if subjects are the effects of social construction, transpeople are specifically socially-constructed as *frauds*. Hence, trans resistance requires that this specific construction be opposed. And the sheer recognition that all the world is a stage on which we all must play (or be) a role itself goes no distance in resisting the view that transpeople, in particular, must play (or be) the role of 'role-player'. We *need* to contest this construction.

Moreover, any trans politics needs to pay careful attention to the dangers of the deceiver/pretender double-bind, particularly with respect to the 'options' of visibility and invisibility. For there is a danger of being ensnared by one side of the bind, while attempting to avoid the other: Multiple, even conflicting, strategies (with respect to visibility and invisibility) would appear to be called for, at least as temporary measures.[39] Consequently the strategies of invisibility, deception, and duplicity must be recognised as welcome supplements to visibility and 'coming out'. Given that we are 'always already' gender frauds and deceivers, a commitment to 'gender honesty' is surely to act out a morality of the oppressor.

Here, it is important to emphasise a notion of the political that is broader than one focused only upon large scale 'social change'.[40] Individual acts of survival (such as 'passing') need to be recognised as subversive (i.e., resistant and political) rather than dismissed because they do not fit a particular political vision. And, I think that it is important to recognise that political resistance more generally might sometimes need to use tactics of *invisibility, silence, secrecy, and duplicity*, particularly in a world that is dangerous.[41] Moreover, it is very dangerous to assume that *only* invisibility is the problem and that *only* visibility is the solution. There are other issues, such as such as forced visibility and the forced animation of negative representations – problems which are ignored by an over emphasis on the importance of visibility as a strategy.

It is also important to recognise that 'coming out' is itself fraught with difficulties which seem to impair its subversive force from the outset. In addition to the problem of *invisibility,* there is also the problem of *'communication breakdown'*. To the extent that we *cannot* 'come out' except in ways that construct us as 'deceiver/pretenders', visibility in dominant mainstream discourse itself becomes largely destructive. In saying this, I do acknowledge the obvious point that 'coming out' can be an important strategy in making the world a safer place for transpeople. This is because the dominant constructions which I have identified are simply *not* monolithic (i.e., they are not embraced by everyone even within such 'mainstream' contexts). It is only because of this fact that visibility ('coming out') remains a viable strategy. My point, however, is that *visibility* needs to be supplemented with an emphasis on the problems of *comprehension.* For visibility is deeply connected to interpretation. And we are simply not always in charge of how we are interpreted – the modalities by which we are visible. How can we get other people to so much as understand our words?

In short, I believe that much more attention needs to be devoted to the deceiver/pretender construction. And the underlying theory matters because it has consequences in terms of political action and lived lives. What grounds the gender appearance – sex reality distinction? Why, exactly, is this connected to sexual violence and accusation of sexual violence? The basic denial of authenticity is an important kind of transphobia, and it needs to be better understood. If what I have said is correct, this understanding may require a significant reassessment of current trans theory and politics. Indeed, it might require a deeper understanding of the nature of the political in the first place. Resistance ought to be valued, even when it is not what is expected. And it ought to be recognised as inherent in *all* trans lives. To do anything less is to succumb to a transphobia that pervades.

Endnotes

*   I wish to express my gratitude to María Lugones. This article is informed by her work and by the conversations that we have had. I am likewise grateful to C. Jacob Hale and Emilia Lombardi for all that I have learned from them, both through their written work, as well as our many conversations, and I thank them for valuable comments on earlier drafts of this paper. I also thank Ann Garry, Rachel Hollenberg, James Singer, and Kayley Vernallis for their helpful comments on earlier drafts. And I give special thanks to Susan Forrest for her editorial assistance in the process of writing several drafts of this paper, as well as her invaluable insights.

1   There are deep concerns about 'transgender' as a colonising discourse and the ways in which transgender politics, queer politics, and medical transsexual discourse are negotiated in terms of complex intersections between race, class, culture, and nation. For a good preliminary discussion of some of these issues, see Namaste, Viviane: *Invisible lives: The erasure of transsexual and transgender people* (Chicago: University of Chicago Press, 2000), pp. 62–64 and Roen, Katrina: 'Transgender theory and embodiment: The risk of racial marginalisation', *Journal of Gender Studies* 10.3 (2001), pp. 253–263. For a more sustained critique of transgender politics as a form of imperialism, see

Namaste, Vivianne: *Sex Change, Social Change: Reflections on Identity, Institutions, and Imperialism* (Toronto: Women's Press, 2005).
2   For an introduction to the notion of 'trans studies' see Prosser, Jay: 'Transgender' in A. Medhurst and S.R. Munt (eds): *Lesbian and Gay Studies: A Critical Introduction* (London: Cassell, 1997), pp. 309–326.
3   The move in this direction is best captured by C. Jacob Hale's 'Suggested Rules for Non-Transsexuals Writing about Transsexuals, Transsexuality, Transsexualism, or Trans____' (1997) at http://sandystone.com/hale.rules.html.
4   See Prosser, J.: *Second Skins: The Body Narratives of Transsexuality* (New York: Columbia University Press, 1998), p. 175; Namaste, Viviane: *Invisible lives: The erasure of transsexual and transgender people* (Chicago: University of Chicago Press, 2000), pp. 9–23, 60–69; Namaste: *Sex Change, Social Change: Reflections on Identity, Institutions, and Imperialism* (Toronto: Women's Press, 2005), Rubin, H.: 'Phenomenology as Method in Trans Studies' in *GLQ: A Journal of Lesbian and Gay Studies* 4. 2 (1998), pp. 263–81; 'Trans Studies: Between A Metaphysics of Presence and Absence' in K. More and S. Whittle (eds.): *Reclaiming Genders: Transsexual Grammars at the fin de siecle,*(London:: Cassell, 1999); Rubin, H.: '*Self-Made Men: Identity and Embodiment among Transsexual Men* (Vanderbilt University Press, 2003) on some of the political and theoretical tensions. Here most of the concerns involve an exclusive affiliation with LGB politics and the understanding of trans-subjectivity within an exclusively queer paradigm.
5   Lombardi, E., Wilchins, R., Preising, D., Malouf, D.: 'Gender violence: Transgender experiences with violence and discrimination', *Journal of Homosexuality* 42 (2001), pp. 89–101.
6   Reback, C., Simon, P., Bemis, K., Gatson, B.: *The Los Angeles Transgender Health Study: Community Report* (West Hollywood, 2001).
7   Lombardi, E.: 'Understanding genderism and transphobia' (Unpublished). While both the *GenderPAC study* (2001) and *The Los Angeles Transgender Health Study* (2001) fail to discuss correlations between race/ethnicity and reported incidence of transphobic abuse and violence, Lombardi finds in her study that African-American transpeople reported the highest levels of discrimination over the past year, while white transpeople reported the lowest.
8   See Gwendolyn Ann Smith's 'Remembering Our Dead' web site at www.rememberingourdead.org. Smith is the founder of the Transgender Day of Remembrance.
9   By 'gender presentation,' I mean not only gendered attire but also bodily gesture, posture, manner of speech (pitch, tone, pattern, expressive range) and socially interactive style. By 'sexed body' I mean physical characteristics such as genitals, presence or absence of breast tissue, facial and body hair, fat distribution, height, bone-width and so forth. I intend for this distinction to admit of some blurriness. By 'gender identity' I mean simply how an individual self-

consciously conceptualises themselves – as a man, a woman, mtf, ftm, trans-man, third gender, non-gender, beyond gender, gender queer and so forth.

10   Namaste, V.: *Sex Change, Social Change: Reflections on Identity, Institutions, and Imperialism*, op. cit., p. 9.

11   The essentiality of genitalia in determining sex is part of what Harold Garfinkel calls 'the natural attitude about sex' – a kind of pretheoretical 'common sense.' The other notions which constitute this attitude include: (1) There a two mutually exclusive and exhaustive categories (male and female); (2) This distinction is 'natural'; (3) Memberships in a particular sex is 'natural' and invariant; (4) Exceptions to the preceding claims may be dismissed as 'abnormal.' See Garfinkel, H.: *Studies in ethnomethodology* (Oxford: Polity Press, 1957), pp. 122–133, Kessler, W. and McKenna, S.: *Gender: An ethno-methodological approach* (New York: John Wiley and Sons, 1978) and Born-stein, K.: *Gender outlaw: On men and women and the rest of us* (New York: Routledge, 1994), pp. 45–51. While some views about gender have changed, the importance of genitalia in determining sex continues, see Kessler, W. and McKenna, S: 'Who put the 'trans' in transgender? Gender theory and everyday life'. *The International Journal of Transgenderism* 4.3 (1978) at the website http://www.symposion.com/ijt/index.htm, pp. 113–4

12   For a more detailed account of this double-bind, see Bettcher, T.: 'Evil deceivers and make-believers: reflections on transphobic violence and the politics of illusion' (Forthcoming).

13   Meyerowitz, J.:. *How Sex Changed; A History of Sexuality in the United States* (Cambridge: Harvard University Press, 2002), pp. 69–73.

14   For a more detailed account, see Bettcher, T., op. cit.

15   Latour, F.: 'Sibling decries murder acquittal: verdict is assault in transsexual's death', *Boston Globe,* 3 May 1997.

16   In the emerging transgender movement of the 1990's, the name 'Brandon Teena' was used, despite the fact that there is not substantial evidence that Brandon (the name this individual used most commonly went by before the murder) actually used 'Teena' as a last name. Ultimately, any name choice is problematic, and possibly pronoun use may be problematic as well. For a thorough and provocative discussion of these issues, see Hale, C. J.: 'Tracing a ghostly memory in my throat', in T. Digby. (ed.): *Men doing Feminism* (New York: Routledge, 1998), pp. 99–129. see also Jay Prosser's discussion of Brandon and his relevance to transgender politics in Prosser op. cit.

17   Hernandez, G.: 'Bittersweet justice: in the wake of the Gwen Araujo trial, activists are grimly aware of how difficult it is to obtain a first-degree murder conviction when the victim is transgender', *The Advocate,* 22 November 2005.

18   O'Bryan, W.: 'Killer Sentenced in Transgender Murder Case: Antoine Jacobs to serve 16 years for the 2003 shooting of Bella Evangelista', *Metro Weekly: Washington DC's Gay and Lesbian Magazine*, 22 December 2005.

19   Hernandez, G., op. cit.

20 For an account of some of the connections between the denial of authenticity and sexual abuse, see Bettcher, T.: 'Transphobia, authenticity, and sexual abuse', in Krista Scott-Dixon (ed.): *Trans/Forming Feminisms* (forthcoming).

21 Locke, M.: 'Defence lawyers claim heat of passion in transgender killing case', *Associated Press,* 3 June 2004.

22 Raymond. J.: *The Transsexual Empire: The Making of the She-Male* (Boston: Beacon Press, 1994), p. 104.

23 Rubin, H.: 'Trans Studies: Between A Metaphysics of Presence and Absence', in K. More and S. Whittle (eds): *Reclaiming Genders: Transsexual Grammars at the fin de siecle,* (London: Cassell, 1999), pp. 190f. Also see Rubin, H., op. cit., pp. 163–165, and Namaste, V., op. cit., pp. 6–10. For a related discussion see Elliot, P. and Roen, K. 'Transgenderism and the Question of Embodiment', *GLQ A Journal of Lesbian and Gay Studies* 4. 2 (1998), pp. 231–261. In addition to an emphasis on the importance of embodied subjectivity, one of the concerns in this article is that by drawing a 'too sharp' distinction between 'gender rebels' and 'gender conformists' one fails to appreciate the permeability of the boundary between the two, while successfully re-inscribing prevailing normative conceptions as ultimately authoritative.

24 Jay Prosser, op. cit., pp. 175, 203 4, questions the subversive force of transgender politics and Stone's notion of a 'posttranssexual'. However, Prosser means to question the subversive potential of positioning oneself outside of binary discourse and claiming a 'dislocatedness' and to argue for the importance of 'gender homes'. For example, Prosser writes, '[...]Teena's death demonstrated the limited capacity of the transitional subject as 'gender outlaw' to change gender conventions' (p. 175). Prosser begs an important question by representing Brandon as a 'transitional subject' (presumably on the grounds that he had not sought out sex-assignment surgery). The problem, however, is how to describe such lives without doing grave violence to them. For example, one may see oneself as 'fully complete' and 'at home' without subscribing to dominant mainstream conceptions of gender/sex. What Prosser disregards, at any rate, in his attempt to point to the 'subversive failure of the gender outlaw' is the fact that *all* transpeople who present themselves in ways that can be taken as at odds with sexed-body (and this includes those who have undergone genital-reconstruction surgery and are living in 'stealth') may be subject to public disclosure, invalidation, and murder. Similarly Viviane Namaste rightfully worries that positioning oneself 'outside the binary' as a political strategy is utopic (see her *Sex Change, Social Change: Reflections on Identity, Institutions, and Imperialism,* op. cit., p. 22). My own concern is that the current politics (regardless of how positions oneself with respect to 'binary oppositions') is in itself insufficient as an account of oppression/resistance.

25 Here I emphasise not lack of adequate language, but rather the facility with which (when negotiating dominant, main stream conceptualisations) our own words (imperfect and inadequate as they are) may be utterly ignored and/or

re-interpreted in hostile ways (i.e., in ways that are contrary to our own under-standings). Hale emphasises the former: 'For those of us on whom the limits of already available discourses press the most closely, it would seem that refusing colonising discourses leaves us in a position of near speechless: reverse discourse' (op. cit., p. 113). The difference, I believe, is only one of emphasis, which may be a function of our different subject locations and projects.

26   See Lugones, M.: *Pilgrimages/Peregrinajes: Theorising Coalition Against Multiple Oppressions* (New York: Roman & Littlefield Publishers, 2003) esp. p. 14). See also Scheman, N.: 'Queering the Center by Centering the Queer: Reflections on Transsexuals and Secular Jews', in D. T. Meyers (ed.): *Feminists Rethink the Self* (Boulder: Westview Press, 1997), p. 125.

27   For other articulations of a politics of visibility, see Kate Bornstein's *Gender Outlaw Gender outlaw: On men and women and the rest of us,* op. cit., and Leslie Feinberg's *Stone Butch Blues: A Novel* (New York: Firebrand, 1993). Also see Jason Cromwell *Transmen & FTMs: Identities, Bodies, Genders, & Sexualities* (Chicago: University of Illinois Press, 1999), Jamison Green: 'Look! No, Don't! The Visibility Dilemma for Transsexual Men' in K. More and S. Whittle (eds): *Reclaiming Genders: Transsexual Grammars at the fin de siecle,* (London: Cassell, 1999), and Roz Kaveny: 'Talking Transgender Politics' in *Reclaiming Genders,* op. cit., pp. 146–158.

28   Stone, S: 'The *Empire* Strikes Back: A Posttransexual Manifesto' in J. Epstein and K. Straub (eds): *Body Guards: The Cultural Politics of Gender Ambiguity* (New York: Routledge, 1991), p. 299.

29   Ibid., p. 296.

30   Ibid., p. 297.

31   Ibid., p. 293.

32   Gabriel, D. A.: 'Interview with the Transsexual Vampire: Sandy Stone's Dark Gift', *TransSisters: The Journal of Transsexualism* 8, Spring (1995), p. 24.

33   Stone, S., op. cit, p. 296.

34   Ibid.

35   Ibid., p. 298.

36   Ibid., p. 296.

37   Gabriel, D.A., op. cit., p. 24.

38   Stone, S., op. cit., p. 295.

39   See Hale, C. J.: 'Are lesbian's women?' *Hypatia* 11. 2 (1996), pp. 94–121 for his development of the view that the 'incoherent' (and effectively 'double-binded') concept of womanhood requires multiple (and apparently inconsistent) strategies.

40   See ibid., p. 2.

41   See ibid., pp. 10–16). See also Scheman, N., op. cit., p. 124.

Felix Ó Murchadha

On Provocation: Violence as Response

Provocations come in different forms. Words, actions, gestures, people, places, artefacts, works of art, cartoons, dress can all be provocative. The response to provocation need not of course always be violent, but from a raised voice to murder expressions of anger, if not rage, inform responses to provocation, and indeed there is a violence – at least latent – in provocation itself. This is so because provocation suspends my intentions, confronts me with that which I[1] cannot ignore and turns me against myself. I am not provoked if I do what I would have done anyway; provocation disrupts my equilibrium and calls on my desire or my anger such that it threatens to engulf me. Characteristic of the power of provocation is the perception of that which provokes as being addressed to myself; the logic of violence in this context is one of response: it articulates a prior affect of being addressed by an other. The response begins before the retaliatory act of violence itself in the sense that it is pre-structured in that affection of being provoked. There are no natural provocations; nothing is provocative *in itself*.[2] For this reason many provocations are unintended and unwitting. To be provoked by something is to perceive it to be disturbing, offensive, possibly degrading. This is an ethical perception, a perception of an act or its products as violating a claim, which I am entitled to make on an other and which an other should respect. As such provocation belongs to the order of society, to the symbolic order in which acts can be interpreted as violations of claims. But the interpretation of such violations is rarely unambiguous: while dependant on the common symbolic meaning of a society it reaches deep into the self-understanding of the one provoked as a singular, ethical being. My ethical perception of the provocation is itself an expression of that self-understanding. I am in a strong sense responsible for such ethical perception: the ethical claims that I make are those for which I take responsibility, they make up who I am as an ethical being. In this sense responsibility comes into play in the provocation itself not first in the question of retaliation. *I am responsible for being provoked.* Responsibility does not mean culpability; my being provoked may be justified. But such justification is never a simple fact of the matter. Nor is the self for whom I take responsibility entirely my own: if provocation comes from an other, my self-understanding is of self which in large measure is not its own origin. I am responsible for my own passivity, for how it is that things in the world provoke me.

If provocation is only possible in relation to the symbolic meaning of a society, by the same token it concerns the law. The legality of violence of any sort is a contentious issue, particularly when the violence in question is not state sanctioned. The plea of provocation is the source of some legal controversy. The reasons for this are clear: It raises the question as to the justification or at least the excusability of some forms of violence. Crucial in this debate among other things is the issue of proportionality: the violence inflicted must be proportionate to the violence suffered. For the provoked the justification of violence lies not (in the first instance at least) in the goals which it might achieve, as in the suffering endured. The source of violence – as far as such justifications/excuses are concerned – is in the passivity of the perpetrator.

The question of the justification of violence poses fundamental issues. If violence is justified, then does that make it right and good? Certainly we can say that violence is wrong 'in itself' so to speak, and that this wrongness is outweighed in certain situations by certain factors. But what is violence *in itself*? How can one abstract violence from the situations in which it arises? Not alone can this not be done, it cannot for a fundamental reason: the situation of the act is – in part – constitutive of its violence. Violence does not receive its justification by reference to extraneous factors, rather either the act of violence is justified due to factors constitutive of it, or it is not. Hence, the question of the rightness or wrongness of violence allows for no general answer, unless of course there are no situations in which violence is justified.

1.   The Legal Debate

In terms of the plea of provocation the legal dispute centres around – assuming the plea to be sound at all[3] – whether the plea should be taken as an excuse or a justification. The normal interpretation of common law tends towards the excusatory in that it sees the plea as relevant only if the act of retaliation took place in the 'heat of the moment', when the defendant had lost self-control.[4] Clearly the loss of self-control is in certain cases excusable, but hardly justifiable. Nonetheless, an element of justification may appear to enter into the second condition, which is that the defendant acted as any reasonable person might have in such circumstances. As presently understood the justificatory element even here is quite thin: the condition is not that the act was reasonable, rather that any reasonable person might be expected to lose self-control and become – temporarily – unreasonable in such circumstances. Nonetheless, the reasonable person test also contains the criteria of proportionality: the retaliatory response must be proportionate to the injury inflicted. This understanding of provocation has recently come under criticism from a number of quarters.

Both conditions of excusability have recently come under attack. The 'heat of the moment' condition, it has been argued, is a rather abstract way of understanding provocation. While in certain cases retaliation may amount to a momentary response to a perceived injury, more usually the anger caused is either a response to a series of incidents, or is a justified response to one incident. The anger is justified. Indeed one contribution to the debate argues that conscience drives us to such anger: anything less would be a 'sign of the actor's paying insufficient regard to his own worth'.[5] This anger leads then to a moral conflict: on the one hand, the sense of outrage, on the other hand, restraint in the expression of this outrage. The moral conflict itself, it is argued, elicits our sympathy and in certain circumstances can supply grounds to excuse the acts concerned, whether or not they occur in the 'heat of the moment'.

Objections have also been raised against the 'reasonable person' condition. Both in relation to the relativity of cultural norms and to gender difference, this condition seems difficult to uphold. Implicit in the concept of the reasonable person, it is argued, is the image of a particular type of person: male, white, privileged. Arguments have been made – some of which have influenced court decisions – that culturally specific sources and degrees of provocation should be accounted for in deciding culpability. Furthermore, in the case of battered women it has been argued that female anger is unlikely to be such as to emerge simply in the heat of the moment, but may rather manifest a long history of resentment and result in a pre-meditated action.[6] The validity or otherwise of these claims is not the present concern. What is crucial is the implicit assumption shared both by the reasonable person condition and its critical modifications that the nature of the person provoked is essential to the issue of provocation and that the culpability of the person depends on what type of person he or she is. The person is to be held responsible for whom he or she is.

It is also evident that as far as the debate on the plea of provocation is concerned the excusability of violence has to do with the injury suffered not with what is to be gained by the act of violence. In this respect the case of provocation seems to go against Hannah Arendt's understanding of violence as justified – if at all – by the ends to which it is a means. [7] Here the account focuses on the suffering to which it is a response. The goal of ridding herself of her tormentor is not the source of the possible excuse or justification, but rather the suffering inflicted on her. Hence, the proportionality of the response is not considered in terms of proportion to an end to be achieved, but to a wrong endured.

2.   Provocation as Motivation

Being affected by a provocation is different in kind from being injured either physically or psychologically. My being provoked depends on the situation in which I am in and what I am in relation to that situation. Depending on that situation a physical injury (e.g. suffered in a boxing fight) or a psychological injury (e.g. that suffered with the death of a one's child) will not be perceived as a provocation. The order here is one of motivation not causality. Provocation is a species of motivation. To be provoked is to be motivated to act in this or that manner. Seen in this way the issue of provocation leads to the question: what is it to be motivated to violence?

According to Edmund Husserl, motivation is an interplay of affection and habitual tendencies.[8] Essentially, there are at play here relations of passivity and activity: for something to be a motivation it must activate an already existing, perhaps forgotten or barely conscious, belief or attitude. Crucial here is that mediating element between passivity and activity namely *receptivity*, which though passive 'includes the lowest level of activity'.[9] It is a lower level because it is not free, in the sense of taking a stand in relation to things, but nonetheless is more than a simple affectedness. The activity of the subject requires a receptivity to stimuli from things, stimuli which excite in relation to underlying tendencies of the subject that make it more or less receptive to them. In other words, the structure of passivity of the subject is in each case unique to the individual subject and is characteristic of him or her. The sources of these tendencies may lie in previous acts which remain unsatisfied, now sedimented, or indeed attitudes and beliefs which are part of the tradition into which the subject was born.

Husserl relates the discussion of the distinction between the passive and active subject to that between rational and instinctive (*triebhafte*) motivations. The ideal of rational motivation is one in which the subject is totally free and motivates himself through his own rational decision. Strictly speaking at this level there would be no place for provocation at all. A purely rational and free subject would be motivated by himself alone and would be deaf to all provocations. Such a subject of course would be one without passivity. The force of Husserl's description is not alone to deny the possibility of such a subject, but indeed to question the possibility of pure motivation at all. Insofar as no subject is characterised by pure activity, and hence is not the self-originator of its own motivations, all motivation is founded on passivity. What this means is that all motivation is itself motivated, has a source in other words either outside the self or in the past of the self. Motivations are in this sense not discrete, they form habits and

constitute the character of the person. The freedom of any particular
motivated act is dependant on such habits and such character.

There is, however, a further point here that brings to the fore
certain tensions, which I wish to explore further in the next section.
The ideal of rational motivation is that of active self-motivation. The
passivity of the subject is in respect of other – or past – motivations
such that the 'I' is always motivated. To be motivated is to be dependant in some way on something else, something other. Husserl distinguishes between this dependence and what he calls 'alien influences'
(*fremde Einflüsse*).[10] While motivation involves being acted upon,
alien influences are thoughts or feelings coming from an alien source
and which are foisted on me as an impertinence (*Zumutung*). Impertinent, it is out of place, it is of alien origin, but yet comes – either
through my own passive acquiescence or through being forced – to be
my own thought or feeling. This is an inauthentic feeling or thought,
one which follows the 'they-self'.[11] Here not alone is the free act of
reason excluded, the tendencies of sensibility are so too. The source of
the feeling or thought is that of an alien one. While Husserl clearly
wishes to uphold the relative autonomy of reason against such alien
influences, one can ask to what extent provocation tends towards
being an alien influence in this sense. Provocation has the structure of
such an impertinent motivation. The source of the provocation is so
out of place, that it places me outside of my normal tendencies. I am
taken over by a feeling which is not my own, a rage which comes over
me, which exceeds those limits of what I can 'put up with', places me
outside of those limits and forces me to confront that which is alien
from me.

Yet that which provokes me in this way is itself directly related
to my own tendencies and dispositions: while my dispositions are
directed towards certain goals and objects this directedness can either
through its intensification or repression by that which entices or
opposes me be brought to a level in which these tendencies and
dispositions become almost unrecognisable. However, although unrecognisable these tendencies are still my own, they form who I am
even though they were not freely chosen even in their more normal
manifestations. As Husserl points out ethical responsibility extends to
the whole self to the extent to which that self acts. In this sense I am

responsible for my motivations, not alone the conscious ones but also those embedded in habitual ways of acting which are susceptible to provocations that lead me to violence.[12]

3. Alien Origins

Being provoked is a relation to an other, a source beyond myself to which I find myself already subject. Through this provocation the other calls me to violence. Violence can only be wrought against an other, against another origin. The other is first and foremost impertinent to me. Hence, reading Husserl's account against the grain one could say that both rational and instinctive motivations are modifications of the prior impertinence of the other. This impertinence is that of a claim, a claim put on me from another place, from a place beyond myself. This claim is not one among others to which I am made subject as it is in each case unique: this other, not simply a general notion of others, makes a claim on me. My response to this claim, and my responsibility in this response, is not relative to my capacity to respond, but rather is experienced as that which overwhelms my capacities. Emmanuel Levinas understands this 'experience' to be one of absolute obligation to and absolute responsibility for the other. But at the heart of such an absolute responsibility is an impertinence, a provocation, a calling forth of violence.[13]

Being affected by the other differs from other affections, in the sense that in this case the affection is in the form of an address or demand, not simply of something which befalls me.[14] Provocation as such an address calls forth a response. As the one provoked I am placed in the situation of a respondent. A response relates to that to which it is responding. What it responds to, however, is not the other as such, but rather the being affected by the other.[15]

This being affected is not ultimately by the blows of the other, or the sound of the words of the other, or by the mute presence of the other. The burning rays of the sun, the sound of the roar of thunder, the fallen tree blocking my way do not affect me as provocations, nor do they appear to me as impertinences (if anything they lead me back to myself as being out of place). It is rather the case that the other affects me by addressing me, by making a claim on me to which I must respond. This claim need not be verbally articulated; in fact the mute presence of a beggar lays as much claim on me as the bantering approaches of a salesman. Levinas understands the source of such affectedness as the face of the other. The face of the other is not simply that which I can see, but rather that which I cannot see, that which sees, looks upon, me. This face gazing upon me refuses me the luxury of being alone in my world, refuses me a life without provocation. The ultimate provocation, that which lies at the core of all provocation, is the provocation to murder, to annihilate that face which calls me to account for myself. This is the ultimate provocation because it calls forth a violence which is from the beginning futile. The only way I can murder the other is to undermine his very otherness, to reduce him to a merely physical thing, a mass of flesh which I can of course destroy. But gaze of the other is irreducible to such mere physicality and fleshiness. The ambiguity of the face of the other in Levinas' account lies in the fact that it both brings murder into the world and declares its impossibility. The other calls forth the ultimate violence, murder, while denying me the power to inflict it. The statement, 'thou shalt not kill', which the other utters without doing so expressly, is in this pre-moral sense as much a dare as an injunction: the other dares me not to kill him, this is the provocation of the other. Where the other is, there can be no peace.[16] This is so because violence arises not in the 'I', not in the realm of the same at all, but precisely in the penetration of the same by the other. This raises at a different level the question posed at the beginning of this paper as to the justification of violence. If there is a obligation in the being of the other – a claim on me –, by the same token there is the invitation to a violation of this claim.[17] This violation is initiated by the other. My powerlessness to kill – understood as an incapacity of my autonomous will – lies in being affected by the initiatory being of the other. My act – or my lack of acting – is a response to this initiation.

Even if the provocation is brutal, inarticulate, it is not a brute fact. A provocation is perceived as being addressed to me and as such as calling for my response. In the face of such an act there are four possible responses: identification, negation, refusal, or retaliation. I take identification to be a masochistic response, negation a stoic response, refusal a pacifist one. Retaliation is the only *openly* violent response. I will go through each in turn.

The first response to provocation is that of identification. In this case I accept the violence of the other on me as justifiable or as not requiring justification. This amounts to a devaluing of the self in relation to the other. Levinas sometimes sounds as if he is describing such a response. But this is a total effacement – to the point of defacement – of oneself in the face of the other. I close myself off from the other by ceasing to be the other's other.[18]

The second response is that of 'apathy' (*apatheia*). Through a disciplining of my own response to my emotions I can allow whatever emotional response I may have to the provocation to simply run its course, but in so doing I separate myself from it. In attaining the state of apathy I still feel the provocation, but in a detached manner: I do not allow myself to be acted upon by it.[19] It is not simply that I do not respond to the other, I negate the other. My own freedom is insulated from the other, such that the other is simply a negative, a non-being, to my own dis-incarnated self.[20] This is a 'non-violence', which in Levinas' terms is not a peace, as it in effect does violence to the other.

The third response to provocation is the Gandhian one. This is truly a response to the other. It recognises the injury caused and the provocation it gives rise to. The point though is not to respond to this injury with more injury.[21] The pacifist response is refusal of this provocation in two senses. On the one hand, it refuses to accept the injury as just, declares the injury to be unwarranted. On the other hand, it refuses to engage in the violence to which the injury calls. Indeed, it attempts to reverse the provocation: by responding in a pacifist manner to the violence inflicted it attempts to provoke a change of heart in the other. What is at issue here is certainly a response to the other, indeed a loving one. The response aims to reach the heart of the other. Implicitly it aims at something like a common humanity. But this response reaches its limits precisely in those encounters with which Levinas begins, namely when faced with the face of the concentration camp guard, the serial killer or the torturer. The reverse provocation of pacifism fails in such cases because its addressee is simply not reached, the provocation fails due to the lack of receptivity of its target.

This brings us to the fourth possibility, namely retaliation. To retaliate is to articulate a response to the provocation. While the Stoic and Gandhian approaches either negate or refuse the address of the other's provocation, retaliation responds to the suffering itself. It perceives the provocation as an address, perceives the message contained in it and articulates a response. The response is both an expression of the anger motivated by the provocation and an articulation of the person provoked. The act of retaliation is not simply a knee-jerk reaction, like hitting away a mosquito. Rather, it is an articulation of the self and of her relation to the other. It is an articulation of the self in the sense that it expresses that self's character and tendencies. The violence of the response is an assertion of that self against the other, a taking of a stand towards the other.

The violence of such a response, however, distinguishes it from the normal motivational structure. The impertinence of the other places the self under alien influences, which take it out of itself, places it in the position of violence. It is this phenomenon which the descriptions in terms of loss of self-control and 'going berserk with rage' attempt to capture. But in these cases too that which triggers this being beside oneself is related to the sedimented tendencies of the self. The act of provocation calls forth violence in me because it exposes me to myself as a being for whom I take responsibility in taking up that for which I am not responsible. This self finds itself responsible for a self the origins and sources of which are other to itself. In confronting the alienness of the provocation it encounters at the same time its own subjection to the other, an other in the self. The self would not be open to such losses of self-control, if its capacity for control were not compromised from the beginning. The other calls my freedom into question, my powers do not extend even over myself. My loss of self-control is an extreme case of my general being subject to that which is alien from me. This being subject begins in my exposure to the other, an exposure to which I am always already articulating a response, the manner of such articulating discloses me prior to the articulations themselves.[22] I am subject to provocation in the very act of responding to it.

4. Anger

The violence of my response is that of my anger. In anger I respond to the provocation of the other. My approach to the other is not a matter of my own freedom, but rather stems from a prior provocation. The violence of that provocation, the hate of the other (subjective and objective genitive), calls forth in me anger as a response to it. But what is anger? Returning to the legal debate discussed in section one we find that at the historical roots of the plea of provocation anger was not understood as loss of self-control, but rather as a more or less proportionate response to provocation. Working with the Aristotelian dictum of 'the man who gets angry at the right things and with the right people, and also in the right way and at the right time and for the right length of time, is commended',[23] the legal question was one of assessing the proportionality of the response to provocation. Anger in this understanding is outrage at an offence either against oneself or against those with whom one shares a special relationship. The good man was one who responded to provocation according to the Aristotelian mean: neither irascible nor lacking in spirit, but patient.[24] Only with the separation of emotion and reason through the influence of Hobbesian mechanistic psychology, did the idea of anger as loss of self-control become dominant, hence transforming the plea of provocation.

The interest of such a genealogy is that it demonstrates the contingency of our legal and psychological notions of anger and provocation. Furthermore, the philosophical bases both of early and late modern views are subject increasingly to fundamental criticism. In the light of this it is important to ask what can be learned from this shift in meaning, which though subtle is decisive. This can be attempted only through finding a point of orientation in the phenomenon of anger.

Anger is an affliction. From *angere* – 'to be troubled' – anger is
the perception of being troubled unjustly. Anger is a pain placing me
before the injustice of the other. My anger responds to the other in
relation to a perceived pain. The pain or affliction does not bring
about anger. Rather, anger is a certain way of being afflicted. It is a
way of being afflicted which suffers the affliction as unjustified in
some sense.[25] Anger is a perception both of being injured and that this
injury ought not to be. The extent of the injury inflicted does not in-
spire anger. It is the perception of this injury as a wrong which is
crucial. This wrong is not just noted, it is suffered. The suffering of
wrong is not the mere injury itself, but rather that injury perceived as
wrong. Anger does not always find expression in action. But it is
directed at the source of the injury suffered. As such, anger is not, or
is only in a marginal sense, a knee-jerk reaction. If I feel a stone hit
against my arm my response is not one of anger unless I perceive the
stone as having been thrown at me. Anger discloses in this sense the
source of my injury as a culpable one. My anger is ranged against
what I perceive to be the culpability of another or others. This culpability may appear to me as outrageous. My anger is not in any
mechanistic sense simply an emotional *reaction* to this outrage, it is
nothing other than my *perception* of this act as outrageous. The restriction in common law to spur of the moment anger fails to
appreciate that the anger in such a perception does not necessarily
dissipate after the moment has passed. In fact to the extent to which
the anger amounts to a perception of wrong(s), then it may just as
easily deepen with time.

The injury is not, however, immediately present to anger. The
injury has been inflicted, is past. Anger retrospectively perceives that
injury as an affront. Anger does not let the injury be past however, but
rather keeps hold of the injury, keeps hold of the affront in the present.
Anger is in this sense a relation to a past which does not slip away
but is kept hold of in the present. It does not give way or give away,
but retains the injury and more fundamentally its own passivity in
relation to that injury. Anger is a mood which discloses the other as
culpable. It discloses a past which is that of the other's initiative, of a
foreign beginning – a past which has been incorporated before and
beyond my conscious control into the biography of my being. Anger

discloses an other's freedom. It discloses that freedom in terms of the self's passivity. Only a vulnerable being can know anger. As such anger discloses myself as subject to the other, as subject above all in my corporeality. Anger discloses my corporeality both as vulnerable and as responsive. Anger is a mood engulfing the whole body, something captured in the phrase 'the heating of the blood'. This phrase, which is well instituted in legal parlance,[26] refers to the way in which anger takes hold of the body, emboldens me to respond, indeed to retaliate for the violence suffered. This phrase tends to go hand in hand with the understanding of action as lack of self-control. This can be understood without recourse to any dualistic account of reason and emotion. The vulnerability of the body means that, while capable of enjoyment, I am also exposed to the other. This exposure does not only mean that I can be subject to violence, the very being exposed itself is a violence: before my will or my own power I am in the position of responding. Response is forced on me and forced on me before I have any say in the matter. This means that I am always already beside myself: my being is one in which I am other than myself. My anger which articulates a perception of wrong, is motivated by sedimented characteristics in myself, points also to a source which I cannot appropriate, a foreign source which nonetheless lies at the basis of my self. That foreign source, which I begin by responding to, is manifest in anger and rage, in the distortions of myself which flow from its impertinence. In my rage I attack that source which, however, is traced in a wound in myself. Anger shows the self as being invaded by the other in its very origins. In this sense anger is closely tied to trauma.

A trauma is the otherness in an experience, an otherness which remains unperceivable in the present but indirectly continues to effect after the event is past. Anger is provoked when the traumatic core of the self is exposed. Although directed at a particular person or persons it is not simply directed at such people. Rather, it is directed also and fundamentally at the dependence on the other as such, the dependence on a source alien to me, the effects of which in a sedimented manner constitute the self. A self which makes ethical claims is a self which has been formed into an ethical being, a self which has inherited and suffered its own nature. Such a self of course also forms itself, but it is only in respect of that which is other than itself that it can respond to the exposure of the sources of itself with anger. Acts of provocation refuse to recognise the claims I make for myself and in so doing demonstrate my dependence on the acknowledgement of an other for my very ethical being. In this sense whether or not the act of provocation directly threatens my physical survival, it does threaten me as an ethical being. But while anger arises out of the traumatic condition of my being, it is not a response to that condition. Rather it is a response to the injury inflicted.

I am responsible for my being provoked, because I am responsible for what I am. But my responsibility is for a being which finds itself exposed in numerous ways to the other, finds itself as always more than that over which it has control. The ideal of self-control in which my responsibility is only for that which my own autonomous reason dictates, is based on a modernist disincarnating of the self, which shows strong Stoic influences. For an incarnate self, however, the past remains beyond its mastery as something which provocation in its full traumatic force discloses. In such an instance the self responds with an anger which may or may not express itself in acts of violence.

The question here is not whether this anger will result in violence; it is itself violent.[27] To perceive the other as culpable is to feel oneself at the other's mercy; to be possessed by a searing rage is already to respond to the other even as it infects myself. Anger is from the beginning such a response. As a response it calls for articulation. Retaliation is one form of such articulation. Retaliation responds to a source of perceived wrong, and as such is always frustrated. It affirms both my responsibility for my being provoked and the initiative of the other, which it cannot undo.

5.   Retaliation

If violence is a response, is it ever appropriate, proportionate? How would one go about measuring such a thing? Court decisions are guided by certain cultural mores: in seventeenth century England to pull a gentleman's nose was an outrageous provocation and if this resulted in a duel in which the provoker was killed, the response was thought to be proportionate.[28] Such judgements are contingent not alone upon such mores, but also upon the taking up of third-party positions from which both sides' actions can be weighed up. But the provocation itself is a form of questioning. It questions my worth, my beliefs, my very existence. A proportionate response would be one which would equal such a questioning, would cancel out the suffering, would make things good again, as the German saying goes (*wieder gut machen*). But retaliation does not equal the provocation but rather always misses its mark. The other who calls forth my violence, remains as other beyond its possible reach.[29] I cannot reach behind the initial offence, my response to this offence is always a responding which the answer – that articulation which is my violence – can never fulfil.

In this sense the futility of revenge lies not so much in it effect of perpetuating a cycle of revenge ad infinitum (as Arendt for example suggests),[30] but in the insatiability of the desire for retaliation that can never fully fulfil its task.

The question of justification, finally, comes always too late. The violence of retaliation, the anger towards the other, expresses the passivity of the self, its ultimate exposure and vulnerability. The source of putative justification lies there in that suffering which calls for response that is not goal directed, but rather seeks to find an answer to the other. There is here a shocking intimacy of violence, the perpetrators obsession with the victim and his own victimisation.

If violence in respect to provocation is a response does this tell us something about violence *tout court*? In other words, is there such a thing as unprovoked violence? Certainly there is violence against people who do not provoke it (intentionally or otherwise). Nevertheless, that does not mean that the violence has not been provoked by some other factor and that the victim is simply standing in for or symbolising the source of the provocation. The source of violence – such is the claim here – is not in an autonomous will seeking mastery, but in an incarnate and vulnerable will which is motivated to violence long before it takes up its weapons of retaliation.

Endnotes

1   The use of the first person singular here and throughout this article is necessary in respect of the phenonenological approach to self and other attempted here. This should become particularly apparent when dealing with anger in section 4.

2   This parallels an understanding of violence as belonging to the 'symbolic order of law, politics and morals' which we find in Benjamin. As Derrida states in his reading of Benjamin: 'there is no natural or physical violence'. See Derrida: 'The Force of Law: The Mystical Foundation of Authority' in Cornell, Drucilla, Rosenfeld, Michel, Carlson, David Gray (eds): *Deconstruction and the Possibility of Justice* (London: Routledge, 1992), p. 31.

3   J. Hordor argues for its abolition, cf. *Provocation and Responsibility* (Oxford: Clarendon Press, 1990), ch. 9.

4   Cf. Mousourakis, G: 'Emotion, Choice and Criminal Responsibility', *Indian Philosophical Quaterly*, 27. 1 & 2 (2000), pp. 63–78.

5   Narayan, U. and Von Hirsch, A.: 'Three conceptions of provocation', *Criminal Justice Ethics* 15 (1996), p. 19.

6   Cf. Baker, B.: 'Provocation as a defence for abused women', *Canadian Journal of Law and Jurisprudence*, 11. 1 (1998), pp. 193–211.

7   Arendt: *On Violence* (London: Allan Lane The Penguin Press, 1970*)*, p. 79

8   Husserl, E.: *Ideas Pertaining to a Pure Phenomenology and to a Phenomenological Philosophy. Second Book,* trans. by R. Rojcewicz and A. Schuwer (Dordrecht: Kluwer, 1989), pp. 223–293; *Ideen zu einer reinen Phänomenologie und phänomenologischen Philosophie. Zweites Buch* ed. by M. Biemel (The Hague: Martinus Nijhoff, 1952), pp. 211–280. I have rendered some key terms differently into English than in the translation.

9   Ibid., p. 225; p. 213.

10   Ibid., pp. 281f.; pp. 268f.

11   There are striking parallels between this analysis and Heidegger's later discussion of inauthenticity and the they-self in *Being and Time*. Although *Ideas* 2 was published only posthumously in 1952 the main years of composi-

tion were 1913 and 1915 and Heidegger was almost certainly familiar with its contents.

12 On this theme see Nenon, T.: 'Freedom, Responsibility and Self-Awareness in Husserl', *The New Yearbook for Phenomenology and Phenomenological Philosophy,* 2 (2002), pp. 16f.

13 Levinas, E.: *Totality and Infinity*, trans. A. Lingis (Pittsburgh: Duquesne University Press, 1969), pp. 198–201.

14 See B. Waldenfels: *Bruchlinien der Erfahrung* (Frankfurt a.M.: Suhrkamp, 2002) p. 148 where Waldenfels distinguishes between *Widerfahrnis* and *Aufforderung*, between that which befalls me and that which claims me.

15 On responsivity see Waldenfels: *Antwortregister* (Suhrkamp, 1995)

16 This may appear to contradict the inner intention of Levinas' philosophy. Yet, peace for Levinas comes not from the other, but from the I. See *Totality and Infinity*, op. cit., p. 304.

17 Cf. St. Paul: *Romans* 4:13 'Where there is no law there is no violation'.

18 Sartre's analysis of the masochistic relation to the other remains the most compelling phenomenological description of such a response. Cf. Sartre, J. P.: *Being and Nothingness* trans. by H. Barnes (New York. Philosophical Library, 1969), pp. 374–379.

19 Cf. Waldenfels, op. cit., p. 105: '*Apathie bedeutet dass man…den Ansprechsbarkeit grad gegen den Nullwert oder einer Gleichgültigkeit tendieren lässt*'.

20 Levinas marks his distance from the Stoics by understanding the will as incarnate, cf. *Totality and Infinity*, op. cit., pp. 229–230.

21 Gandhi's first and second rule for a civil resister are significant in this regard: '1. A civil resister will harbour no anger. 2. He will suffer the anger of the opponent'. *Selected Political Writings*, ed. by D. Dalton (Indianapolis: Hackett, 1996), p. 81.

22 Cf. Levinas, E.: *Otherwise than Being or Beyond Essence*, trans. by A. Lingis (Pittsburgh: Duquesne University Press, 1998), p. 49.

23 Aristotle: *Nichomachean Ethics*, trans. Thomson, J. A. K. & Tredennick, H. (London: Penguin, 1953), 1125b32–33.

24 Ibid., 1108a4–8.

25 Arendt, op. cit., p. 63: 'only when our sense of justice is offended do we react with rage'.

26 Cf. Horder, J., op. cit., pp. 69, 85, 109f.

27 Gandhi sees this clearly. He states: 'When a person claims to be non-violent, he is expected not to be angry with one who has injured him', op. cit., p. 44.

28 Cf. Horder, J., op. cit., p. 30.

29 Sartre again sees this clearly in his discussion of the death of the negro Christmas in Faulkner's *Light in August*. Cf. *Being and Nothingness*, op. cit., pp. 405f.

30 Arendt, H.: *The Human Condition* (Chicago: University of Chicago Press, 1998), ch. 5.

Felix Ó Murchadha

Afterword

An afterword is not a conclusion; it does not tie up loose ends. Rather, it is a word of reflection looking back on the course of a book. The aim is to bring the contributions to this volume into dialogue with one another. This task is all the more pressing because of the different styles of discourse and of approach evident in this volume. Such difference reflects the diversity of voices within the philosophical debate on violence. The task of this Afterword is to show how fruitful a debate between such voices might be.

The contributions to this volume are diverse both in their thematic focus and methodological approach. Nonetheless, over and over again issues of responsibility, vulnerability, security, belonging and identity arise in these articles. Furthermore, the contributions to this volume can be usefully discussed in terms of the relative emphases they place on the position of the perpetrator, the victim and the witness of violence.

I will begin this Afterword with a discussion of Ted Honderich's contribution. Honderich offers a not alone a justification of violence, but of a particular form of violence, which – in the Western world at least – is generally considered unjustified and unjustifiable. Starting from his position we may come to see some of the fundamental issues which this interplay of violence and discourse, the use of force and its justification and condemnation, gives rise. I will begin therefore with a fairly lengthy discussion of his article (1) before going on to discuss victimhood and the place of the witness in violence, widening out the discussion to include the issue of the place of the philosopher in respect of violence (2). To be a victim (or witness) of violence is to be vulnerable in some way. Such vulnerability is addressed in many of the contributions, particularly in relation to embodiment. That will form the theme of the third section (3). The final part will draw the discussion to a close by focusing on the paradoxical interrelation of intimacy and impersonality in violence (4).

1. Honderich on Terrorism

Ted Honderich's recent writings on terrorism have sparked heated debate. This is particularly true in Germany where the leading publisher Suhrkamp withdrew the translation of *After the Terror* because of charges that it was anti-Semitic in its defence of suicide bombing. The latter charge is without foundation and merely serves to foreclose debate on the position Honderich articulates.[1] The main points of that position are contained in his contribution to this volume.

The key concept which structures this argument is announced in the title 'terrorism for humanity'.[2] Any meaningful engagement with Honderich's argument must first consider that notion and the consequent position he articulates on innocent victims. It is only in the light of such considerations that the defence he offers of the actual practice of suicide bombing by Palestinian terrorists can be discussed.

It must be acknowledged at the outset that any notion of 'terrorism for humanity' is a provocative one. For one thing terrorism is generally considered to be against humanity, even by those who may defend it in certain instances. Specifically – and this is a point to which I will return – terrorism is considered dehumanising, both to its victims and its perpetrators. Victims in this case do not just include those who are directly injured, but also those who suffer under the terror of imminent attack.[3] Terrorism cannot be identified with revolutionary violence – the fact that it is generally so used is as Michael Walzer puts it 'a small victory for the champions of order, among whom the uses of terror are by no means unknown'.[4] The current 'war on terror', with its implications that terrorists are the other side, those set on undermining the state (albeit with the help of so-called 'rogue states'), follows the logic of this 'small victory'. Honderich clearly rejects this identification and makes no distinction in principle between revolutionary and state terror. Of course the fact that states can act in a terroristic manner does not in itself lead to the conclusion of indifference between the two. I will return to this point later. Important in this context is that whether practiced by the state or by revolutionary groups, terrorism is generally considered as demeaning to humanity in a way that war is not or at least in a more profound way than war usually is. The analogy to war is not accidental as Honderich himself makes use of just war type arguments.

While up to recent times the rules – if not the practice – of military engagement were clear about the distinction between combatants and non-combatants, this distinction has become very blurred with the rise of total war in the past century or more.[5] Terrorism functions precisely through a denial of such a distinction. It is true that terrorist groups do still speak the language of 'legitimate targets', but when the field of legitimate targets becomes so wide as to include practically anybody, then we can say that the term has lost all meaning – rarely at any rate are such definitions of legitimate targets commensurate with combatants alone. When we still distinguish between combatant and non-combatant the target of attack is being recognised in terms of his position or his actions. In the case of terrorism the person injured or killed is not a victim due to his or her actions or position, rather his or her suffering is a 'message' delivered to the opposing side. That suffering has no other meaning. The victim is reduced to a suffering or lifeless mass of flesh. The aim is to reduce often a whole people to something close to the state of the actual victims: dismembered, confused, disorientated, unfit for any relations of human solidarity or the pursuit of the good.[6] In contrast the aim of a battle commander may be simply the gaining of certain territory, with as few casualties as possible.[7] While we may be sceptical of the glory of wounds of war, those who feel pride in military service do so because they fought bravely in what they understand to have been a just war; the person who loses an arm in a car bomb has no such human values to comprehend his victimhood. We need have no romantic views of warfare to see a difference here and one which pertains to the humanity of the victim. To kill an innocent person is to kill someone not because of his who she is – her actions and position, but simply because of what her suffering represents. The 'innocent' person by definition does not play any active role here; she is useful only for the screams of agony and/or the splattering of her blood and the crumbling of her bones.

Honderich would wish to question the use of innocence here. In one sense this may seem peripheral to his argument as he defends the killing of innocents in the case that the greater good – the good of humanity – is served. But, if I am not mistaken, part of the strength of this argument rests on his account of half-innocents. Half-innocents are in his terms non-combatants, i.e., are not in the army, police etc., but 'are by choice or consent benefiting or profiting from wrongful killings by their state or their people' (26). The power of Honderich's argument for this goes back to a position worked out in his famous essay, 'Our Omissions, their Violence' (republished as 'Our Omissions, their Terrorism').[8] Here Honderich argues for the moral equivalence of omissions and acts. He further argues that the terrorist's response of *tu quoque* is not without validity. If by our omissions we contribute to the misery against which they are fighting, we are implicated in the violence we are condemning. Non-combatants are thus redefined as half-innocents. They are innocent in the sense that they do not actively engage in acts which contribute to the misery of those on whose behalf terrorism is taking place, but by 'choice or consent' they benefit from those acts and omit to take any action to alleviate this misery. It is hard to see how anyone – with the exception of children and people mentally incapable of moral responsibility can escape from this category of half-innocence (except into a more culpable one). Hardly a day passes in the life of a reasonably prosperous citizen of a western country that he or she does not benefit or profit from wrongful killings or at least degradations. To say that one benefits without consent would need a strong quasi-Stoic defence, which I do not think Honderich would accept. If the aim of terrorism is the good of humanity, and this means some degree of equal access to human goods, then all deliberate deprivations of these goods seem relevant in defining half-innocents. In this case, as Honderich makes clear, most of the West falls under the category of half-innocents and terrorist actions on behalf of the peoples of Sub-Saharan Africa would be potentially justifiable on Honderich's terms.

A half-innocent may respond that he certainly cannot claim innocence, but that his 'guilt' is more a matter of what he *is* than what he has *done*. He was born into the prosperous North and benefits from this birth, but this does not make him responsible for it. He may or may not play his own small role in helping to change the situation. He cannot be expected however, to give away all the benefits of his birth. To expect this would be to expect an act of exceptional moral rectitude. If we are to take Honderich at his word, then the expectation of such exceptional moral rectitude is the outcome of moral reasoning, specifically the generalisability of such reasoning. But unless we are to throw out the principle 'ought implies can', then there are difficulties here. This is so because before any act there is a 'guilt' which no action can undo. So long as to be white for example means to be privileged then nothing short of self-annihilation can undo this situation. A white person might struggle to achieve a global society with equal access to the primary human goods, but until that goal is achieved she remains a legitimate target of terrorist attack. For all practical purposes this amounts to a legitimation of a reign of terror into the foreseeable future, provided that the reasonable chance of success has been demonstrated. But this latter qualification is vague enough to allow for a quasi-permanent terrorist war. Honderich's argument leads to a parallel claim to the advocates of the 'war on terror': the justification of a struggle without foreseeable end, potentially consisting of an ever spiralling cycle of violence. This is not to place the two positions on the same moral level, but it is rather to suggest that Honderich has grasped philosophically the nature of the present situation in a manner, which points to a horrifying future. All critique of Honderich to one side, there seems to be a truth to his analysis, the full horror of which he himself has not perhaps fully seen.

Honderich has a further argument for the justifiability of the killing not alone of half-innocents, but also of innocents. The argument has I think two components. The first acknowledges the emotional force of the horror occasioned by terrorist (specifically suicide-bombing) attacks. Honderich is clear that such emotional responses are not at all out of place here; in fact they are necessary in making moral judgements.[9] But at the same time he insists that to fixate on such emotions, and to ignore both the suffering out of which these attacks emerge and the emotional responses exposure to such suffering gives rise to, is a culpable blindness. What the latter emotion teaches us is that inequalities and injustices are outrages, which should be responded to with vigorous action. If terrorist violence is in certain situations the only possible response to this situation, then such violence is at least potentially justifiable. But even assuming that there are such cases, where there is no other option but for physical violence,[10] then we must nonetheless ask whether or not there are limits – quasi-absolute limits – to what violence is justifiable. If there is a logic of retribution, in which misery is to be repaid with equal misery, that seems again understandable, but hardly justifiable or even viable.

The second argument is a more consequentialist one: if the killing of some innocents will lead to greater good then it may be justifiable. It is certainly the case that 'we ourselves' (i.e., Western nations) have justified such killings during the first and second world wars (and most recently during the Iraq war) on this basis, as Honderich argues (28f.). But it is not clear even on the terms in which they were made that these arguments were correct. Arguably modern terrorism began with the bombings of Dresden and Cologne and the destruction of Hiroshima and Nagasaki in World War Two. But for Honderich the argument is deeper. For him it is a question of ends and those ends he attempts to describe in terms of a 'morality of humanity'. Such a morality is based on the principle that 'we must take actually rational steps, which is to say effective and economical ones, to get people out of defined lives of wretchedness and other deprivation.'(31) Certain acts of terrorism, Honderich claims, have or may have such an aim. And to the extent to which they do they are at least candidates for being right.

Faced with a choice to kill an innocent person or let hundreds die, the tendency of the consequentialist argument is to say that the killing of an innocent person is or may be justified. In the standard type of consequentialist scenario the killing of an innocent person has a *specific* and *direct* consequence of the saving of others. Honderich, however, can offer no such case. In the situation in question, Palestinian suicide bombing, the consequence is a *possible* alleviation of living conditions, a *possible* step towards equality of access to human goods, which however is not certain and is definitely not immediate. In other words, not alone does 'a world go out of existence' (28), but there is no clear expectation of a new world coming into being with every life taken in such attacks. In fact the immediate consequence is more death, namely the death through reprisals by the Israeli army. Obviously, that is not the direct responsibility of Hamas or whichever group is engaged in the bombing, but it is surely a consequence, which must play a part in the thinking of those who engage in these attacks.

The present, in short, is being sacrificed for an indefinite future. In a sense this is characteristic of much of human action and indeed much political and military violence: in the interests of peace and happiness in the future, war and terror are practiced in the present. The higher the goal being aimed at the higher the threshold of acceptable violence to reach it. This has a paradoxical effect:[11] not alone does the ideal being aimed at justify violence in the present, but the extent of that violence undermines the very possibility of that ideal. This is not an argument that violence never achieves anything, which is manifestly false. Rather, it is an argument to the effect that if that which is to be achieved is understood such as to trump all other considerations – as the principle of humanity appears to do – then the argument against acts of violence to achieve that goal are progressively undermined. In that case no level of violence seems too great to achieve this end. But the ideal being aimed at is one of equality and hence of nonviolence that, however, requires levels of civility and solidarity, which limitless violence makes less and less possible.

Honderich is claiming that the avowed end of certain terrorist organisations is to bring certain populations up to the level of common human aspirations. In doing so they are depriving others of access to their aspirations, indeed in differing measures to all six of the human aspirations which he lists. This includes those who are innocent of causing suffering or benefiting from it. While a simple equation of violence or suffering ignores the political realities of oppressor and oppressed, at the same time suffering cannot in itself justify the infliction of suffering. Terrorism must both aim to reduce the levels of suffering in the world and be capable of achieving this end, if it is to be a candidate for goodness. Let us accept the first part of the proposition in the case of at least some terrorist organisations.[12] The second part is much more difficult to defend. By targeting innocent and half-innocent people the terrorist organisation is making a clear statement: nobody is safe. What this challenges is a basic tenet of the state, namely that one of its major functions is to give security to its citizens. The response of the state is almost always to become more repressive. The repression of the state further justifies the terrorist organisation and a cycle of violence and counter-violence threatens to spiral out of control. Once this happens the danger of a collapse into a quasi-Hobbesian state of nature is very real. This is so because terrorism does not so much take the killing of innocents as an unfortunate consequence of its actions; it is based on such killing. This is the lesson from Dresden and Hiroshima: for terrorism to work there can be no boundaries between innocent and non-innocent. Once this is accepted then all are guilty and all are targets. To accept this consequence is to undermine the basis of democracy itself.

Elsewhere, Honderich argues for the compatability of democracy and terrorism on the basis that terrorism generally is involved in the coercion of persuasion not of force.[13] In effect terrorism does not force governments to change policy, what it does do is give those who are without influence more influence than they would have otherwise. Certainly Honderich is right to point to the context of inequality of influence in the origins of terrorism, and right also to pour scorn on the defences of our democracies' claims to fostering equality; it nonetheless seems to conflate matters to describe terrorism as a force of persuasion. Persuasion Honderich understands as leaving room for reflection and decision. More positively, however, persuasion within a democracy requires a belief in the relative safety of the citizen and the again relative (i.e., within certain limits) freedom to persuade and be persuaded. Terrorist organisations tend to undermine both.

This brings us to Honderich's comparison of the cases of the Hamas suicide bomber and the crew member in an Israeli helicopter gunship (38–41). He claims that there is no moral difference between the killing of a passer-by in the one case and the killing of an innocent civilian in the other. I think Honderich is right in this, but I think that there is a *political* difference, which has some moral bearing. Both of these acts I take (with Honderich in the case of the latter, against him in the case of the former) to be morally wrong, because in both instances innocent people are killed and in neither case can such taking of innocent life be justified in the interests of a greater good. Honderich is right to deny the relevance of intention here: the helicopter crew-member by shooting a rocket into a crowded street knows or should be expected to know that this act may bring about the deaths of innocent civilians. The suicide bomber brings about such deaths as well. If the helicopter crew member could have brought about the death of the Hamas leader without killing innocent civilians he would supposedly have done so, but so too, Honderich retorts, the suicide bomber would have acted in an other manner to bring about her ends, if they were available to her (39f.).

There is a disanalogy here though. The political judgement in one case is that the Hamas leader should be killed, in the other is that suicide bombing of civilian targets should be practiced. Once that political judgement is made then questions arise as to what are the moral constraints on such actions. In the second case those moral constraints cannot involve not killing civilians, in the former case they can. Is this significant? It cuts both ways. On the one hand, those who ordered the helicopter attack may retain their political judgement and still not on this particular occasion engage in the attack because it would involve the death of civilians. Hence, by going ahead with the attack they are unnecessarily breaking a moral precept. The same cannot be said in the case of the suicide bomber, whose political judgement entails the death of civilians. On the other hand, the political judgement of the Israelis is not necessarily morally repugnant, while in the case of the suicide bomber it is (assuming the death of innocent civilians is *prima facie* wrong). The political decision to destroy the leadership of Hamas may or may not be either morally right or politically far sighted, but that political decision does not entail the deaths of innocents.

Certain other political decisions of the Israeli state in relation to water, economic development etc., however do entail the deaths of innocents. Both sides are waging war on innocents, and, to repeat, the distinction must be upheld between the violence of the oppressor and the oppressed. But in waging this war both are undermining the basis of any political order this side of totalitarian terror. This is so because none of us are innocent. But the legitimacy of our security cannot simply be gainsaid. This is not simply in our interests, but in the interests of humanity itself.

I remain then unconvinced by Honderich's arguments. They represent however a powerful attempt to justify violence and to do so on consequentialist grounds. Furthermore, as I have suggested, Honderich's analysis is depressingly realistic: the alternatives to terrorist violence, the possibilities of peaceful coexistence seem more remote in today's world. While Honderich wishes us to re-think our use of 'innocence', at the same time he invites us to widen our view of the victims to include the terrorists themselves and the communities which they represent.

2.   Victims and Witnesses

If one of Honderich's principle contributions to the debate regarding terrorism is to problematise the notion of innocence and show how it is ideologically employed, in doing so he brings to light the dynamic relation between violence, victims and justifications. In effect the justification of violence rests on the claim to victimisation. Violence, it is claimed, is a justifiable response to that victimisation in certain circumstances. In this sense the victim plays a pivotal role: while the suffering of the victim tends to discredit attempts to justify it, the suffering of other victims tend to do the opposite. It would be too easy to speak here of vicious circles. The attempts at justification – on the part of the perpetrators of violence themselves and on the part of philosophers reflecting on their acts – are, however, not simply after-thoughts. The act of violence is so rupturing of human relations that its perpetrators, victims and witnesses are driven to discourses of explanation, if not justification. Philosophical approaches to violence are likewise so driven, driven it might be said out of their natural homes in rational discourse to take account of that which ruptures such discourse, which points to circumstances where such discourse is not enough or is not perceived to be enough. There is after all another innocence that of the rational being ignorant of the fury and the despair which may drive someone to acts of great violence. Such an innocence must itself be questioned not alone as a condition, but also as an ideal state to be aimed at. Since the ultimate justification of violence is non-violence, that is the state beyond victimhood to which violence must aim if it is to be anything other than an expression of that fury, the very ideal of non-violent rational agreement itself functions ironically as a justification of, if not a catalyst to, violence.

Bernhard Waldenfels closes his contribution with a quote from the Spanish author Jorge Semprun: 'There are just wars, but no innocent armies' (91). Waldenfels cautions against what he terms the 'over-rationalisation of violence' through which violence is justified. As he puts it 'one relies on a *felix violentia* which, similar to the *felix culpa*, is on the path towards a non-violent order and derives its justification from this fact'(89). Justifications of violence, according to Waldenfels, function by making violence in some sense felicitous because it is claimed it will bring about an ultimately non-violent order. Such justifications increase violence in the interests of non-violence. Waldenfels is here articulating a concern which relates to the very place of the philosopher himself reflecting on violence. Between him and Honderich there appears to be a fundamental difference in the understanding of the place of the philosopher, one which is more or less reproduced in some of the other contributions to this volume corresponding, perhaps, to the distinction between analytic and continental philosophers. While Honderich understands the question of violence for the philosopher to do mainly with arguments as to its justification or otherwise, Waldenfels sees the phenomenon of violence as already saturated with attempted justifications. For the latter the philosopher's role is not to add to these justifications, but rather to understand them as belonging to the very phenomenon which is to be understood. The philosopher needs to bring out the meaning of this phenomenon to, as Waldenfels himself puts it, 'question [...] how violence appears, how it invades the field of experience and how it is expressed in language' (74). There is a clear methodological difference here, but one which is rooted in something more fundamental: for Waldenfels the place of the philosopher is as witness,[14] for Honderich it is the role of the defence or prosecution lawyer as his analogy of the law court makes clear. As witness the philosopher is no *mere* observer. She experiences the harm done by violence as calling forth an account which does not so much try to make sense of the violence as testify to its horror, its disruption, its destruction. This amounts to two different models of engagement one based in a confidence in the power of a justificatory reason,[15] the other suspicious of such reason as constitutive of the very violence that is being investigated. For the philosopher who follows the latter course there can be no clear line between his place as a philosopher and that of the violence he is discussing. Language too does violence, the language about violence can blur into the language *of* violence (75). The philosopher can in this respect claim no special innocence.

This difference though is not as clear-cut as may at first appear. Despite Honderich's appeal to the place of defence and prosecutor, by arguing for a responsibility which knows no degrees, he in effect places the philosopher too in the place of witness. It is striking how continental philosophers such as Levinas, Derrida and Waldenfels on the one hand, and analytic philosophers such as Honderich, Glover and Harris on the other, have thematised the issue of conflicting responsibilities and have come to equally 'excessive' conclusions. According to the latter theorists, there are instances where omitting to act is as morally culpable as acting. But in that case what of the philosopher writing his books, say about omitting actions? In choosing to write a book and not say spend that time volunteering for Oxfam, is he not guilty of an omitting act? There is not a clear-cut answer to this question, but the question does raise again the issue of responsibility: how responsible are any of our actions, even those of doing philosophy.

Vittorio Bufacchi in his contribution attempts also to negotiate the claims to absolute responsibility. Arguing against what he sees as a 'moral absolutism' inherent in the positions of Harris, Honderich and Glover, Bufacchi defends a moral gradualist thesis. According to Bufacchi there are degrees of responsibility, which are determined by the nature of the omitting act itself. This in effect means that there are degrees of innocence: while omitting to help someone may in certain circumstances be morally equivalent to harming them, this is not always the case. Where conflicting responsibilities emerge – as (to use Bufacchi's own example) between my duty as a spouse to provide a holiday for my partner and my responsibility for the starving in the Third World – then I may act in a manner which (by failing to help) actually leads to harm without being morally culpable for that. This is not to say that I am innocent in respect of the starving in the Third World, but it is to say that *whatever* my actions may be, innocence is not going to be my reward. Although Bufacchi does discuss cases where the omitting act is that of a perpetrator – as in the case of the son withholding medical treatment from his dying father – his main focus is on the place of the witness. He focuses on the example of bystanders of the holocaust. Bufacchi argues that the level of culpability of bystanders varies in this case to the extent to which they were asked to help Jews fleeing the Nazis or were not asked. There are in short degrees of responsibility and hence degrees of innocence on the part of witnesses.

The intuition which Bufacchi's attempts to defend is that our responsibilities to those with whom we are in direct relationship may, and in many cases do, outweigh our responsibilities to total strangers (once being asked to help, then the potential victim is not longer an anonymous 'Jew', but a particular individual or set of individuals). This is a common intuition. Bufacchi defends it by claiming that while it would be viable for example to spend the money he was going to use to take his wife on holiday on third world relief, to do so would be to fail in his duty of being a good husband. One might of course argue that what he should really do is convince his wife that the need of the hungry for aid is greater than hers for a holiday, but we can see where such an argumentation eventually breaks down: the richness of our lives comes – in part, perhaps in large part – from the intimacy of our personal relations, to sacrifice them would be to sacrifice what makes life worthwhile. But what is the moral standing of such relationships, what makes them – morally speaking – anything other than a form of egotism?

Just as Bufacchi tackles the moral absolutism of Honderich et al., Burkhard Liebsch addresses the claims regarding absolute responsibility which we find in Levinas and Derrida. The reduction of 're-sponsibility to different orders of responsibility which [...] allow us to measure, to calculate and distribute it' is, he says, the 'dream of "every good conscience"' (147). This, however, Liebsch contends is precisely a dream. Responsibility allows for no such limitations. Drawing on the work of the French philosopher Emmanuel Levinas, he suggests that the implication of this is not unlimited freedom, but rather unlimited responsibility for the other. To the extent to which I exist, I take a place which ultimately I do not deserve, I have asserted myself above the other, I am in a relation of violence towards the other. I have referred already to the quasi-Hobbesian state of nature in which Honderich seems to transport us and which Starr contends leads us to increasing levels of violence (63); in his contribution Liebsch addresses the manner in which Hobbes has changed the moral universe in a way which again undermines the stability which our 'good consciences' demand. Once we no longer accept a teleological system of goods as exemplified by Aristotle and contemporary Neo-Aristotelians, then our responsibilities to the other are no longer limited by his or her place in the moral universe. Rather, the demand of the other is unrestricted to levels of intimacy, friendship or belonging. Such a demand is operative even if I reject it. My freedom as an ethical subject begins with my response to this demand on me. This demand as we can see is indeed unlimited. At every moment there are strangers who are suffering, who need to be cared for. My excessive responsibility is to respond to all these demands. But of course the problem is that I cannot. To respond to such an excessive responsibility would be precisely to do nothing, because in any action I might make I am choosing to help one person rather than an other. If the demand of the other is unlimited then I can never do justice to it (146). My freedom is precisely manifest in how I answer these demands: 'Unlimited responsibility calls for restricted responsibility in order not to collapse in irresponsibility' (ibid). The issue for Liebsch is how to negotiate between this unlimited responsibility, on the one hand, and my concrete social and political responsibilities, on the other. This, as Liebsch sees it, leads to new and perplexing questions of violence. While Levinas is right, he claims, to reject an abstract opposition of freedom and responsibility, he failed to see the 'unexpected forms of violence' which arise once freedom is conceived in the way he does. 'An excessive demand of the other can only be answered by way of a forcible restriction which seems to be doomed to do violence to the unlimited appeal of the other' (149). This for Liebsch means that there is always a violence in the ethical itself and this violence is tied up with the imperative to decide between competing demands. What this entails is that the self is always violent in its relation to the other, through a rejection of the other's claims, a rejection which in the end is without reason and arbitrary.

In relation to the other the self responds but inevitably and simultaneously determines the limits of that response. The self determines himself in relation to the other and such self-determination does violence against the other. Diane Enns quotes the following from the introduction of an influential collection edited by Sam Weber and Hent de Vries:[16] 'violence would come to pass not in the passage *from* self to other, much less in that from other to self, but perhaps in the very attempt to delineate the border that separate self *from* other' (173, n. 8). In other words, the origins of violence lie prior to my self-defence or 'their' attack, but precisely in the way in which this distinction between me/us and them is made. If this is so, then the claim to innocence is based on a forgetting of the setting of such distinctions and their ultimate lack of sufficient basis.

While it is not possible to respond to everyone, the one cut off and left alone loses the capacity to make such differentiations, the whole world becomes hostile because the whole world was of no help when the victim needed help the most. Degrees of responsibility matter not at all to the victim. The victim of violence is often faced with what appears to be a total irresponsibility and indifference. The world, once experienced as a safe and secure place, becomes an alien realm in which the very ties of love and friendship, which Bufacchi emphasised (108), become hollow and empty. Enns in her contribution examines cases in which violence undoes the identity of the victim. This undoing is directly related to the lack of help of others, hence not alone the perpetrator's actions but the bystanders/witnesses inactions (both during and in the aftermath of the violence) contribute the victim's trauma. This does not just refer to actual inaction: that once one can be displaced from the human community means that it can occur again, the future becomes seen as unpredictable and potentially hostile. The event of violence which fragments and disrupts the identity of the victim actually reveals a truth about the contingency of any such identity. In this way such events are not simply to be expelled and undone: they disclose a vulnerability to violation which is at the basis of any human community. In that sense acts of violence reveal fundamental truths about human relations. The overcoming of trauma amounts to the recognition of such truths, which in the case of particularly horrific events makes recovery extremely difficult. But there is no avoiding such recognition in any facile attempt to conceive of violence as some sort of reversal to nature which can be overcome.[17]

Common to the investigations of Enns and Waldenfels is the recognition that the question of violence directly concerns the order of human relations. Violence is not simply to be pressed to the margins of human relations as irrational animality or as a contingent part of human history. Rather, the very contingency of the order of human relations, a contingency which is distinctive of relations of identity and belonging in human societies, means that violence is constitutive of those relations. The order of human relations is inherently contestable. It is so because every such order is a contingent, historical development. How we relate to one another is not written in stone nor is it inscribed in our human nature, but rather is the result of an instituting of orders of relations between people and such an instituting never takes place without violence. To speak concretely, why should women in many parts of the world look after the home and children, why should some people live in mansions and others on the street, why are parts of the world wealthy and other parts of the world poor, why are homosexuals generally discriminated against, why is there a separation of church and state, why in some countries is there no such separation. To all these questions there is no answer in terms of human nature, but rather answers in terms of contingent historical developments through which a certain order of things was imposed and is kept in place by violence. Not indeed by violence alone, but none of those or other developments would have been possible without violence and their maintenance demands at least the potential use of violence. The violence here is two-fold: on the one hand, the very instituting and maintaining of an order of things is violent in the sense that there can never be a good enough reason for such instituting or such maintenance. Where reasons run out there is nothing left but arbitrary decision which imposes on people a certain way of being. This way of being may not be experienced as violent; it may seem the most natural thing in the world. But if it is experienced as violent then the second element of violence in such institutionalisation becomes evident: when people resist by questioning and challenging the place they have been allotted in the social, political, economic order then they are almost invariably met with overt violence of some sort. The place of victims and witnesses of violence is not marginal to human relations, but rather is at the very core of those historically contingent orders, which are challenged and defended with more and more ferocious violence depending on the stakes involved.

3.   Vulnerability, Embodiment, Identity

Human relations are characterised by their vulnerability. Precisely the extent of the human capacity to develop and mould the interrelations of social, economic, political life, as well as the nature of class, gender and ethnic relationships, disclose the contingency of these arrangements and the vulnerability of those who uphold and who subvert them. The very possibility of human interrelations is based on vulnerability; so too is the violence which disrupts them.

Pretensions to immunity from violence are ungrounded. Introducing the topic of violence, Waldenfels employs the language of infection. Violence, he says, is like a foreign body (78). This captures something important about violence, that it seems to come from outside, that it disrupts and disturbs. Violence targets a vulnerability. Only a vulnerable being can be the victim of violence (and possibly only such a being can be its perpetrator). Importantly, vulnerable being is an embodied being. The suicide bomber and his victims are all embodied beings but through the detonation of the bomb their embodiment is transformed, the fragile unity of their bodily beings is revealed. So too is something else. An embodied being is a lived body, in Merleau-Ponty's terms, he acts and lives through his body.

This is the body of the 'I can', again to employ Merleau-Ponty's terms.[18] But this capacity of the body is transformed in violence. The capable body is also the body, which is affected, which suffers. But violence by making the body suffer cannot alone kill and maim it, but can reduce it to little more than suffering, little more than screaming, searing flesh. This transformation into flesh (*not* in the later Merleau-Ponty's sense) is detailed by Diane Enns in relation to the victim of rape and the victim of the concentration camps. While recognising the differences, Enns (cf. p. 162) stresses the common process here of a stripping away of everything that makes human life what it is and a revealing through such a stripping away of a brute, physical facticity, characterised only by pain. This stripping away consists not alone in discrete acts of violence, be they physical, sexual, psychological or whatever, but rather in disorientation in the world. The world is no longer a secure place, but a constant source of penetration and infection. As embodied beings we live necessarily in dependence on the world around us and we depend on a certain constancy in that world for our well-being. The 'pain of violation' of which Enns speaks is primarily the trauma of infection through which the world in which we belong becomes no longer the place of nourishment, but the source of infection.

Such a characterisation of violence as violation runs as a common theme through the contributions of Waldenfels, Liebsch and Enns. To engage in an act of violence in this conception is to violate someone. Once we see things in those terms, we are faced with is a pre-legal, pre-moral claim of the other on us. To violate such claims is to violate a person, it is to invade that person. That invasion can itself be constitutive, can form our bodies, as, to use Waldenfel's example, through forced labour (82). This forms a relation of self and other, a relation of violation and resistance.

Enns – following the Italian philosophy Giorgio Agamben – is pointing to the unrealisability of any ultimate belonging as revealed by cases such as those of Susan Brison. But there are degrees here of belonging and not belonging. Violence can serve to totally exclude whole sections of people from society, most radically in the case of genocide, but also insidiously by a refusal of their identities. The latter is the case outlined by Talia Bettcher. As she points out in her contribution, violence can be as much about identity enforcement as of undoing identity. The case she is examining is that of transgendered people, those who dress and act as a gender opposite to their sexual organ identity. A common form of violence against such people consists in (or begins with) forced sexual identification by which their genitals are exposed in order to determine their 'true' identity. Not alone do such people not accept such identification, but they are caught in what Bettcher calls a double bind: either disclose who one is and be seen as a pretender/masquerader or refuse to disclose and run the risk of enforced disclosure and run the risk of being exposed as a liar (187). Identity, as Bettcher makes clear, is a matter of visibility and invisibility: to have an identity is to be identifiable to an other, to be 'visible'[19] to that other. But at least as concerns sexual identity, that visibility cloaks an invisibility: outer appearance hides genital identity, but points to it, communicates it. Transgendered people cannot be visible in this sense: their visible appearance understood in terms of the binary opposition of gender based on genital 'reality', can only deceive or mislead. As Bettcher puts it: 'given the gender appearance – sexed body reality contrast, one is always already a liar' (189). What Bettcher points to is a dissonance between authenticity and honesty. If honesty is understood in terms of being what you appear, then it is literally impossible for transpeople to be what they appear (at least in our society). As she states:

> To what extent does the tactic of self-revelation, when represented as unproblematically valuable, require of transpeople an oppressively impossible honesty? Surely secrecy, duplicity, and deception ought to be recognised as important tactics in not only personal survival, but in resistant politics more generally (189).

The term 'oppressively impossible honesty' should make us pause here: in the context in which Bettcher is speaking the difficulty she is pointing to is clear. But – without diminishing the specificity of Bettcher's concerns – is it not the case that all social relations require something less than total honesty? If our reflections upon violence lead us to consider it anything other than marginal in human relations, we need to ask what does violence disclose about human relations? For Bettcher, identity is secured through a notion of visibility in which authenticity is understood as the isomorphism between visible appearance and invisible reality. It is striking that the accounts of violence from which Enns draws, Jean Amery and Susan Brison, both stress the need for concealment, both could share the suspicion expressed here of 'oppressively impossible honesty'. If the world can be infectious as much as nurturing, perhaps deception is a necessary part of the human 'immune system'. As embodied beings human beings are subject metaphorically as well as literally to viruses, viruses of violence in respect to which the other, no matter how intimate remains a stranger.

4.   Violence both Intimate and Impersonal

There is in violence both a cold impersonality and a shocking intimacy. In exposing the vulnerability of his victim the perpetrator strips away the layers of mediation between social agents, in pain the victim can often do nothing else than plead to the person of her attacker; yet in that very intimacy the perpetrator refuses the personhood of the victim – in Levinasian terms refuses her face – and reduces her to screaming flesh. Of course, as Waldenfels points out, the level of impersonality can be taken to such extremes that the victim is far distant from the perpetrator, who presses a button to launch a missile (85). Furthermore, as Starr points out, anonymity can provide an important condition for violence (62). Nonetheless, such a perpetrator to the extent to which he recognises his actions – understands that is the difference between launching a missile and playing a computer game and that his victim is not simply a stranger 'places' himself with the victim.

  Eve Garrard in exploring the relations between violence, cruelty and evil suggests that evil is characterised by a moral blindness of the perpetrator as to the moral reasons for not acting the way he does. It is this which captures the sense in which evil acts are not alone wrong, but 'evoke[s] from us a particular kind of horror' (116). This horror discloses something outside of the normal fallibility of human actions and intentions; it discloses that which cuts the perpetrators of such acts off from normal human relations. If one of the moral reasons for not acting is the vulnerability of the victim, that is the wrongness of taking advantage of that vulnerability and possibly of causing pain through that vulnerability, then the perpetrator is blind to what that vulnerability says to him. The vulnerable body of another calls to the perpetrator not to cause it suffering. That is the ambiguity of vulnerability, it both invites and prohibits violation. The lack of sensitivity to this ambiguity in the response of the perpetrator is I take it – in part at least – what makes up the state of mind of the perpetrator of an evil act. A similar lack of sensitivity is essential to cruelty. Essential to cruelty for Garrard is a 'taking pleasure in [...] the serious and unmerited suffering of the victim' (127). Violence is not always evil and cruelty is not always violent. Nevertheless, the paradigmatic cases of evil involve violence (118f.). This is, as Garrard states, not accidental (129).

That evil in paradigmatic cases involves violence is not accidental for reasons which I think Enns' and Waldenfel's analysis make clear: violence is a violation of the vulnerability of the victim, who stripped of all else appeals through that very vulnerability in a strange intimacy to the perpetrator to respond to him not as a friend or an enemy, a combatant or a non-combatant, an innocent or a half-innocent, but as an other person whose appeal is beyond all categories which serve to regulate responsibility and in that moment at least calls on the absolute responsibility not to harm. This appeal may or may not be responded to. It may not be responded to with justification: a Hitler, a Pol Pot, a Stalin would appeal to us in the same way. But the appeal tells us something about violence and why it is both ubiquitous and for the most part wrong.

Violence erupts often unexpectedly in all forms of human relations. It is a phenomenon which seems to know no set limits either in scale or in scope. As such it calls into question many of our deepest held assumptions about innocence, responsibility, and security. The authors gathered in this collection pursue these questions rigorously and open up the new and fascinating avenues of future research and debate.

Endnotes

1   On this debate see the report on the *Deutsche Welle* at the website: www.dw-world.de/dw/article/0,,943605,00.html. For Honderich's response to this debate see his '*After the Terror*: The Fall and Rise of a Book in Germany' at the website: http://www.ucl.ac.uk/~uctytho/BrumlikSumbyTH.html

2   Significantly he has issued a new edition of his book *Violence for Equality* under the title *Terrorism for Humanity – inquiries in political philosophy* (London: Pluto Press, 2003).

3   Honderich himself does not consider the causing of fear to be essential to the definition of terrorism, as he tends to equate political violence and terrorism. However, in the case of Palestinian terrorism is intended to cause terror. Cf. Honderich: *Terrorism for Humanity*, p. 154f.

4   Walzer, M.: *Just and unjust wars: a moral argument with historical illustrations* (New York: Basic Books, 1992), p. 197.

5   On the bombing of civilian targets during World War Two cf. Glover: Humanity: a moral history of the twentieth century (London: Pimlico, 2001), pp. 69–88.

6   E.g. Jerusalem at the height of the suicide-bombing campaign

7   I am not in any way attempting to romanticise war and I am well aware that terrible atrocities occur in war. My point is, however, that the aims of war are generally to achieve a certain territorial advantage, the cost in lives is irrelevant to that aim; the aim of a terrorist (in the case of no-warning attacks) is to do nothing other than to cause injury and death.

8   *Violence for Equality* (London: Routledge, 1989).

9   See ibid, pp. 7–8.

10   This seems to me to be a questionable assumption, at least when we consider terrorist violence over an extended period. While there may be situations in which violence is the only option, frequently the continuation of violence has much to do with struggles for power within the oppressed community.

11   Waldenfels makes a similar point in his contribution to this volume, cf. p. 91.

12   The goals of terrorist organisations such as Hamas, IRA, Tamil Tigers, El Queda, etc. are more varied in fact than Honderich gives them credit for. A terrorist organisation, however, is concerned not with humanity as a whole but with a certain section of humanity. It seems naïve to claim even that it is concerned with the whole of a certain section, say the Palestinians, or Northern Irish nationalists. Generally – and in both these cases – they oppose others within their community and turn their terroristic methods on them when it serves their interests. (Witness the public hangings of 'informers' in Palestinian controlled territory and the knee-capping of 'anti-social elements' by the paramilitaries in Northern Ireland.) But Honderich is hardly claiming that the members of these organisations are angels or that they are consistent.

13 Honderich: 'On democratic terrorism', in *Terrorism for Humanity*, pp. 148–171.

14 This is not strictly true as the role of the witness is itself a topic of philosophical reflection for Waldenfels. But the philosopher for him does not have the elevated place of the judge nor the adversarial place of the lawyer (speaking now in terms of common law court), but rather the place of one who is both implicated in and reflecting upon the situations of violence.

15 Honderich is not unaware of the problem of overconfidence, if not arrogance, on the part of the philosopher, cf. this volume, pp. 52f.

16 de Vries, H., Weber, S.: *Violence, Identity and Self-Determination* (Stanford, CA: Stanford University Press, 1997), p. 2.

17 Waldenfels warns against the temptations of such a view. See his contribution to this volume, pp. 79f.

18 Merleau-Ponty: *Phenomenology of Perception* trans. by Colin Smith (London: Routledge, 1989), part one.

19 I am using visible here in a wide even metaphorical sense of being apparent to another.

Notes on Contributors

Dr Talia Mae Bettcher is an Assistant Professor of Philosophy at California State University, Los Angeles. Her research interests include early modern philosophy, the philosophy of self, and gender and sexuality studies.

Dr Vittorio Bufacchi is Lecturer in Philosophy at University College Cork. He has published on the topics of social justice, equality, democracy, exploitation, moral motivations and applied philosophy. His main publications include: *Italy Since 1989: Events and Interpretations* (2001), co-authored with S. Burgess, and *Democracy and Constitutional Culture in the Union of Europe* (1995), co-edited with R. Bellamy and D. Castiglione. In Preparation: *A Theory of Violence* and *Theories of Violence: An Anthology*.

Dr Diane Enns is Assistant Professor of Philosophy at McMaster University in Hamilton, Ontario, Canada. She is the author of *Speaking of Freedom: Philosophy, Politics and the Struggle for Liberation* (Stanford University Press, forthcoming) and is currently working on a book-length manuscript concerning ethnopolitical violence, victimisation and survival.

Ms Eve Garrard is a Senior Lecturer in the Centre for Professional Ethics at Keele University. Her main publications include 'Bodily Integrity and the Sale of Human Organs', *Journal of Medical Ethics* vol. 22, 1996 (jointly with Stephen Wilkinson); 'The Nature of Evil', *Philosophical Explorations* January, 1998; 'Mapping Moral Motivation', *Ethical Theory and Moral Practice,* April 1998 (jointly with David McNaughton); 'Slote on Virtue' *Analysis,* July 2000; 'Evil as an Explanatory Concept', *The Monist* vol. 85 no. 2, April 2002; 'Forgiveness and the Holocaust' *Ethical Theory and Moral Practice,* vol. 5 no. 2, June 2002; 'In Defence of Unconditional Forgiveness',

Proceedings of the Aristotelian Society November 2002 (jointly with David McNaughton); *Moral Philosophy and the Holocaust,* Aldershot: Ashgate, 2003 (co-editor with Dr Geoffrey Scarre); 'Passive Euthanasia' (jointly with Stephen Wilkinson) *Journal of Medical Ethics* 2005.

Prof. Ted Honderich has been Grote Professor of the Philosophy of Mind and Logic at University College London, and a visiting professor at Yale and the City University of New York. He is now visiting professor at the University of Bath. His theory of the nature of perceptual consciousness – Radical Externalism, also called Consciousness as Existence – is a nearly-physicalist alternative to recent orthodoxy in the philosophy of mind. A short book on determinism, *How Free Are You?*, a summary of *A Theory of Determinism: The Mind, Neuroscience and Life-Hopes*, is the most translated book on the subject. He is editor of the single-volume reference work *The Oxford Companion to Philosophy*. His book *After the Terror* caused controversy in Germany and elsewhere for its moral defence of Palestinian terrorism. He is also the author of a philosophical autobiography, *Philosopher: A Kind of Life*.

Dr. Burkhard Liebsch is Professor of Philosophy at the Ruhr-Universität Bochum. His publications include: as sole author, *Spuren einer anderen Natur* (1992); *Verzeitlichte Welt* (1995); *Geschichte im Zeichen des Abschieds* (1996); *Vom Anderen her* (1997); *Geschichte als Antwort und Versprechen* (1999); *Moralische Spielräume* (1999); *Gastlichkeit und Freiheit. Polemische Konturen europäischer Kultur* (2005); *Zerbrechliche Lebensformen. Widerstreit – Differenz – Gewalt* (2001); as editor, *Sozialphilosophie* (1999), *Hermeneutik des Selbst – Im Zeichen des Anderen. ZurPhilosophie Paul Ricours* (1999), *Vernunft im Zeichen des Fremden* (ed. with M. Fischer, H.-D. Gondek, 2001); *Trauer und Geschichte* (ed. with J. Rüsen, 2001); *Vom Sinn der Feindschaft* (ed. with C. Geulen, A. v. d. Heiden, 2001); *Gewalt Verstehen* (ed. with D. Mensink); *Handbuch der Kulturwissenschaften. Bd. 1, Grundlagen und Schlüsselbegriffe* (ed. with F. Jaeger, 2004).

Dr. Felix Ó Murchadha is Lecturer in Philosophy at the National University of Ireland, Galway. His publications include *Zeit des Handelns und Möglichkeit der Verwandlung. Kairologie und Chronologie bei Heidegger im Jahrzehnt nach 'Sein und Zeit'.* (Würzburg: Königshausen und Neumann, 1999); 'Being and Ruination. Simmel and Heidegger on the Phenomenology of Ruins' *Philosophy Today. SPEP Supplement* 2002; 'Glory, Idolatry, Kairos: Revelation and the Ontological Difference in Marion' in E. Cassidy & I. Leask, (eds): *Givenness and God. Questions of Jean-Luc Marion* (New York: Fordham University Press, 2005).

Prof. Bill Starr is Associate Professor of Philosophy at Marquette University, Milwaukee, USA. His publications include *Moral Philosophy: Historical and Contemporary Essays* (Milwaukee: Marquette University Press, 1989 (co-edited with Richard Taylor)); *Ethics Across the Curriculum: The Marquette Experience* (Milwaukee: Marquette University Press, 1991 (ed. with Robert Ashmore)); *Moral Philosophy: An Interdisciplinary Approach* (Milwaukee: Marquette University Press, 1994 (ed. with Robert Ashmore)).

Prof. Bernhard Waldenfels is Emeritus Professor in Philosophy (esp. practical philosophy) at the Ruhr-Universität Bochum and Visiting Professor in Paris, New York, Rome, Louvain-la-Neuve, Prague Vienna and Tbilis. He was Co-founder and Vice-President of the German Society for Phenomenological Research (1970–76) and its President (1994–96). He is the author and editor of numerous books. His main publications are as follows: *Phänomenologie und Marxismus* 4 vols. Frankfurt a.M.: Suhrkamp, 1977–79 (English translation: Routledge & Kegan Paul, 1984) *In den Netzen der Lebenswelt.* Frankfurt a.M.: Suhrkamp, 1985; *Ordnung in Zwielicht.* Frankfurt a.M.: Suhrkamp, 1987 (English translation: *Order in the Twilight.* Ohio University Press, 1996); *Antwortregister.* Frankfurt a.M.: Suhrkamp, 1994 (English translation: *Registers of response.* Evanston: Northwestern University Press, 2003). *Bruchlinien der Erfahrung,* (Frankfurt: Suhrkamp, 2003).

Index